BUGATTI
Type 57 Grand Prix
– A Celebration

Neil Max Tomlinson

Also from Veloce Publishing

Those Were The Days ... Series
Alpine Trials & Rallies 1910-1973 (Pfundner)
American 'Independent' Automakers – AMC to Willys 1945 to 1960 (Mort)
American Station Wagons – The Golden Era 1950-1975 (Mort)
American Trucks of the 1950s (Mort)
American Trucks of the 1960s (Mort)
American Woodies 1928-1953 (Mort)
Anglo-American Cars from the 1930s to the 1970s (Mort)
Austerity Motoring (Bobbitt)
Austins, The last real (Peck)
Brighton National Speed Trials (Gardiner)
British and European Trucks of the 1970s (Peck)
British Drag Racing – The early years (Pettitt)
British Lorries of the 1950s (Bobbitt)
British Lorries of the 1960s (Bobbitt)
British Touring Car Racing (Collins)
British Police Cars (Walker)
British Woodies (Peck)
Café Racer Phenomenon, The (Walker)
Don Hayter's MGB Story – The birth of the MGB in MG's Abingdon Design & Development Office (Hayter)
Drag Bike Racing in Britain – From the mid '60s to the mid '80s (Lee)
Dune Buggy Phenomenon, The (Hale)
Dune Buggy Phenomenon Volume 2, The (Hale)
Endurance Racing at Silverstone in the 1970s & 1980s (Parker)
Hot Rod & Stock Car Racing in Britain in the 1980s (Neil)
Last Real Austins 1946-1959, The (Peck)
Mercedes-Benz Trucks (Peck)
MG's Abingdon Factory (Moylan)
Motor Racing at Brands Hatch in the Seventies (Parker)
Motor Racing at Brands Hatch in the Eighties (Parker)
Motor Racing at Crystal Palace (Collins)
Motor Racing at Goodwood in the Sixties (Gardiner)
Motor Racing at Nassau in the 1950s & 1960s (O'Neil)
Motor Racing at Oulton Park in the 1960s (McFadyen)
Motor Racing at Oulton Park in the 1970s (McFadyen)
Motor Racing at Thruxton in the 1970s (Grant-Braham)
Motor Racing at Thruxton in the 1980s (Grant-Braham)
Superprix – The Story of Birmingham Motor Race (Page & Collins)
Three Wheelers (Bobbitt)

Biographies
A Chequered Life – Graham Warner and the Chequered Flag (Hesletine)
Amédée Gordini ... a true racing legend (Smith)
André Lefebvre, and the cars he created at Voisin and Citroën (Beck)
Chris Carter at Large – Stories from a lifetime in motorcycle racing (Carter & Skelton)
Cliff Allison, The Official Biography of – From the Fells to Ferrari (Gauld)
Edward Turner – The Man Behind the Motorcycles (Clew)
Driven by Desire – The Desiré Wilson Story
First Principles – The Official Biography of Keith Duckworth (Burr)
Inspired to Design – F1 cars, Indycars & racing tyres: the autobiography of Nigel Bennett (Bennett)
Jack Sears, The Official Biography of – Gentleman Jack (Gauld)
Jim Redman – 6 Times World Motorcycle Champion: The Autobiography (Redman)
John Chatham – 'Mr Big Healey' – The Official Biography (Burr)
The Lee Noble Story (Wilkins)
Mason's Motoring Mayhem – Tony Mason's hectic life in motorsport and television (Mason)
Raymond Mays' Magnificent Obsession (Apps)
Pat Moss Carlsson Story, The – Harnessing Horsepower (Turner)
Tony Robinson – The biography of a race mechanic (Wagstaff)
Virgil Exner – Visioneer: The Official Biography of Virgil M Exner Designer Extraordinaire (Grist)

Toys & models
Britains Farm Model Balers & Combines 1967-2007, Pocket Guide to (Pullen)
Britains Farm Model & Toy Tractors 1998-2008, Pocket Guide to (Pullen)
Britains Toy Models Catalogues 1970-1979 (Pullen)
British Toy Boats 1920 onwards – A pictorial tribute (Gillham)
Diecast Toy Cars of the 1950s & 1960s (Ralston)
Ford In Miniature (Olson)
GM In Miniature (Olson)
Plastic Toy Cars of the 1950s & 1960s (Ralston)
Tinplate Toy Cars of the 1950s & 1960s (Ralston)

General
1½-litre GP Racing 1961-1965 (Whitelock)
AC Two-litre Saloons & Buckland Sportscars (Archibald)
Alfa Romeo 155/156/147 Competition Touring Cars (Collins)
Alfa Romeo Giulia Coupé GT & GTA (Tipler)
Alfa Romeo Montreal – The dream car that came true (Taylor)
Alfa Romeo Montreal – The Essential Companion (Classic Reprint of 500 copies) (Taylor)
Alfa Tipo 33 (McDonough & Collins)
Alpine & Renault – The Development of the Revolutionary Turbo F1 Car 1968 to 1979 (Smith)
Alpine & Renault – The Sports Prototypes 1963 to 1969 (Smith)
Alpine & Renault – The Sports Prototypes 1973 to 1978 (Smith)
Anatomy of the Works Minis (Moylan)
Armstrong-Siddeley (Smith)
Art Deco and British Car Design (Down)
Autodrome (Collins & Ireland)
Autodrome 2 (Collins & Ireland)
Automotive A-Z, Lane's Dictionary of Automotive Terms (Lane)
Automotive Mascots (Kay & Springate)
Bahamas Speed Weeks, The (O'Neil)
Bentley Continental, Corniche and Azure (Bennett)
Bentley MkVI, Rolls-Royce Silver Wraith, Dawn & Cloud/Bentley R & S-Series (Nutland)
Bluebird CN7 (Stevens)
BMC Competitions Department Secrets (Turner, Chambers & Browning)
BMW 5-Series (Cranswick)
BMW Z-Cars (Taylor)
BMW – The Power of M (Vivian)
British at Indianapolis, The (Wagstaff)
British Cars, The Complete Catalogue of, 1895-1975 (Culshaw & Horrobin)
BRM – A Mechanic's Tale (Salmon)
BRM V16 (Ludvigsen)
Bugatti Type 40 (Price)
Bugatti 46/50 Updated Edition (Price & Arbey)
Bugatti T44 & T49 (Price & Arbey)
Bugatti 57 2nd Edition (Price)
Bugatti Type 57 Grand Prix – A Celebration (Tomlinson)
Caravan, Improve & Modify Your (Porter)
Caravans, The Illustrated History 1919-1959 (Jenkinson)
Caravans, The Illustrated History From 1960 (Jenkinson)
Carrera Panamericana, La (Tipler)
Chrysler 300 – America's Most Powerful Car 2nd Edition (Ackerson)
Chrysler PT Cruiser (Ackerson)
Citroën DS (Bobbitt)
Classic British Car Electrical Systems (Astley)
Cobra – The Real Thing! (Legate)
Competition Car Aerodynamics 3rd Edition (McBeath)
Concept Cars, How to illustrate and design (Dewey)
Cortina – Ford's Bestseller (Robson)
Coventry Climax Racing Engines (Hammill)
Daily Mirror 1970 World Cup Rally 40, The (Robson)
Daimler SP250 New Edition (Long)
Datsun Fairlady Roadster to 280ZX – The Z-Car Story (Long)
Dino – The V6 Ferrari (Long)
Dodge Challenger & Plymouth Barracuda (Grist)
Dodge Charger – Enduring Thunder (Ackerson)
Dodge Dynamite! (Grist)
Dorset from the Sea – The Jurassic Coast from Lyme Regis to Old Harry Rocks photographed from its best viewpoint (Belasco)
Dorset from the Sea – The Jurassic Coast from Lyme Regis to Old Harry Rocks photographed from its best viewpoint (souvenir edition) (Belasco)
Draw & Paint Cars – How to (Gardiner)
Drive on the Wild Side, A – 20 Extreme Driving Adventures From Around the World (Weaver)
Dune Buggy, Building A – The Essential Manual (Shakespeare)
Dune Buggy Files (Hale)
Dune Buggy Handbook (Hale)
East German Motor Vehicles in Pictures (Suhr/Weinreich)
Fast Ladies – Female Racing Drivers 1888 to 1970 (Bouzanquet)
Fate of the Sleeping Beauties, The (op de Weegh/Hottendorff/op de Weegh)
Ferrari 288 GTO, The Book of the (Sackey)
Ferrari 333 SP (O'Neil)
Fiat & Abarth 124 Spider & Coupé (Tipler)
Fiat & Abarth 500 & 600 – 2nd Edition (Bobbitt)
Fiats, Great Small (Ward)
Ford Cleveland 335-Series V8 engine 1970 to 1982 – The Essential Source Book (Hammill)
Ford F100/F150 Pick-up 1948-1996 (Ackerson)
Ford F150 Pick-up 1997-2005 (Ackerson)
Ford GT – Then, and Now (Streather)
Ford GT40 (Legate)
Ford Model Y (Roberts)
Ford Small Block V8 Racing Engines 1962-1970 – The Essential Source Book (Hammill)
Ford Thunderbird From 1954, The Book of the (Long)
Formula 5000 Motor Racing, Back then ... and back now (Lawson)
Forza Minardi! (Vigar)
France: the essential guide for car enthusiasts – 200 things for the car enthusiast to see and do (Parish)
Funky Mopeds (Skelton)
Grand Prix Ferrari – The Years of Enzo Ferrari's Power, 1948-1980 (Pritchard)
Grand Prix Ford – DFV-powered Formula 1 Cars (Pritchard)
GT – The World's Best GT Cars 1953-73 (Dawson)
Hillclimbing & Sprinting – The Essential Manual (Short & Wilkinson)
Honda NSX (Long)
Inside the Rolls-Royce & Bentley Styling Department – 1971 to 2001 (Hull)
Intermeccanica – The Story of the Prancing Bull (McCredie & Reisner)
Jaguar, The Rise of (Price)
Jaguar XJ 220 – The Inside Story (Moreton)
Jaguar XJ-S, The Book of the (Long)
Jeep CJ (Ackerson)
Jeep Wrangler (Ackerson)
Karmann-Ghia Coupé & Convertible (Bobbitt)
Kris Meeke – Intercontinental Rally Challenge Champion (McBride)
Lamborghini Miura Bible, The (Sackey)
Lamborghini Urraco, The Book of the (Landsem)
Lambretta Bible, The (Davies)
Lancia 037 (Collins)
Lancia Delta HF Integrale (Blaettel & Wagner)
Land Rover Series III Reborn (Porter)
Land Rover, The Half-ton Military (Cook)
Lea-Francis Story, The (Price)
Le Mans Panoramic (Ireland)
Lexus Story, The (Long)
Little book of microcars, the (Quellin)
Little book of smart, the – New Edition (Jackson)
Little book of trikes, the (Quellin)
Lola – The Illustrated History (1957-1977) (Starkey)
Lola – All the Sports Racing & Single-seater Racing Cars 1978-1997 (Starkey)
Lola T70 – The Racing History & Individual Chassis Record – 4th Edition (Starkey)
Lotus 49 (Oliver)
Marketingmobiles, The Wonderful Wacky World of (Hale)
Maserati 250F In Focus (Pritchard)
Mazda MX-5/Miata 1.6 Enthusiast's Workshop Manual (Grainger & Shoemark)
Mazda MX-5/Miata 1.8 Enthusiast's Workshop Manual (Grainger & Shoemark)
The book of the Mazda MX-5 Miata – The 'Mk1' NA-series 1988 to 1997 (Long)
Mazda MX-5 Miata Roadster (Long)
Maximum Mini (Booij)
Meet the English (Bowie)
Mercedes-Benz SL – R230 series 2001 to 2011 (Long)
Mercedes-Benz SL – W113-series 1963-1971 (Long)
Mercedes-Benz SL & SLC – 107-series 1971-1989 (Long)
Mercedes-Benz SLK – R170 series 1996-2004 (Long)
Mercedes-Benz SLK – R171 series 2004-2011 (Long)
Mercedes-Benz W123-series – All models 1976 to 1986 (Long)
MGA (Price Williams)
MGB & MGB GT– Expert Guide (Auto-doc Series) (Williams)
MGB Electrical Systems Updated & Revised Edition (Astley)
Micro Caravans (Jenkinson)
Micro Trucks (Mort)
Microcars at Large! (Quellin)
Mini Cooper – The Real Thing! (Tipler)
Mini Minor to Asia Minor (West)
Mitsubishi Lancer Evo, The Road Car & WRC Story (Long)
Montlhéry, The Story of the Paris Autodrome (Boddy)
Morgan Maverick (Lawrence)
Morgan 3 Wheeler – back to the future!, The (Dron)
Morris Minor, 60 Years on the Road (Newell)
Motor Movies – The Posters! (Veysey)
Motor Racing – Reflections of a Lost Era (Carter)
Motor Racing – The Pursuit of Victory 1930-1962 (Carter)
Motor Racing – The Pursuit of Victory 1963-1972 (Wyatt/Sears)
Motor Racing Heroes – The Stories of 100 Greats (Newman)
Motorsport In colour, 1950s (Wainwright)
N.A.R.T. – A concise history of the North American Racing Team 1957 to 1983 (O'Neil)
Nissan 300ZX & 350Z – The Z-Car Story (Long)
Nissan GT-R Supercar: Born to race (Gorodji)
Northeast American Sports Car Races 1950-1959 (O'Neil)
Nothing Runs – Misadventures in the Classic, Collectable & Exotic Car Biz (Slutsky)
Pass the Theory and Practical Driving Tests (Gibson & Hoole)
Peking to Paris 2007 (Young)
Pontiac Firebird (Cranswick)
Porsche Boxster (Long)
Porsche 356 (2nd Edition) (Long)
Porsche 908 (Födisch, Neßhöver, Roßbach, Schwarz & Roßbach)
Porsche 911 Carrera – The Last of the Evolution (Corlett)
Porsche 911R, RS & RSR, 4th Edition (Starkey)
Porsche 911, The Book of the (Long)
Porsche 911SC 'Super Carrera' – The Essential Companion (Streather)
Porsche 914 & 914-6: The Definitive History of the Road & Competition Cars (Long)
Porsche 924 (Long)
The Porsche 924 Carreras – evolution to excellence (Smith)
Porsche 928 (Long)
Porsche 944 (Long)
Porsche 964, 993 & 996 Data Plate Code Breaker (Streather)
Porsche 993 'King Of Porsche' – The Essential Companion (Streather)
Porsche 996 'Supreme Porsche' – The Essential Companion (Streather)
Porsche Racing Cars – 1953 to 1975 (Long)
Porsche Racing Cars – 1976 to 2005 (Long)
Porsche – The Rally Story (Meredith)
Porsche: Three Generations of Genius (Meredith)
Preston Tucker & Others (Linde)
RAC Rally Action! (Gardiner)
RACING COLOURS – MOTOR RACING COMPOSITIONS 1908-2009 (Newman)
Rallye Sport Fords: The Inside Story (Moreton)
Roads with a View – England's greatest views and how to find them by road (Corfield)
Rolls-Royce Silver Shadow/Bentley T Series Corniche & Camargue – Revised & Enlarged Edition (Bobbitt)
Rolls-Royce Silver Spirit, Silver Spur & Bentley Mulsanne 2nd Edition (Bobbitt)
Runways & Racers (O'Neil)
Russian Motor Vehicles – Soviet Limousines 1930-2003 (Kelly)
Russian Motor Vehicles – The Czarist Period 1784 to 1917 (Kelly)
RX-7 – Mazda's Rotary Engine Sportscar (Updated & Revised New Edition) (Long)
Singer Story: Cars, Commercial Vehicles, Bicycles & Motorcycle (Atkinson)
Sleeping Beauties USA – abandoned classic cars & trucks (Marek)
SM – Citroën's Maserati-engined Supercar (Long & Claverol)
Speedway – Auto racing's ghost tracks (Collins & Ireland)
Sprite Caravans, The Story of (Jenkinson)
Standard Motor Company, The Book of the
Subaru Impreza: The Road Car And WRC Story (Long)
Supercar, How to Build your own (Thompson)
Tales from the Toolbox (Oliver)
Tatra – The Legacy of Hans Ledwinka, Updated & Enlarged Collector's Edition of 1500 copies (Margolius & Henry)
Taxi! The Story of the 'London' Taxicab (Bobbitt)
Toleman Story, The (Hilton)
Toyota Celica & Supra, The Book of Toyota's Sports Coupés (Long)
Toyota MR2 Coupés & Spyders (Long)
Triumph TR6 (Kimberley)
Two Summers – The Mercedes-Benz W196R Racing Car (Ackerson)
TWR Story, The – Group A (Hughes & Scott)
Unraced (Collins)
Volkswagen Bus Book, The (Bobbitt)
Volkswagen Bus or Van to Camper, How to Convert (Porter)
Volkswagens of the World (Glen)
VW Beetle Cabriolet – The full story of the convertible Beetle (Bobbitt)
VW Beetle – The Car of the 20th Century (Copping)
VW Bus – 40 Years of Splitties, Bays & Wedges (Copping)
VW Bus Book, The (Bobbitt)
VW Golf: Five Generations of Fun (Copping & Cservenka)
VW – The Air-cooled Era (Copping)
VW T5 Camper Conversion Manual (Porter)
VW Campers (Copping)
You & Your Jaguar XK8/XKR – Buying, Enjoying, Maintaining, Modifying – New Edition (Thorley)
Which Oil? – Choosing the right oils & greases for your antique, vintage, veteran, classic or collector car (Michell)
Works Minis, The Last (Purves & Brenchley)
Works Rally Mechanic (Moylan)

For post publication news, updates and amendments relating to this book please visit www.veloce.co.uk/books/V4789

www.veloce.co.uk

First published in May 2015 by Veloce Publishing Limited, Veloce House, Parkway Farm Business Park, Middle Farm Way, Poundbury, Dorchester DT1 3AR, England. Fax 01305 268864 / e-mail info@veloce.co.uk / web www.veloce.co.uk or www.velocebooks.com. ISBN 978-1-845847-89-0 / UPC 6-36847-04789-4 © 2015 Neil Max Tomlinson and Veloce Publishing. All rights reserved. With the exception of quoting brief passages for the purpose of review, no part of this publication may be recorded, reproduced or transmitted by any means, including photocopying, without the written permission of Veloce Publishing Ltd. Throughout this book logos, model names and designations, etc, have been used for the purposes of identification, illustration and decoration. Such names are the property of the trademark holder as this is not an official publication. Readers with ideas for automotive books, or books on other transport or related hobby subjects, are invited to write to the editorial director of Veloce Publishing at the above address. British Library Cataloguing in Publication Data – A catalogue record for this book is available from the British Library. Typesetting, design and page make-up all by Veloce Publishing Ltd on Apple Mac. Printed in India by Replika Press.

BUGATTI
Type 57 Grand Prix
– *A Celebration*

Neil Max Tomlinson

Table of contents

Acknowledgements & Dedication 6
Foreword & Author's Introduction 7

1. T57G Overview 10
   Depression in France. 10
   A Buick made in Molsheim and a Grand Prix Car 11
   Depression in Germany 11
   Type 59 fades 12
   Fonds des Course and a Sports Car Formula 13
   New sports car planned 14
   Type 57S 14
   Chassis and engine revised 17
   T57G Tank 18

2. 1936 Testing at Montlhéry 20
   Rehearsal 21
   A model for future sports cars 22
   Streamlined body 23
   Tank described.. 23
   Types 57S & 59 combined. 25
   Escalating industrial unrest 25
   Creeping discontent 26
   Factory strike and exile 26
   Paris facilities 26

3. 1936 Grand Prix de l'ACF 28
   Practice 28
   The race 32
   Great success 32

4. 1936 Grand Prix de la Marne 35
   The race 36
   Honorary starter 39
   A great victory 41

5. 1936 Class 'C' World Records. 42
   Modifications 47

6. 1937 Le Mans 48
   1931 misadventure 48
   Father-son comparison.. 48
   Le Mans Tanks described.. 49
   Technical inspection 52
   Roger Labric.. 52
   The race 52
   Tragedy 55
   The race went on 55
   New record and analysis 55

7. 1937 T57S45 Tanks 59
   Erroneous history 59
   Revised history 60
   T57S45 Tank described. 61
   Body details 64
   Disqualification 65
   Mystery.. 68
   Fate 68

8. 1937 T57 'Sport' 69
   57248 69
   1935 Brooklands 500-Mile Race 69
   1936 Comminges Grand Prix 74
   Criticism and overhaul 74
   1937 Pau Grand Prix 76
   The race 76
   1937 Montlhéry 400,000f prize 78
   1937 Tunis Grand Prix 79
   1937 Bône (Annaba) Grand Prix 79
   1937 Marseille 3-Hour Race 79

1937 Marne Grand Prix. 82
The race 82
Criticism, revision and disposal.. 82

9. 1939 Le Mans 86
Only one car.. 86
1939 Tank described 87
Special engine 88
Gearbox 89
Advanced streamlining 89
Star driver.. 92
The 1939 Le Mans Story by Robert Aumaître 92
The race 93
Controversy 97

10. 1939 – Friday, August 11 98
Tragedy 98
Debate 98
Historical facts 99
Reconsideration. .. .. .100
Robert Aumaître's response .. .. .101
Interment and memorial. .. .. .102

11. The surviving Tank.. .. .. .103
Patch panels.. .. .. .106
Damage. .. .. .106
Sold .. .. .106
Restoration .. .. .108
Exhibited .. .. .110

12. The Type 57G engine.. .. .. .111
Special cylinder block .. .. .111
Top end. .. .. .114
Bottom end .. .. .114
Performance.. .. .. .114
Froude records 114
Summary .. .. .115

13. T57G Tank chassis detail .. .. .116
Series 1 T57S frame – gondola.. .. .. .117
Series 2 T57S frame .. .. .118
Narrow firewall .. .. .119
Cut-down long frame. .. .. .121
Clutch .. .. .121
T57G synchromesh gearbox.. .. .. .121
T57S45 Tank gearbox .. .. .124
De Ram dampers .. .. .127
Racing wheels .. .. .127
Carburettors.. .. .. .130

14. Evolution – Grand Prix Type 59 to Type 57 Grand Prix .131
T59 origins.. .. .. .131
Bugatti's first straight-eight .. .. .133
Advantages .. .. .134
Technical advances .. .. .134
Dynamic balance and 2-4-2 .. .. .134
Torsional vibrations .. .. .135
4-4-Type 59 .. .. .135
Revised crankcase .. .. .138
Racing debut. .. .. .138
3.3-litre capacity .. .. .138
Factory mechanics' notebooks.. .. .. .139
Racing Department disbanded.. .. .. .140

15. The Type 57 Grand Prix emerges.. .. .. .142
Trade plates .. .. .142
T57 engine revised. .. .. .142
T59 engine revised .. .. .143
Faster supercharger .. .. .144
T57G engine is trialled .. .. .144
Ulster TT .. .. .145
BARC 500 146
San Sebastian, Brno, East London and Pau .. .. .146
Lightened crankshaft and pistons.. .. .. .146
Paris-Nice Rally 146
La Turbie, Monaco, Tunisia and& Spain 147
New carburettor .. .. .147
T57G Tank debut .. .. .148
Spa, Deauville and Nürburgring 148
Outrage at St Gaudens.. .. .. .149
T59/57G .. .. .149

16. Three Tanks or four .. .. .150
Enthusiastic research. .. .. .152
Bodywork studies.. .. .. .152
Froude records .. .. .154
Crashed car .. .. .154
Scrap or repair .. .. .155
Coachwork practice .. .. .157
Timeline 157
Weight differences. .. .. .158
Two dashboards .. .. .158
Veyron car 159
Shooting star 160
Summary .. .. .160
Who was driving?.. .. .. .161

17. Tail lights 162

18. Bibliography & further reading .. .. .169

Index 175

Acknowledgements & Dedication

ALTHOUGH THEIR PEDIGREE WAS sourced from and influenced by the artist and artisan Ettore Bugatti, this work is a celebration of the Type 57 Grand Prix cars, being predominantly the creation of his eldest son, Jean Bugatti, between 1932 and 1939.

The story of the T57G is quite complex, and has taken more than 40 years to study, evaluate and draw together. The late celebrated marque historian, Hugh G Conway wrote in his seminal and authoritative work *Bugatti – Le pur sang des automobiles*, that, after 1935; "Bugatti's racing programme became involved and very confusing to the humble historian without accurate factory records."

Many early assumptions have been dismissed, and a number of conventional beliefs challenged, so the findings of these studies may not agree with everyone, but have been influenced by the dedicated research of numerous automotive historians.

This composition has also been inspired by what were once dismissed as unremarkable factory documents, their importance being formally revealed to marque supporters by Hugh G Conway in 1967.

In particular, I would like to thank all past and present staff of the The Bugatti Trust study centre at Prescott. Its very existence would not have been possible without the outstanding generosity of the Trust's enthusiastic international founders and supporters. The Study Centre contains one of the world's most significant collections of material about the amazing creations of Ettore Bugatti, his son Jean, and the Bugatti family. Little gems are still being discovered.

Dedication

Dedicated to the memory of the late (Ronnie) RC Symondson, AFC, who encouraged my enthusiasm for Bugatti Type 57G sports racing cars, and who, many years ago, probably should have written this book.

Also to Gill for her patient support.

Cover illustration painted by the late Alan Williams.

VISIT VELOCE ON THE WEB – WWW.VELOCE.CO.UK
All current books • New book news • Special offers • Gift vouchers • Forum

Foreword & Author's Introduction

Foreword

From the earliest days of the twentieth century, the Bugatti automobile has epitomised innovative engineering and style. It is surprising, therefore, that of all the many books that have been written about the company, little of the story of the 57 racing models has been told.

An explanation for this may be that a simple historian would have been discouraged by the fact that, by the mid-1930s, the Bugatti company was in serious financial difficulty. France was in turmoil, and Ettore Bugatti had, more or less, left the running of the motoring side of the company to his talented son, Jean. Furthermore, Grand Prix racing had become dominated by the state-sponsored German teams, against which Bugatti had no chance of competing. As a consequence, Bugatti racing models had little opportunity to excel.

The Author has taken the view that another explanation can be found in the fact that Jean was considering the Type 59 as a racing version of the 57. In considering the two models together, a logical development sequence can be established. The Author has offered a radical explanation into the known history of the racing models at that time.

Sadly, Jean was killed whilst at the peak of his career, and then the Second World War intervened, so it is a subject that may never reach a definite conclusion. However, the story of the company and the racing models in the late 1930s needs to be told.

Today, we are fascinated by the history of the Bugatti family, the cars and the brand. A book that sheds further light on a little known area of activity, and adds to our knowledge of the history of the Bugatti car, is to be welcomed.

HRG Conway
Chairman – The Bugatti Trust

Author's Introduction

My late father was of that generation born during the declining years of horse-drawn transport and the rise of the motorcar, being always very enthusiastic about car development, as well as having a strong affection for the veteran car movement. My family lived in Surrey, and, as a child during the 1950s, I was privileged to have regularly attended the London to Brighton route to cheer the pre-1904 cars as they made their way south. One year, after they had all passed by, my father drove his 1937 SS Saloon to a large triangular village green close to an ancient public house amongst a group of non-Brighton-run early cars. That day, one car in particular engraved its famous nameplate into my seven-year-old memory after I was permitted to sit in it, and to hold its massive steering wheel. It was Peter Hampton's 'Black Bess,' the 5-litre, chain-driven 'Garros' car. Whether the inspiration was the car's dark looks or the visceral raw power of its engine I cannot say, but it left me hooked on Bugattis forever.

For my next birthday I received a wooden SMEC kit of a Bugatti Type 59 that was really far too advanced for my age, although I survived carving it with very little blood loss and all my fingers intact. After that, it was a die-cast Lesney Yesteryear Type 35B, followed by a French RAMI Type

Bugatti Type 57 Grand Prix – A Celebration

35C; all still in my possession. Since then I have become a keen collector of Bugatti books, scale models and toys, and a reasonably accomplished model maker when some of the more interesting prototypes were not commercially available. In my youth, I managed to acquire copies of WF Bradley's *Ettore Bugatti – A Biography* and the Eaglesfield/Hampton's *The Bugatti Book*. As an adult in the early 1970s, this general interest in Bugattis began to focus closely on the rather ferocious beauty of the Type 57G streamlined racing cars known as 'Tanks.' This culminated in an enthusiasm for compiling photos, illustrations, facts, figures, stories, and even rumours about these historically important cars, as well as to explore their presently mysterious origins and development.

Derived from their 'Touring' brothers, these amazing super sports cars appeared to spring to success from nowhere in 1936, winning two major Grands Prix, and securing 14 Class 'C' World Records, before winning the Le Mans endurance races of 1937 and 1939. This was an astonishing result from a manufacturer which had been tottering on a financial precipice for many years. The Tanks' successes also represented a great triumph for the French Nation, where, almost immediately, enterprising makers reproduced their futuristic, Art Deco – 'Flash Gordon' – looks in a number of toys. These ranged from simple and inexpensive 'plaster and flour' offerings sold from trays in their thousands, to clockwork-powered tinplate and celluloid miniatures.

To some people, a toy or model of a racing car is merely a futile object: a plaything for a child, a bauble or a trinket; to others they have a much deeper significance. Rex Hays, a highly acclaimed professional model maker of the immediate post-World War II period, characterised the nature of model racing cars rather concisely, writing:

"Models are trophies in tribute to the many different facets of the sport of motor racing." Additionally, "Their purpose is to perpetuate the memory of some notable or victorious car, great achievements, famous personalities, thrilling or tragic situations associated with each."

This interpretation seems to be absolutely right, where such objects, whether sculptures or toys, appear to be endowed with the capacity to invoke the spirit of the car as well as to inspire the imagination of the viewer. This high esteem has endured to the present day, where enthusiastic manufacturers from all parts of the world continue to celebrate the achievements of the Bugatti Type 57G cars, producing models of them in every popular scale, from 1/87 to 1/8. Consequently, I have included several photographs of Bugatti T57G toys and models from my collection.

Under the new 1936 Automobile Club de France (ACF) sports car regulations, the successes of the Type 57G Tanks influenced the renaissance of the Bugatti marque during the latter half of that decade. Yet ironically, the successful Le Mans T57C Tank of 1939 played a pivotal role in the demise of the factory, when its heir, Jean Bugatti, died tragically in the car just a few days before the outbreak of World War II. These dual calamities effectively sealed the fate of this great car manufacturer, which had created some of the most exciting and sought-after cars in the world. Fortunately for enthusiasts, the 1937 Le Mans winning Type 57G Tank survived the conflict, despite the efforts of the British Royal Air Force to bomb its storage facility at Bordeaux. Many enthusiasts consider the car to be the most successful and unique Bugatti in existence.

In this compilation I've endeavoured to collate the trivial detail differences between the Tanks and their derivatives in relation to their particular competition events that might be of interest to enthusiasts and scholars alike, as well as model makers. Moreover, I trust these observations will be an aid to dating period photographs related to these great cars. The official factory records are a little sparse with regards to the T57G, with many gaps in knowledge, so I also attempt to describe and interpret the Tanks' development and progress in conjunction with known facts, contemporary drawings and photographs, as well as some necessary speculation to tie it all together.

In summary, this book attempts to celebrate every aspect of the Bugatti T57 Grand Prix racing cars: their origins, triumphs, failings, trivia, trinkets, and something of the personalities behind the cars, interwoven with the social and political events that influenced those times. That is my personal accolade to these magnificent racing cars and their creators.

VIVE LA MARQUE!

Neil Max Tomlinson
Minera

Foreword & Author's Introduction

Model Bugattis developed from 1950s SMEC 1/32-scale wooden kits. Clockwise from top left: Type 36, Type 57G, Type 59, and Type 51. (Courtesy NMT Collection)

VISIT VELOCE ON THE WEB – WWW.VELOCE.CO.UK
All current books • New book news • Special offers • Gift vouchers • Forum

T57G Overview

THE BUGATTI TYPE 57G 'Tank' racing car of 1936 was essentially a Grand Prix version of the 3.3-litre T57S sports car exhibited in October 1935, which, in turn, had evolved from the T57 touring car debuted in October 1933, and was being supplied by March 1934. The T57 touring model was the zenith of a long line of earlier models to have emerged from the factory in Molsheim, in the Alsace region of France. Specifically, though, the T57 was developed to replace the outmoded single-camshaft Type 49, but was arranged on a longer, 3.3m wheelbase chassis. However, unlike its predecessors, which had been principally directed by the hand of Ettore Bugatti, the T57 was fashioned under the supervision of his highly talented eldest son, Jean, who, at the age of just 23, had been given a very high level of autonomy to produce a more modern, luxurious, state of the art, fast touring car that would secure the future of the family business. Jean seems very young to have been handed this important duty, until one considers that his father established himself as a motor manufacturer at the tender age of just 19.

Whilst the parentage of the Type 57 is familiar, its composition differed dramatically from all of Ettore Bugatti's earlier practices, where the only material T49 element shared with the T57 was the rear axle; and that was for the first season only. However, the T57 engine retained the T49's 3.3-litre capacity, 72mm x 100mm bore/stroke aspect, better-balanced 2-4-2 crank timing, and a firing order of 1.6.2.5.8.3.7.4.

Now with a valve-included-angle of 96°, and valves operated through low-inertia fingers, the twin overhead camshaft engine was a totally new design from end to end. It produced almost 50% more power, and was the quietest and most flexibly ranged ever made by Automobiles Bugatti. This new power unit was able to span commercial utility from luxury town carriage to Grand Prix racing car. The T57 was fitted with a completely new constant mesh gearbox, which, for the very first time at Molsheim, was in unit with its engine. The design office was clearly under new management. Here, Jean's undertaking was necessarily tempered by an urgent need to apply a more economic approach to manufacture and marketing, in order to meet the challenging world financial slump that swept into France at the beginning of that decade.

Depression in France

The Wall Street Crash of October 24, 1929, and the subsequent world depression, did not noticeably affect France until the summer of 1931. However, once this belated slump took hold, car production throughout the country quickly dwindled to a third of its earlier output. For Automobiles Bugatti, this meant an urgent rationalization of a wide range of enterprises that included its racing activities as well as car manufacture. Before long, the workforce of around 1200 was reluctantly halved, with the remainder limited to a 24-hour-week subsistence wage. Providentially for those employees and the company, welcome respite came in the form of French government intervention that granted contracts to several French motor companies, including Bugatti, to design and build advanced high-speed railcars for the state-owned railways.

In the spring of 1932, whilst still retaining overall responsibility

1 T57G Overview

for the factory, Ettore Bugatti set up a design office in Paris with his principal designer, Noel Domboy, and immersed himself enthusiastically in this project. He left the automobile side of the business in the more than competent hands of Jean. Subsequently, many of Bugatti's employees were re-tasked, and so far as can be determined, almost all those laid-off earlier were re-engaged to establish railcar production facilities at Molsheim. This necessary yet unavoidably ruthless transition appears to have been managed quite efficiently during that twelve-month period. Extraordinarily, by May 1933, Ettore Bugatti's outstanding team of talented artisans and craftsmen had designed, built and tested a prototype railcar on the tracks. Remarkably, this venture was probably one of the most successful and profitable projects ever undertaken by Bugatti, for, during the following five years, some 76 railcars were constructed.

A Buick made in Molsheim and a Grand Prix Car

With his new position at the factory, for which he had been nurtured from childhood, Jean took full advantage of his relative independence. It was an unprecedented opportunity for him to create his personal vision of a modern Bugatti motorcar. Sadly, this notion was not one shared by his father, who never accepted Jean's creation with full approval. Its overall concept had broken-free from many of his expensive, time-consuming and eccentric 'Bugatti' practices. Instead, the Type 57 was a practical, economical and relatively more mass-production oriented car. In letters to his son, Ettore often expressed this dissonance by referring to the T57 as "... a Buick made in Molsheim," so it should have hurt Jean deeply to have his efforts put down by his father like this. Apparently, though, such unkind criticism did not seem to bother Jean greatly, for he had never concealed his admiration for the style, theory and practice of American motor makers.

This high esteem may be seen expressed in his bodywork styling exercises, as well as the conspicuous adoption of the 'Harry Miller' cylinder head design for the Types 50 and 51 in 1930, for which he was largely responsible, reprised for the Type 57 in 1932. Consequently, his sense of humour and positive psyche undoubtedly interpreted his father's criticism as a compliment. Nonetheless, with the Type 57, Jean had liberated the imagination of his designers to create a car that better suited the economy, style, and the contemporary age of the thirties, and for Automobiles Bugatti, a truly classic example of the right car at the right time.

The Type 57 power unit also inspired the basis of a new Grand Prix car in 1932 known as the Type 59, although from the outset, the car was technologically old-generation. Whilst having a brand-new chassis frame, it was essentially a low-weight racing version of the Type 57, with dry-sump lubrication and a 4-4 crank array in Bugatti Grand Prix tradition, and a firing order of 1.5.3.7.4.8.2.6.

As we shall see, the T57 and T59 engines were very closely related, so were natural for hybridised improvement. The handsome T59 racing car was campaigned in 1933 even before the T57 touring model was officially exhibited; the latter embargoed because surplus stocks of the T49 model had to be sold off first. Whilst some elements of the new racing car were quite advanced, it was soon obvious that the T59 was no match for the state-sponsored and technically-advanced German Grand Prix cars. These were new-generation racing machines that quickly dominated European circuits at the time. Besides, the financial support necessary for racing activities and development was being urgently curtailed in order to keep Automobiles Bugatti afloat. Indeed, as soon as the new Type 57 went into full production, other models and expensive projects were quickly shelved, before being later sacrificed, including the embryonic Type 50S Spéciale.

Depression in Germany

Germany, too, had been affected by the world slump, but when Adolf Hitler became Chancellor in 1933, the Reich's propaganda machine decided that technological superiority was a means to world power, and would be demonstrated through the medium of Grand Prix racing. Advances in engineering knowledge could be applied advantageously to the apparatus of future belligerence. Financial support of 450,000 Reich marks (£41,500) per year was offered to any German company which would co-operate toward such an objective, with extra bonuses for race success. Understandably, Mercedes-Benz and Auto Union were seduced by such an incredible opportunity, each sharing around half of the subsidy, and almost straight away began building extremely innovative cars.

The dark political motives that inspired this machinery should not necessarily taint admiration for their novel design, execution and amazing performance. In competition, these unique new vehicles soon began to overwhelm all the

Bugatti Type 57 Grand Prix – *A Celebration*

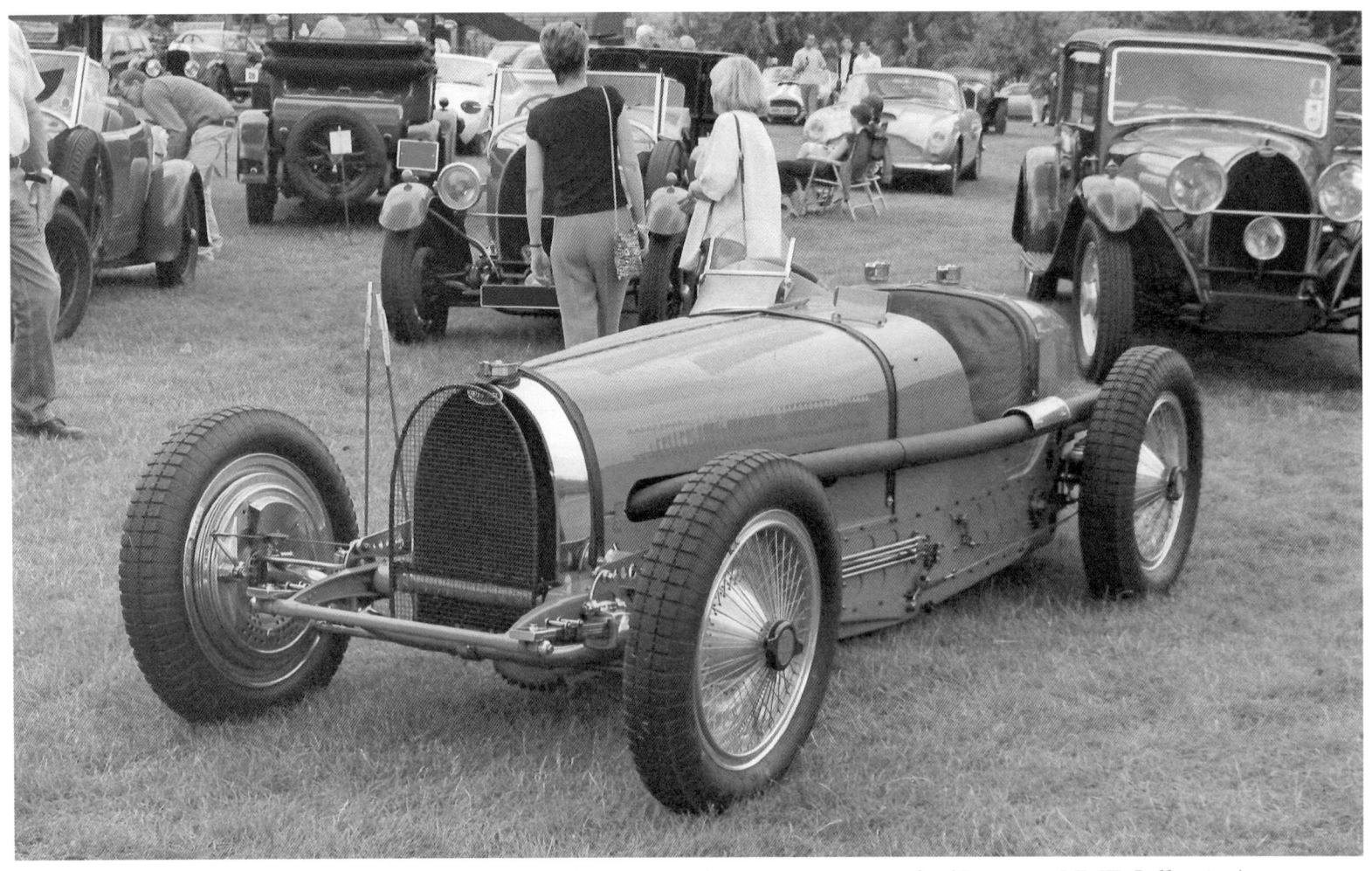

Type 59 racing car. One of the most handsome Grand Prix cars ever made. (Courtesy NMT Collection)

opposition, despite the valiant efforts of some brilliant drivers in technically inferior machines. As a result, by the end of the 1934 racing season, most of the French racing car makers, including Bugatti, knew they lacked the financial reserves to compete effectively against these challengers.

Type 59 fades

The Grand Prix Type 59 was, and still is, considered to be one of the most handsome racing machines ever created, where an original car is highly valued and sought after. Unfortunately, beauty contests do not qualify in competition when racing. Weighing rather more than the 750kg regulation limit, and producing 230bhp at 5100rpm, the bitter truth is that, in its day, the T59 was surpassed by the lightweight, technologically advanced chassis design and extraordinary engine power of the Auto Union and Mercedes racing cars. The T59 utilised some very innovative and advanced ideas, but, compared with the almost 'no expense spared' German cars – which liberally used cutting-edge and sometimes exotic materials, as well as expensive manufacturing techniques – the T59 was technologically obsolete even before it first raced.

At the end of the 1934 season, several drivers had left, and the Bugatti racing department formally disbanded. In addition, four of the five previously active Team Type 59s were sold to British amateur drivers in March and April 1935. Such draconian measures from a previously successful racing car manufacturer shocked the motoring public at the time.

The sensational Type 57GR, first seen at the Paris Salon in 1934. (Courtesy Bugatti Trust)

Fonds des Course and a Sports Car Formula
Unsurprisingly, Bugatti was not the only French automobile maker to suffer in the rather bleak economic situation. National concerns, too, were such that, in November 1934, the Federation Nationale de Clubs Automobiles de France initiated a fund to support French Grands Prix. In fact, shortly after the Bugatti racing department's disbandment, this fund was taken over by a Government-sponsored committee, later known as 'Fonds des Course.' Parallel to these end-of-season deliberations, the Automobile Club de France (ACF) unofficially consulted several French car makers, including Bugatti, to discuss the future direction of French motor sport. Before long, the ACF's frustration with other European clubs, over the conspicuous superiority of new generation German racing cars, developed into a serious schism. The emerging anger finally erupted during the Grand Prix de l'ACF in June 1935, embarrassingly confirming that the French were well out of the running. Within days, the ACF decreed that the 1936 Grand Prix would be for un-supercharged sports cars, and straight away petitioned the Alliance Internationale des Automobile Clubs

Bugatti Type 57 Grand Prix – A Celebration

Reconnus (AIACR), governing body, to produce international regulations. These were published just three months later, on Sunday October 13, 1935. As the late Anthony Blight put it so concisely, the French sports car revolution had begun.

New sports car planned

The project shop had been working on the T57GR (Grand Raid) version of the long-framed car quite early on, where Desin 31, dated September 6, 1933, shows the original chassis layout. It had its radiator, bonnet line and steering column arranged 80mm lower than the touring T57. Curiously, this is the same period during which the Type 59 was being developed, so perhaps Jean was already contemplating fitting the T57GR with a de-tuned, dry-sump T59 engine and lowered transmission train. It may be more than coincidental that the Type 59 engine crankshaft centre line lies 81.5mm lower in the chassis than the T57 engine, enabling a similarly-lowered bonnet profile. Therefore, it is feasible that such reasoning inspired the Types 57GR and later T57S.

Nevertheless, a year later, an exciting two-seat roadster was presented at the Paris Salon de l'Automobile at the Grand Palais in October 1934. The car was styled with camelback headrests, pigskin upholstery, and spats over the rear wheels. Its bodywork carried Jean Bugatti's classic two-tone paint finish in black with a yellow blaze. Whilst it looked terrific, with a lowered profile and go-faster flash, it was a heavy vehicle whose engine was little better than standard. On the other hand, it is clear that the T57GR was a temporary hybrid that would act as a bridge between the T57 and the 'marvel' that Jean planned for the future; the T57 'Super Sports Car.' Moreover, Jean must have also considered his options as to what he might do with the, soon-to-be-redundant T59 racing car. After all, his handsome and successful T55 Supersports of 1932 was basically a composite of former Types 47/54 Grand Prix chassis frame sides, Type 49 and slightly de-tuned Type 51 racing engine.

The main advantage the German cars had over everyone else was clearly related to engine power and high-pressure supercharging, where such inequalities could not be easily redressed. Retrospectively, of course, it's evident that the discussions between the ACF and Bugatti at the end of 1934 must have been mutually advantageous, with a potent hint that the 1936 season might be for un-supercharged sports cars. Hence, it was an opportunity for Jean to seriously concentrate on the development of the Type 57, combining a shorter and lighter chassis with attributes of the technically-wilted Grand Prix T59. The earliest drafts of the new 'S' model are dated December 1934, and, by early 1935, Jean was in a position to formally announce to the press that the 'Ultimate' Bugatti sports car would be created to succeed the 2.3-litre Type 55 model. The new car would have similar chassis dimensions, so by interpretation, suggested a two-seater sports model with a relatively short, Type 55-like, wheelbase.

Type 57S Torpedo, 1935.

Type 57S Torpedo, 1935. Note the rear end showing the 'gondola' chassis. (Courtesy Bugatti Trust)

14

1   T57G Overview

Illustration of the 1935 Type 57S Torpedo by John Dunscombe. Note the 'gondola' chassis. (Courtesy Bugatti Trust)

The futuristic Type 57S Aérolithe at the Paris Salon, 1935. (Courtesy Bugatti Trust)

Type 57S

Later that year, Jean Bugatti exhibited his first Type 57S 'Competition' models during the Paris Salon in October, then two weeks later for the London Motor Show at Olympia. He presented a Torpédo open-bodied car, alongside the spectacular and bizarrely-styled (and star of the show) closed Coupé Spéciale. The press dubbed it l'Aérolithe (Meteorite). Both cars were arranged on a 2.98m wheelbase chassis.

Interestingly, the specification leaflets for even the most expensive models were the smallest issues ever: 210x140mm, very simply printed in black and white, and with a pale yellow Bugatti badge. This minimalist approach to marketing may be seen as a conspicuous statement from Automobiles Bugatti regarding its acutely precarious economic situation at that time.

The T57S Competition models were fashioned with the newly designed surbaissé (lowered) frame, using 3.5mm thick steel sheet, instead of the 5mm of the touring model. Being lower and much lighter, with additional strength and stiffness, it had very deep sections at the rear, with large openings through which the axle passed. These prototypes used the 'waisted' or 'gondola' chassis frames designed August 7, 1935; drawings 57S.CH.1 to 10. In plan, the frame sides curved to follow traditional Grand Sport torpedo bodywork, similar to the Type 43. As a result of this characteristic, it had a narrow firewall, and, like the Type 57GR, used a flat radiator similarly lowered by 80mm. However, by December 14, 1935, the chassis design was revised with parallel rear sidemembers; as per drawing 57S.CH.72. Additionally, the radiator became V-shaped, with an even more reduced fitted height – 112mm lower than the Type 57 – accentuating its stylish and sleek sports car image. It appears the V-radiator was designed for the Type 57S45 4.5-litre touring car, published in a leaflet dated November 15, 1935, although, in turn, this was adopted from the aborted 4.9-litre Type 50S Spéciale of 1934. Curiously, four narrow firewalls, later widened with extension pieces, have been identified in existing cars. This tends to suggest that four prototype gondola chassis were originally created before being revised; Bugatti wasted little.

The production version of the 1936 T57S chassis. Note the depth of the frame at the rear, with large apertures through which the axle passes. (Courtesy Bugatti Trust)

1 T57G Overview

modified to accept early T59 compound pumps. Although not as wide, these sumps were little shallower than those on the standard T57, being difficult to identify with confidence when seen side on. Prototype engines were trialled in long T57GR chassis frames, although, with their rear mounting arms cut and ground away to clear the steering box, normal T57 crankcases could have been modified to fit prototype T57S frames.

Nevertheless, a dedicated T57S crankcase and sump, Nos 57S.MOT.1 and 57S.MOT.2 dated October 9, 1935, was designed for the new 'S' frame. This was well conceived to suit wet or dry sump models, having reinforcements, and also facilitated a housing for a supercharger drive. The clever design included short front mounting arms to accept either solid or flexible engine bracket mounts, as well as Bugatti-made casings for De Ram damper internals. The latter was subject to a French patent, number 808.447 in October 1935, and which fed damping forces into the inert mass of the engine. The rear engine mountings used a diaphragm plate, sandwiched between the clutch casing and gearbox adaptor. This innovative design enabled solid or flexible options, too.

Overall, this revision could now be applied universally to future T57, T57S, T57SC, and, eventually, T57C models; 'C' meaning Compresseur (supercharger). At least two prototype T57S engines using the new crankcase have been identified, these being: 226S and 235S for the Paris Salon cars. Barrie Price, in his excellent book *57-The Last French Bugatti*, submits that the new crankcase was used from number 225 onward. Even so, earlier T57 crankcase stock continued to be used up first where practicable, hence some overlap and confusion. This sequence was from the T57 list, and it seems a decision was soon made to initiate a committed T57S register, where some were actually renumbered. As an example, engine 226S became 2S, now in the ex-de Rothschild Atlantic 57374; likewise, engine 235S was renumbered 1S, now in the Atalante 57384. A completely new twin-plate clutch assembly and synchromesh gearbox was also developed for the T57S model, though the latter was abandoned for production models, and only ever used for the T57Gs.

It may be noted that the T57 engine had by now combined some of the attributes of the T59 power unit in order to become the T57S. In doing so, these new realizations were some of the fastest production sports cars of their time, being received with great acclaim and enthusiasm by the motoring

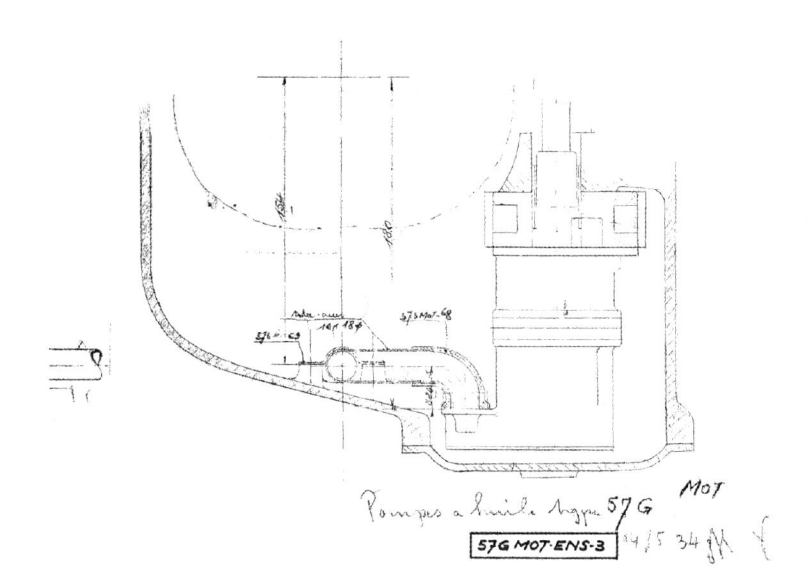

Drawing of the prototype dry-sump arrangement for T57GR, dated May 14, 1934. (Courtesy Bugatti Trust)

Chassis and engine revised

It's not formally recorded why the chassis design changed, although factory minutes report issues with frame precision and an increase in the man-hours necessary to re-work them to specification. Consider, by reducing the complex compound curvature of the original form, the revised design would simplify manufacture, and reduce cost and weight. Intriguingly, the amended drawing details were not finalised until late January 1936; yet, on December 5, 1935, 20 left-hand and 20 right-hand T57S side frames in 3.5mm thick steel were requisitioned from the Brunon-Vallette forge, with a specified delivery rate of four per month. Absurdly, this timeline suggests the frames were ordered before the drawings were actually finished. Surely though, the stimulus for this must have been the 1935 deadline dictated by the new AIACR sports car competition regulations in October. These required that a minimum of 20 of the type had to be built (or laid down) between January 1 and July 1, 1936. Given these particulars and the timetable, it seems unlikely that the first batch order of four frames could have been delivered much before the end of February 1936, yet, all 20 could be adequately supplied and 'laid down' by July 1, 1936.

The Type 57S engine evolved from dry-sump lubricated T57GR progenitors under development since May 1934, using standard T57 four-arm mounted crankcases and special sumps

Bugatti Type 57 Grand Prix – A Celebration

Cigarette card – T57S Torpedo – which states: "Probably the fastest un-supercharged standard car in the world." (Courtesy NMT Collection)

press. A well-known British tobacco firm illustrated the Bugatti T57S Torpedo in its collector's cigarette card series, number 9, declaring: "Probably the fastest un-supercharged standard car in the world." However, the spectacular performance of the Grand Prix racing Tanks developed along side them was something else altogether; now entirely combining the most effective racing features of the Type 59 with the Type 57S. When they first appeared in May 1936, the Bugatti Type 57G Tank sports racing cars were considered one of the most futuristic and exciting machines to have ever emerged from the Molsheim factory.

T57G Tank

The name 'Tank' appears to have been coined by the motoring press because of its all-enveloping bodywork. This recalled an earlier venture into aerodynamics by Bugatti in 1923 for the Type 32 French Grand Prix cars at Tours, also referred to as 'Tanks' by the media. *The Autocar's* European correspondent and Ettore Bugatti's 1948 biographer, William F Bradley, wrote that the idea for the Tank body originated from Ettore Bugatti himself, who urged they should be regarded as Grand Prix racing cars, rather than Touring models. Unique and advanced for their time, the super streamlined shape of the Tanks would not appear out of place a generation later.

The factory initially designated the new project 'Type 57 Grand Prix,' but later abbreviated it to T57G, although it should be emphasised that the cars were always referred to as T57S in promotion and publicity material. This evidently suggests that the appellation 'T57G' noted on drawings, really only refers to the exclusive parts and modifications necessary to convert the T57S to T57 Grand Prix specification. Whilst always officially a Type 57S, fitted with a 3.3-litre, straight-8 cylinder, twin overhead camshaft engine, these new sports racing cars were by now radically different from the large and heavy touring models that had emerged two years before.

The Molsheim project shop began work on the new cars

1   T57G Overview

The T57G Tank prototype on test around Molsheim. Note the plain-sided rear wheel covers, and the absence of rear jacking bars. (Courtesy Bugatti Trust)

more than a year before their formal announcement at the end of May 1936. Yet the Tank's development during 1935 was an exceptionally well-guarded secret, where unusually, they are never specifically mentioned in the monthly factory reports. In retrospective analysis, the T57G engine's progress began from those early 1934 T57GR concepts linking one or two elements of the T59 and T57 power units; eventually amalgamating them totally; all executed with very limited material resource and a closely constrained budget. In addition, I believe a key factor to consider in the evolution of the T57G lies in the systematic and technical transformation of the Grand Prix T59 engine during the period 1934 to 1937. These details are discussed in a later chapter.

Nevertheless, despite the secrecy, a prototype 'Tank' was eventually observed during road testing on the highways around the factory, so the 'cat was out the bag,' and its existence was formally notified to the French motoring press. Whilst dining in Paris with *L'Auto* journalist Maurice Henry, Bugatti's acclaimed racing driver-cum-sales director Robert Benoist, acknowledged:

"Yes, it's true, we are building four cars of the current 57S model, and you will see three of them at the Grand Prix next month."

Accordingly, a notice was published in the May 25 edition of that journal. However, within a few weeks, one of the Tanks surfaced for testing at the Montlhéry Autodrome creating a great deal of interest and excitement.

2

1936 Testing at Montlhéry

THE LINAS-MONTLHÉRY AUTODROME and road circuit is positioned on the Plateau St Eutrope, 25km (15.5 miles) south of Paris, close to the villages of Montlhéry and Linas. The track was opened in 1925 to be the permanent home of the Automobile Club de France (ACF), where, with a circuit distance of 12.5km (7.8 miles), it utilised a large segment of the banked autodrome as well as very long straights that ran out through serene hills and forests. At weekends this peaceful

Front aspect of the prototype Tank. Note the high tyre cooling slot position, and the shape of the bonnet lip.
(Courtesy Bugatti Trust)

20

2 1936 Testing at Montlhéry

Rear view of the prototype Tank. Note the single, central fuel filler cap, and the absence of jacking bars and rear cooling slots. (Courtesy Bugatti Trust)

countryside was disturbed by the ferocious snarl of high-performance motorcars as they wound their way around the circuit. Jean Bugatti hired the track from mid-day Monday 8 until Tuesday June 9 in order to carry out extensive functional and performance tests on one of his streamlined T57G Tank prototypes. Only a few trusted members of the motoring press were invited as observers. Just three weeks away, the French Grand Prix was only the second race of the season to be run under the brand-new ACF sports car rules. It was essential that the new T57G streamliner should take advantage of its aerodynamics in the high-speed sections of this circuit, especially given its greater overall weight and smaller capacity engine in comparison to most of its rivals.

Rehearsal
Driven in rank by Robert Benoist, William Grover-Williams, Pierre Veyron and Baron Philippe de Rothschild, they rehearsed the 1000km (about 620mile) ACF race distance at blistering grand prix speeds, before impudently adding a further 50km (about 30mile) to it. Pit stop times, fuel consumption, brake and tyre wear were all extensively explored and analysed, and it was clear that the new car ran superbly. Its amazing performance was verified with a fastest lap of 134.33km/h (just under 84mph). During the afternoon of the Tuesday, Veyron ran the car around the Autodrome bowl for an hour, during which time he travelled 203km (almost 127 miles) at an average speed of 208.5km/h (130mph). Along the short straight sections he exceeded 215km/h (135mph). Then, after bringing the car into the pits, Benoist again took over the wheel and positively flaunted the T57G's extraordinary performance by resuming this same gruelling pace for a further 30min. The new car had been superbly prepared and ran like a dream, which clearly revealed to its rivals in the forthcoming ACF that the Bugatti Tanks would be formidable opponents.

21

Bugatti Type 57 Grand Prix – A Celebration

The prototype Tank at Montlhéry during test on June 8-9, 1936. Note the plain-sided rear wheel covers, and the absence of rear jacking bars. (Courtesy Bugatti Trust)

Some important advantages were noted by the project team during this severe trial, recognising that some essential modifications would need to be carried out, too. They found the streamlined body clearly beneficial to the car's top speed and fuel consumption, which suggested a potential for unique race strategies; in particular that the car could travel much further before refuelling. Nonetheless, they also discovered that these same benefits adversely affected the performance of the brakes. The higher speeds, with reduced air resistance under retardation, meant that the brakes needed to work much harder to slow the car into corners, which, in turn, generated far more heat. What's more, this energy was not as easily dissipated under the fully enclosed bodywork as it might be with an open-wheeled car, so heat was building up. This culminated in the brakes overheating and fading, as well as heat-expanding the hubs, making removal of the rear wheels extremely difficult. Here, the motoring press noted mechanics furiously hammering off the heat-seized hub nuts during pit stops. These issues aside, this futuristic-looking car thrilled the media and spectators with its exciting and fashionable 'half-airship' profile, as well as its stunning and clearly reliable performance. Whilst Bugatti's supporters positively salivated over the new sports car, his critics scoffed, evoking the streamlined Type 32 Tanks trialled at Tours in 1923, never to be seen again.

A model for future sports cars

Back in 1923, the science of aerodynamics was fairly new, and often misunderstood. For some, it was equated with 'dark arts' that frequently appeared more dangerous than beneficial. The effect of frontal area on streamlining, or 'windage' (sic), was well understood from early flying machine development, whereas drag remained less so. Dubbed 'Tanks' by the press, observers at Tours noted that the experimental Type 32 racing cars raised far less dust than their competitors. In modern comprehension, this suggests an extremely low drag coefficient. Yet, even then, these cars appear to have suffered major brake overheating problems, now understood to be as a direct result of streamlining with fully enclosed bodywork. Two of the cars dramatically lost control and left the road at the end of a major fast straight, injuring several spectators in the process. An intolerant and

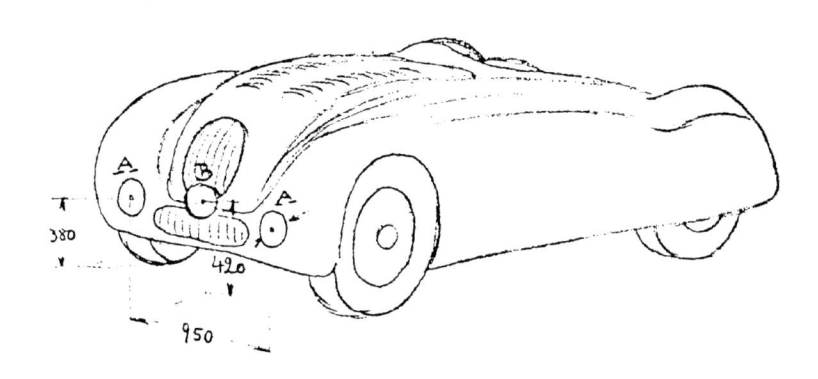

2 1936 Testing at Montlhéry

amongst Italian sports car makers. Furthermore, it memorably enthused Britain's William Lyons, who produced Jaguar cars. The Tank's outline became an Art Deco icon of recognised aerodynamic efficiency, and famously inspired Sir Nigel Gresley in his design of the 4-6-2 Pacific steam locomotives; even its two-tone colour 'flash.' On July 3, 1938, LNER Class 4468 'Mallard' became the World Speed Record holder for steam locomotives at 202.58km/h (125.88mph).

Streamlined body

As related earlier, WF Bradley wrote that the idea for the 'Tank' body originated from Ettore Bugatti himself. Conversely, documents at The Bugatti Trust show the bodywork was primarily drafted by the hand of Antonio Pichetto; a highly talented designer who joined the company in November 1931. The streamliner's prescribed coachwork drawing, number 1078, is dated January 10, 1936, and was finalised by bodywork department leader Joseph Walter. However, the T57G sports racing car clearly reveals the influence of both Ettore Bugatti and his son Jean in its detail. Particularly notable is a subtle souvenir of the classic Grand Prix Bugatti outline, defined in the form of raised panel-work, thereafter stylised with Jean's distinctive 'Arrowhead' flash element, set in two-tone light and dark blue paint. Remarkably, this prominent raised panel-work might also be seen to precisely follow the contours of the 'gondola' chassis in plan, revealing its simultaneous derivation.

Careful consideration was made to achieve smooth, streamlined bodywork on all surfaces, including a full-length under-shield. The rear wheels were faired in, as were the headlamps, which reinforced the car's aura as a futuristic super sports car. Even the spare wheel was stowed away neatly inside the bodywork, vertically next to the passenger's seat and sleekly panelled over. In this pristine condition, it may be noted from the photos taken on June 8 and 9, that the rear wheel covers are smooth, without louvres, and there are not yet rear quick-lift jacking bars or leather bonnet straps either; just standard retaining clips. The prototype also featured a single fuel-filler cap, and lacked a driver's access door. Later, however, the practicalities of competition would soon disfigure Antonio Pichetto's vision of aerodynamic perfection, imposing a number of untidy, yet indispensable modifications.

Tank described

The lightweight, wafer-thin, aluminium alloy bodyshell was

Antonio Pitchetto's sketch of the Type 57G Tank. (Courtesy Bugatti Trust)

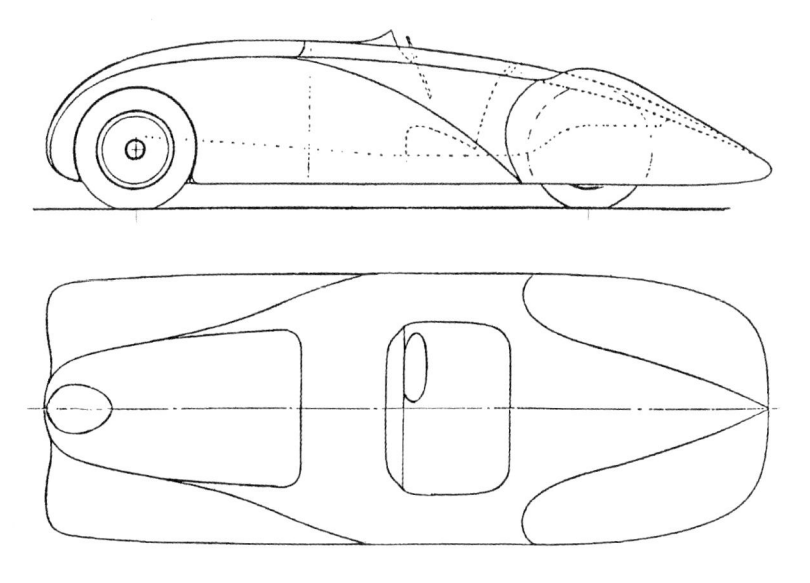

Coachwork drawing of the Tank, Design 1078. (Courtesy Bugatti Trust)

very unforgiving press termed the new T57G cars 'Tanks' as well, so 'Tanks' they have remained.

Despite the harsh criticism, *Motor Sport* magazine recognised something rather superior and predicted "A model for future sports cars?" This prophecy was, of course, correct. The T57G bodywork was so advanced for the time it influenced a whole generation of designers, where this distinctive profile endured as a style trend for more than 20 years, especially

Bugatti Type 57 Grand Prix – A Celebration

mainly secured to the chassis frame by means of a substantial crescent-shaped bulkhead, constructed between the engine compartment and driver. In common with usual Bugatti practice, such robust structures took most of the bodywork inertia forces, although panels and brackets either side of the engine and behind the driver's seat also directed loads into the chassis. Leather cushioning was stitched around the rim of a simple cockpit, exposing a minimal instrument panel that presented a single large tachometer to the right of the steering column, with small-diameter oil and fuel gauges to the left. At this time, a 100-litre (22-gallon) fuel tank was arranged behind the rear axle, providing a range of 400km (250 miles), then fitted with a single, centrally located filler cap just forward of the rear spring crossbeam. A 25-litre (5.5-gallon) dry sump oil tank was secured to the left-hand chassis frame. Its filler cap was concealed behind a hinged flap on the upper edge of the scuttle. The oil tank was counterpoised with an electric battery mounted on the outside of the right-hand frame, just below the driver's seat. An aircraft type, 'elephant's ear' oil cooler stack, was mounted between the chassis rails, below and just in front of a uniquely-designed T57G radiator. A long rectangular alloy tube was arranged from the lower radiator opening to duct cold air to the carburettor. The large bonnet, with 242 louvres set in six rows, opened from the front like a gaping alligator, which at that time had to be raised just to obtain access to the radiator cap.

The chassis was arranged with a wheelbase of 2.98m, although the precise detail of the frame is subject to a number of conflicting opinions. These will be discussed in more detail later, although briefly, the chassis of this prototype has been contended to be either a shortened T57 touring frame, or one of two possible versions of the T57S surbaissé. The car's suspension used T57S springs, but with leaves reduced in number, and specially stiffened, in conjunction with T59 racing car components; in particular, their complicated and exotically expensive De Ram hydraulic-friction dampers. The front axle was standard T57S with a track of 1.35m; hollow-forged for lightness and split in the centre. This was prepared with Grand Prix T59 stub axles and hubs. The unique 19-inch diameter, radial-spoke wire wheels with 360mm diameter brakes and deeply-finned 450mm drums were also directly from the Grand Prix T59. These were shod with Dunlop 28 x 5.50in racing tyres on the front and 28 x 6.00in at the rear.

The T57G engine may be considered to be a Grand Prix

Model of the prototype Tank: front view.
(Courtesy NMT Collection)

Model of the prototype Tank: rear view.
(Courtesy NMT Collection)

version of the standard T57S, using a specially-modified cylinder block and lightened crankshaft, as well as T57S pistons and connecting rods with adjusted clearances. It also used specially-machined T57 camshafts, ground with lift profiles similar to those of the T59, operating 45mm diameter valves. The cams were driven using the narrow and lighter gearwheels from the T59. The engine was equipped with a fabricated exhaust manifold that swept back in two bunches of four into one. Original Froude dynamometer test results show good low-end torque with flexibility, for example, recording 107bhp at 3000rpm, ranging in uniform increments to 166bhp at 5250rpm. Another test result in March 1936, gave 183bhp at 5600rpm. A year earlier, the high-efficiency Harry Ricardo experimental sleeve valve engine gave a best output of 54bhp per litre at 5000rpm, showing that the Bugatti T57G was surprisingly comparable in power output, even if not as fuel-efficient. The power was transmitted through a T57S twin-plate dry clutch to a specially-modified T57S gearbox. This was arranged with a close-ratio gear set and synchronising cone clutches on second, third and top, enabling fast changes up and down. The propeller shaft universal and flexible joints were essentially as specified for the T59. The rear axle used T57 final drive ratios, later set in a lightweight reinforced alloy casing, but employed higher specification steel half-shafts and special T57S axle-tube trumpets modified to accept T59 hubs, brake components and wheels. Available final drive ratios ranged most of the T57, T57GR and T57S fractions: 12:54-4.5:1, 11:46-4.18:1, 12:50-4.16:1, 12:47-3.9:1, 12:44-3.67:1 and 14:42-3.00:1.

Types 57S & 59 combined

Whilst the T57G Tank was different compared to the T57 Touring model, it would be wrong to suggest that its chassis and power train were all that dissimilar to the T57S sports car. The Type 57G was based upon existing elements, but either strengthened or lightened as required, or otherwise adapted to suit racing components from, what was basically by then, the obsolete Grand Prix Type 59 racing car, whose inspiration, lineage and succession always lay in the original Type 57.

As previously mentioned, the AIACR governing body's new sports car regulations required that at least 20 similar cars must have been manufactured, or laid down, before July 1, 1936, but given that only six T57S were actually made by that time, the rules seem to have been liberally interpreted. However, the letter to the Brunon-Vallette forge in December 1935, ordering 20 left-hand and 20 right-hand frames, was probably deemed by the AIACR as satisfactory evidence of having been 'laid down.' Here, the nautical equivalence with laying down the keel of a ship seems to equate with part-assembled bare chassis frames with front and rear crossmembers. The bare chassis undoubtedly represented one of the less-expensive components of the car.

Escalating industrial unrest

WF Bradley wrote that Ettore Bugatti had always regarded himself to be a master craftsman who employed skilled artisan assistants. At *Automobiles Bugatti*, managers did not have formal titles as such. Even Jean Bugatti, during his apprenticeship from the age of 12, was moulded to this mind-set. His sister, L'Ébé, wrote that, "Jean's technical and practical education was undertaken at the factory, growing at the rhythm of the worker's labour, and he knew all their trades." During this period, Jean was treated just as any other apprentice or worker. By tradition, the Master Craftsman always wore a bowler hat, which was an image Ettore Bugatti frequently adopted. Accordingly, there was an unspoken bond of mutual respect and harmony that existed within the workplace. This was totally different to the man-management relationship utilised by dedicated industrialists and their relatively less-skilled, mass-production methods. These directors, of course, would have worn a more authoritarian top hat.

Nonetheless, as Master Craftsman and Le Patron, Ettore Bugatti conducted himself in an extremely conspicuous manner, reminiscent of a feudal overlord. Several visiting customers to Molsheim recalled their impression that, "in this beautiful part of Alsace, they had discovered a small principality of a 'seigneur' of the Italian Renaissance; displaced to the industrial age." Ettore Bugatti was usually seen around the factory in boots, jodhpurs, riding jacket, bowler hat and gloves; often on horseback; a persona no-doubt cultivated in his youth, circa 1901, whilst under the patronage of the Counts Gulinelli, near Ferrara. Yet, like the celebrated horseshoe radiator, this was a façade, an element of Bugatti marketing; Le Pur Sang des Automobiles; comparing his cars to equine thoroughbreds. Nevertheless, such exhibitionism, real or contrived, was not helpful during the socio-economic revolution that swept through 1930s France.

Creeping discontent

Lowered moral standards and political hoaxes were endemic during the Depression episode that affected the whole of the country. Several manufacturers were unfairly accused of taking advantage of the level of unemployment in order to exploit workers. Such callousness led to resentment and, by 1936, culminated in escalating industrial unrest, strikes and serious antisocial conduct within the motor industry. Here, effigies of a number of industrialists, amongst them leading car makers, were dragged through the streets of Paris before being publicly burned. Unrest grew to the point where even the annual Le Mans endurance race, to be held on June 13 and 14, was postponed, before being cancelled altogether. Despite EB's generally benevolent rapport with his skilled craftsmen, this creeping discontent eventually affected Automobiles Bugatti.

Recalling 1932, when Ettore Bugatti was developing the railcar project, many of his automobile employees had been reassigned to the railcar shop instead of being laid off due to the slump in the car market. It seems some were transferred under duress and resentfully, even though it was obvious that it was the only work available to them at the time. Besides, whilst Bugatti appears to have treated his staff with compassion and kindness in contrast to the norm of the time, as the railcar project expanded, around 150 extra skilled workers were taken on. Amongst these were militants, dedicated to pressing changes in employees' rights and working conditions. Subsequently, the factory became ever more industrialised, and then, in 1936, the People's Front won national elections. This situation was intensified by the ever busy, yet often absent, EB in his Paris design office. Too long away from Molsheim, he had begun to lose touch with his workforce, and then to the genuine consternation of an unusually insentient Ettore Bugatti, the fragile situation suddenly blew up in his face.

Factory strike and exile

On Wednesday, June 17, just a week after the successful T57G trials at Montlhéry, Bugatti's workforce went on strike and occupied the Molsheim Works; even the red flag was raised. This was bad enough in itself, but on Saturday, June 20, whilst in Paris, Ettore Bugatti was totally aghast to discover he had been locked out of his own factory. The incident came as a considerable shock; compounded by Jean becoming seriously ill and hospitalised with peritonitis during this period. Clearly distracted by personal circumstance, it was a situation he had sincerely misjudged, but his almost theatrical reaction to it was to feel utterly betrayed by his workforce. In reality of course, it was nothing more than an exceptionally radical process that was engulfing the whole of a, now socialist-governed, France. However, with his extremely conservative beliefs, EB took it personally, perceiving it as an affront to his dignity. It affected him more deeply than most of us could comprehend in this modern age of employment rights by law. In Ettore Bugatti's reasoning, the subjects of his little Molsheim fiefdom, over whom he had ruled for so many years, had essentially deposed him.

Almost immediately afterwards, Ettore publicly announced that he would be leaving Molsheim, his Works, and his home. The place that had so many successful and happy memories for him was now blemished, and would never be the same again. He then resolutely established himself in offices near his Paris showrooms on Avenue Montaigne in a self-imposed exile, scarcely ever visiting the factory afterwards. As Bradley put it, "Molsheim, once the pride of his life, had become an open sore." Jean, of course, when he recovered, was more than competent to take on the job of running the factory, for he was nurtured for the task, being experienced and highly proficient in administration, as well as suave in man-management and negotiation. Yet, the strike clearly affected him deeply, too. L'Ébé wrote that a sparkle noticeably left him, and afterwards he always treated his employees far more formally, including his previously close circle of working colleagues in the design office. An era had ended.

Paris facilities

Bizarrely, during the June 20, 1936 strike and heavily picketed lockout at the Works in Molsheim, dynamometer records suggest 'business as usual.' The archives show that Type 57G engines 1, 2, 3 and 4 were tested respectively on June 21, 22, 23 and 24. On the other hand, consider that the factory in Molsheim was not the absolute heart of Bugatti operations. Here, for cars entered at both Montlhéry and Marne, it was customary that the racing team was based in the Paris area, just 25km (15.5 miles) north of l'Autodrome and 130km (82mile) west of Reims. In 1937 and 1939, Paris was also the base from which the Bugatti Le Mans cars departed, driving the 190km (120 miles) southwest by road. Since the Tanks were being tested at Montlhéry on June 8 and 9 in preparation for the ACF on the 28, it is entirely rational to expect the Tanks to remain in

2 1936 Testing at Montlhéry

the Paris area during this whole period; turbulent or otherwise.

The Paris Bugatti showrooms at 46 Avenue Montaigne had their own local well-equipped garage facilities in Avenue Carnot, as well as experimental workshops at Rue du Débarcadière, where T50B engines were under development and test from early 1936 onwards. Many of Bugatti's customers lived around the capital, where it appears Paris resources included engine test-bed facilities and even a rolling-road dynamometer. Consequently, these documented tests must have been carried out in Paris, rather than at Molsheim, 410km (260 miles) away. Fuel shortages and strikes were challenging at this time, too, but Bugatti used specialised fuel blends for racing, so would have had his own stocks, storage facilities and tanker support. As a result of the social disturbances throughout France, it's entirely feasible that Bugatti's Chateau d'Ermenonville estate, near Senlis, north of Paris, was used to secrete his racing fuels in mobile tankers, just as he concealed the prototype P100 aircraft, T41 Royale Coupé and several horse carriages from the Germans during World War II. Nonetheless, the important ACF competition was approaching, and Automobiles Bugatti knew that race success was crucial to generating sales of the Type 57S in the depressed market.

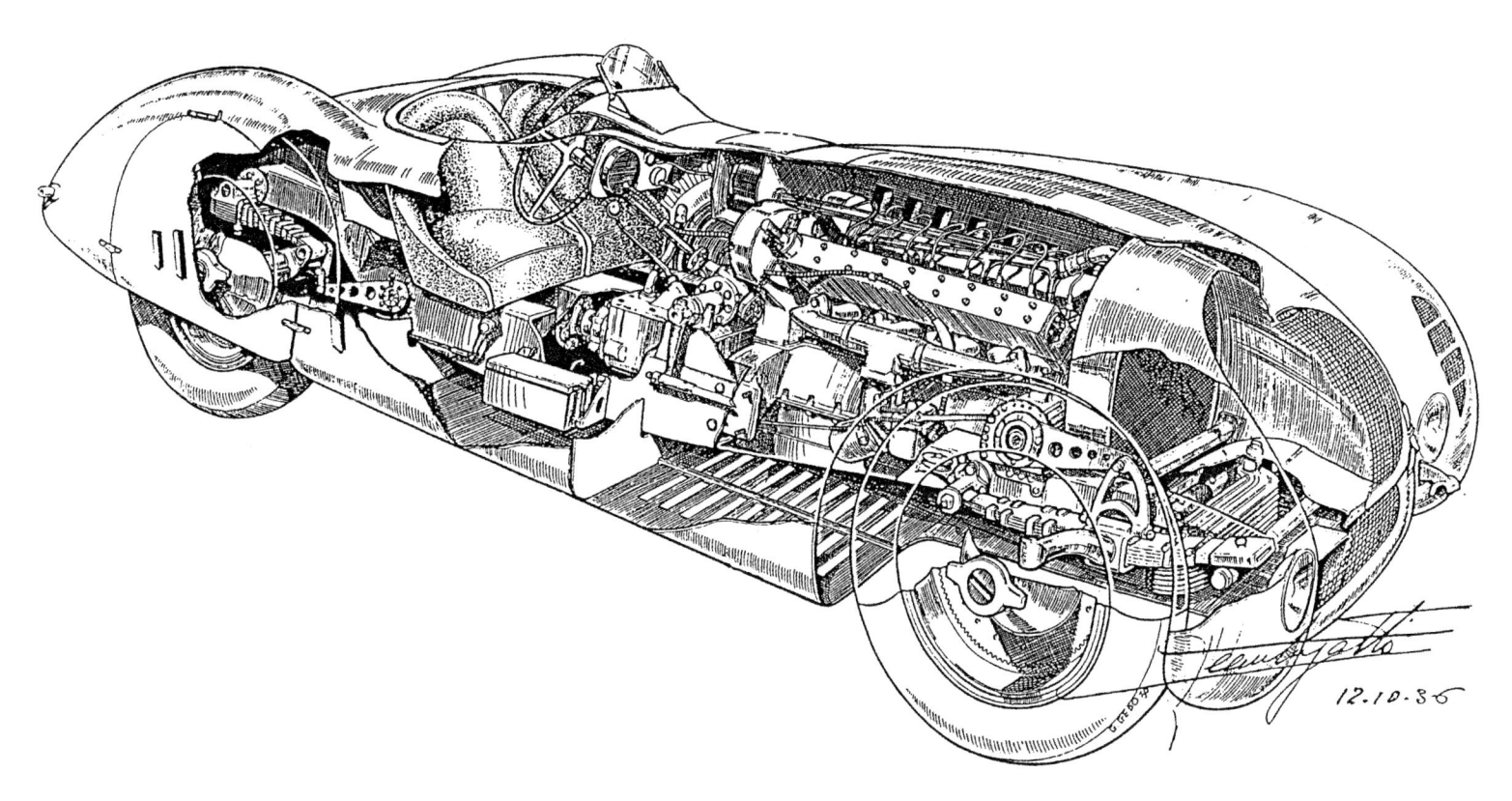

Copy of the artwork by G Gedo, dated and signed by Jean Bugatti 12.10.36, originally published in *Le Auto* and *Speed* issues of September 1936. (Courtesy Bugatti Trust)

3

1936 Grand Prix de l'ACF

AS PREDICTED BY BENOIST, three Tanks appeared in public at Montlhéry on Saturday, June 27, 1936, for practice prior to Sunday's Grand Prix de l'ACF. That same day, Henri Pracht, Bugatti's accountant, formally allocated three chassis Nos: 57454, 57455 and 57456 respectively for insurance purposes. Conversely, however, the Race Committee allocated four places in the pits, with 'Bugatti 88,' 'Bugatti 86,' 'Bugatti 84,' and 'Bugatti 82' race numbers on the board above the pit counter. Such provision clearly indicates the three Tanks as promised – plus a spare car, yet oddly, car number 88 was not seen, and historians have never accepted the existence of the fourth car referred to in the *L'Auto* notice in May. Additionally, as discussed, dynamometer records show four T57G engines tested prior to the race, each yielding around 157bhp at 5000rpm.

Nonetheless, under the new sports car formula, the race would run 80 laps of the extended circuit, and the winner would receive a purse of 60,000f (£857). In car number 82 the drive was shared by Robert Benoist and Philippe de Rothschild; car number 84 by Jean-Pierre Wimille and Raymond Sommer, with car number 86 driven by Pierre Veyron and Willy Grover-Williams. As a guide to income, the ambitious and talented junior driver Wimille was given a generous new contract for 1936, dated October 21, 1935. Although not signed until November 7, he would be paid 4000f (£57) per month, plus 20% of the purse won by the Bugatti Team. As a result, in this race alone, he had an incentive to earn three months' salary for a win.

Practice

Impressively, during Saturday practice, Benoist was able to achieve the fastest lap in a time of 5min 41sec, three seconds faster than Dreyfus' Talbot. Veyron worked just as hard for his place, too, although the apparently nonchalant Wimille seemed reluctant to stress his T57G. In the final line-up of 37 cars, the Bugattis were arranged one, four and 14 on the starting grid. Interestingly, a small, hand-written note found amongst factory Test House records details the fuel composition used for this race: Essence 64%, Benzole 18%, Alcohol 18%. Derived from coal, Benzole blends well, has high carbon content, and increases the highest useful compression ratio (HUCR). As alcohol contains oxygen, the fusion confers to formulate a high-calorific 80 Octane-blend. Bugatti also added a small proportion of castor oil as an upper engine lubricant.

An observation: the six Bugatti drivers that day were paired up in rank, dressed in two shades of overalls. This was

Opposite top: Practice day at Montlhéry, June 27. Robert Benoist gestures in car number 82 as he passes Pierre Veyron's car in the foreground. (Courtesy Bugatti Trust)

Oppsite: Cockpit of the Veyron/Grover-Williams car, number 86. The dashboard is very basic at this time. (Courtesy Bugatti Trust)

Far right: Illustration based on the same photograph, better showing the spare wheel stowage position. (Courtesy NMT Collection)

3   1936 Grand Prix de l'ACF

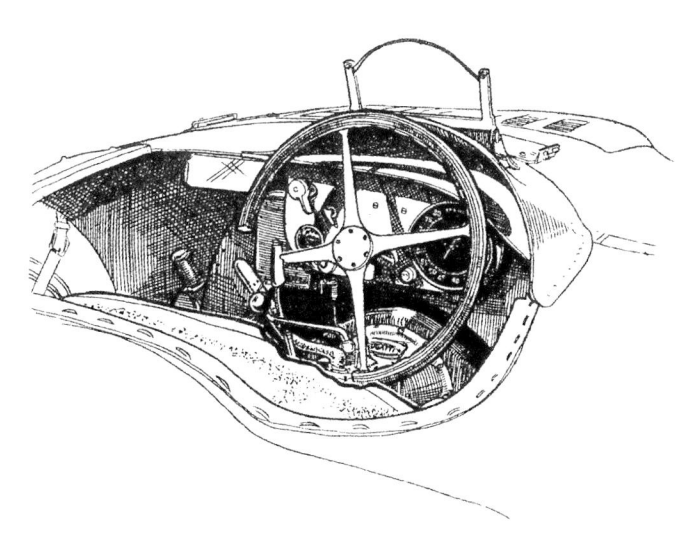

Bugatti Type 57 Grand Prix – A Celebration

The Wimille car, race number 84, warmed up and ready to race. (Courtesy Bugatti Trust)

probably in order to help officials and reviewers identify them during the race as drivers changed places. In car 82, Benoist wore white overalls, and his partner in the car, de Rothschild, wore brown (or a darker shade than white, in black and white photos). In car 84, Sommer wore white, Wimille wore brown, and in car 86, Veyron wore white, Grover-Williams brown.

Although similar to look at, the sharp-eyed will notice slight variations between each car, especially around the bonnet lip and the position of their respective retaining clips and straps, as well as the more obvious brake-cooling air intakes on the front wings. There were several changes visible to all three cars in comparison with the prototype seen three weeks earlier; development had continued right up to the last minute. Long ventilator shutters were now fitted on both sides of the body, just behind the engine firewall, along with two small flaps arranged on the top of the bodywork on each side of

3　1936 Grand Prix de l'ACF

The Veyron/Grover-Williams car, number 86, brought out for pre-race warm-up. (Courtesy Bugatti Trust)

the scuttle. Five louvres were also cut into the rear wheel covers, with lozenge-shaped exit holes in the back of the wheelarches to help cool the wheels and brakes. Additionally, at the rear of the car, the fuel tank capacity was increased to 150 litres (33 gallons), and now had twin filler caps higher up to speed replenishment. This modification appears to have been achieved by attaching an additional 50-litre tank on top of the 100-litre original. Also, an enlarged row of holes at the rear took advantage of air pressure differences to assist with the venting of engine exhaust fumes that could be drawn back into the body and build up. Moreover, quick-lift jacking points at the rear of the car were provided in the form of a wide, light-alloy tubular beam that protruded through both sides of the bodywork behind the rear wheels, secured by brackets fixed to the chassis frame. Two tiny lamps were mounted symmetrically on the tail that could illuminate the rear race

Bugatti Type 57 Grand Prix – *A Celebration*

number. In addition, small slots were cut into the bonnet to allow the retention of leather straps to augment the original retaining spring clips for added security. A token, full-width folding windscreen was added in order to comply with ACF competition regulations.

The race

For the brand new sports car formula, race day weather faired well with brilliant clear-blue skies and delightful flaming June sunshine, yet, the reduced public attendance for the new Grand Prix was a disappointment for the ACF Committee. Nevertheless, the organizers had clearly made a consummate effort to promote a good attendance of 24 French and 13 other-nation challengers under the new AIACR regulations. These included the three Bugatti Tanks, nine Delahaye T135CSs, four Talbot T150Cs, three BMW 328s and ten British cars; one of them a big Lagonda. Sympathetically, the ACF organisers even arranged a sports car 'run-start' for the benefit of those entrants who had missed out in the cancelled 24-Hour Le Mans race.

The cars got away at 10.00am with a run-start from the centre of the road opposite the pit counters. René Dreyfus took the lead immediately in his Talbot, with Benoist's car number 82 in hot pursuit, whilst Wimille's car, number 84, coolly followed around in eleventh place, at least until the end of the first lap. However, by the end of the third, Benoist held a 15-second lead over Dreyfus, and Wimille, now warmed up, quickly advanced into third place, leaving Veyron, number 86, in fifth. Wimille took the lead two laps later when Benoist made the pits for a necessary spark-plug change, his engine barking loudly. By the tenth lap, Wimille was half a minute ahead of Brunet's Delahaye, with Veyron's 57G chasing him in third place.

The major tactical advantage the Tanks had over their rivals was their streamlining, which essentially enabled them to cover a greater distance for the same amount of fuel. On the 24th lap, the Delahayes went in to replenish, allowing the Bugattis to maintain first, second and third places, although this position changed when they came in for their own pitstop. Refuelling went very quickly, but, being such a hot day, the heat under the Tanks' enclosed bodywork had not easily dispersed. The Bugatti mechanics had a repetition of overheating brakes and hub nuts, and were observed struggling hard to remove the rear wheels before changing overcooked brake shoes.

Furthermore, as a direct result of high under-bonnet temperatures, this grand effort was immediately followed by extreme difficulty in re-starting the engines due to vapour-locks as fuel boiled in the feed lines. The Bugatti drivers were seen sluicing water about under the bonnet in order to help cool down their fuel lines and engine compartments. Frustratingly for the Bugatti team, most of the previous advantage was lost, and when Grover-Williams pitted, his car, too, was suffering with overheated brakes. Mercifully, these problems were not exclusive to the Bugatti pit, for, with the fast straights, slow corners, and the glorious summer heat of that day, practically every race entrant was suffering some form of temperature problem or heat-related brake difficulty. Nevertheless, reporters quickly detected the poorly-prepared Bugatti pit management. In reality, pit management was almost non-existent, because Jean Bugatti remained hospitalised, and Ettore was at his bedside. Jean was critically ill, suffering from peritonitis, reportedly due to acute appendicitis.

By the time the Bugattis re-joined the race the Delahayes were holding the first four places. Now having swapped drivers, Sommer gradually regained his position, so that by lap 50, Tank number 84 had taken the lead. Benoist was also working his car hard, breaking the circuit record on lap 52 and gaining thirteenth place before refuelling. This pitstop took five excruciating minutes for brake shoe changes, though; again, because of seized hub nuts. Sommer broke Benoist's circuit record just two laps later, before coming into the pits to refuel for the second and final time. Switching drivers again, Wimille quickly got back out on the circuit in just 4min 41sec, now just one lap behind the leader. He then consistently opened up the pace round after round, passing car after car, until by lap 68 he finally overtook the fastest Delahaye and was back in the lead. Wimille continued this extraordinary progress so that by lap 80, the race officials formally announced that the car had completed the 1000km (620-mile) regulation distance, so at last his car was able to descend the high eastern banking to win the race. It was extremely unfortunate that this crucial success had to be missed by the Bugatti family as a result of Jean's illness.

Great success

Jean-Pierre Wimille and Raymond Sommer's car, number 84, had averaged an incredible speed of 125.6km/h (78mph). Car number 86, driven by Veyron and Williams was sixth, having

3   1936 Grand Prix de l'ACF

The ACF began with a Le Mans start from the edge of the Autodrome apron, with the Benoist/de Rothschild car in pole position. (Courtesy Bugatti Trust)

Wimille leaps into his car, number 84, a second behind Léoz, having been delayed by a confused start countdown. (Courtesy Bugatti Trust)

Bugatti Type 57 Grand Prix – A Celebration

The people of France immediately fell in love with the victorious 'Tanks,' where enterprising manufacturers around Paris quickly began replicating the looks of the cars as popular children's toys. They included surprisingly durable solid replicas made from a humble mixture of plaster of Paris and grey flour, cast in simple open rubber moulds and sold very cheaply from trays in their thousands; very few survive today. Clockwork toys of the cars were also made from tinplate as well as celluloid. The Tanks' great success and fame spread throughout the country, and undoubtedly had a significant impact on France by providing the populace with a common focal point of national pride and optimism. We now recognize this as 'feel good factor.' This was especially important at this time when so many French people were still terribly divided by the political and social instability caused by the Depression.

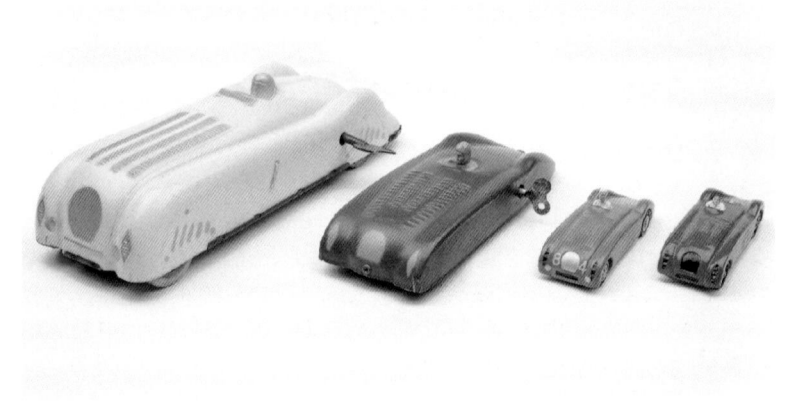

Robert Benoist slops water around under the bonnet, cooling the engine compartment and fuel lines in order to reduce vapour locks. (Courtesy Bugatti Trust)

covered 78 laps of the circuit, and car number 82, driven by Robert Benoist and Philippe de Rothschild finished thirteenth with 73 laps. After four years of Grand Prix pessimism the win was a great triumph for France, and the extraordinary performance of the Tanks had plainly silenced Bugatti's critics. The ACF Committee must have been relieved, for it had been completely justified in its decision to promote a Sports Car Grand Prix formula. Gratifyingly, the *Autocar* wrote of the new challenge: "It was all that a race should be."

Toy Bugatti T57Gs, left to right: Polichinelle, JRD, JRD and CIJ copy by Jean Pastre Cars. (Courtesy NMT Collection – photo by D Roberts)

VISIT VELOCE ON THE WEB – WWW.VELOCE.CO.UK
All current books • New book news • Special offers • Gift vouchers • Forum

1936 Grand Prix de la Marne

FOLLOWING THE INCREDIBLE SUCCESS of the Tanks in the ACF, the cars remained at Montlhéry overnight for technical endorsement, so the triumphant Bugatti team restrained its celebrations. Besides, Jean had previously hired the superb facilities of l'Autodrome for car preparation prior to the Grand Prix de la Marne at Reims, for which the team would be signing-in a few days later. By noon, Monday, June 29, Robert Aumaître's small, hard-working team of mechanics had serviced the cars and changed the rear axle ratios to suit the ultra-fast and triangular Circuit de Gueux. Photographs taken that day show the famous line-up of cars, and illustrate in detail that, although very similar to look at, each has unique identifying features when viewed from the front. The most obvious is that one car has high tyre-cooling air intakes in the front wings, whereas the other two have low. There are also detail differences in the shape of their respective bonnet lip edges and retainers, as well as the two-tone flash. Rear brake overheating had created significant issues for Bugatti at Montlhéry, so soon there would be a further bodywork alteration to help deal with this.

It was early afternoon by the time the mechanics finished preparations. The first driver to take his car around the oval banked circuit was Bugatti's senior, Robert Benoist, who was particularly keen to make up for his relatively inferior performance the day before. In an amazing reinstatement, he completed 130km (81 miles) around the concrete bowl at an average speed of 211km/h (132mph) where, without doubt, this was an unofficial Class 'C' (5-litre) World Record. If formally recognised, it would have invalidated that set in 1929 by Kay Don in his 4-litre Sunbeam. After a brief stop for fine-tuning, Benoist went out a second time, eager to set an even faster single lap, whereupon on the third circuit he broke the Montlhéry record yet again, with a remarkable speed of 223.74km/h (138.94mph). Pierre Veyron took the next nine laps around the Autodrome, achieving a best lap speed of 219.66km/h (136.41mph). Co-ACF winner Raymond Sommer followed, but even before he had warmed the engine, a sudden cloudburst forced him warily back through the heavy downpour to the rapidly flooding pit counter, tremendously disappointed. Nonetheless, the motoring world was completely overawed by the success of the Tanks, which had far exceeded the usual standard of sports car performance for the period.

Given that the T57G had essentially evolved from a T57 touring model, these performance figures were outstanding for a normally-aspirated, 3.3-litre sports car. Without doubt, the Bugatti Tank was exhibiting all of the 'ultimate' super sports car traits that Jean Bugatti had predicted fifteen months earlier, and its display of speed with reliability must have been a fantastic publicity exercise for the new Type 57S model. However, it is quite reasonable to suggest that the car's superbly efficient streamlined body was primarily responsible for this feat. Furthermore, the streamlined Tanks' overwhelming domination on the track must have been extremely troubling for Bugatti's challengers, so very close to the Marne Grand Prix itself. The astonishing achievement of the new Bugatti super sports cars even affected the usually elaborate remarks of Maurice Henry of *L'Auto*, for he wrote quite modestly, "It was an unprecedented display."

Bugatti Type 57 Grand Prix – A Celebration

Three Tanks line up at Montlhéry on June 29, 1936; the day after the ACF. Note the differences in bonnet lip shape and their retainers. (Courtesy Bugatti Trust)

The race

Three Tanks were entered for the ninth Marne Grand Prix at Reims, run on Sunday July 5, 1936, to cover 51 laps and a distance of 400km (248 miles). Wimille drove car number 12, Benoist number 14 and Veyron number 44. Just west of Reims, the ultra-fast 7.8km (4.85-mile) triangular track ran through gently rolling countryside, in effect consisting of three, long, high-speed straights linked by three bends. Whilst being one of the fastest great race circuits in the world, it spanned three otherwise unremarkable two-car width public roads; Route Nationale 31, the CD27, and CD26, where some sections were perilously narrow in places for overtaking at racing speeds. There were 22 starters altogether, but competing against the Tanks in the 3- to 5-litre class were ten Delahayes, three Talbots and a Lagonda. Friday's technical scrutiny was notable for its enforced regulation to weigh-in the cars. Rain had been very heavy all-day Friday, so nobody got out for a test-run. This meant that Saturday's dry-road practice became congested,

4   1936 Grand Prix de la Marne

A fine view of Wimille's Tank. Note the simple dashboard, the rear jacking bars, tail lamps, and fuel filler caps. (Courtesy Bugatti Trust)

Line-up of Tanks for the Marne Grand Prix on July 5, 1936. Compare bonnet lip and other details with the ACF line-up. (Courtesy Bugatti Trust)

Bugatti Type 57 Grand Prix – A Celebration

Car number 12 from above. Note the small flaps on top of the scuttle, the flap over the oil filler, as well as Ettore talking to a friend. (Courtesy *Motor*)

4 1936 Grand Prix de la Marne

Excellent view of Wimille's Tank. Note the additional louvre in the bodywork ahead of the rear wheelarch to aid cooling. (Courtesy Bugatti Trust)

if not exceedingly lively for the competitors. Of little surprise, the hard scuffle during practice resulted in René Dreyfus' Talbot taking pole position, with Wimille's Tank between him and Morel's Talbot, leaving the other two Tanks lined-up in the second row.

The recognition differences between the cars previously noted in the line-up confirm that the drivers appointed for the Reims race were in the very same cars they raced at Montlhéry. Noteworthy, Wimille's car number 12 received some minor collision damage, front and rear during Saturday's fracas; repairs taking the form of quickly knocked-out dents. Other than race numbers, the most obvious visual change to the cars since the ACF was a single large louvre opened-up in the side of the bodywork, just forward of each wheelarch. This additional cooling slot was much larger than those already existing on the wheel cover, but sized in proportion to them. The under-shield usually covering the rear axles appear to have been deliberately omitted altogether to aid cooling of the rear brakes. Of significant interest, the three cars were different masses when weighed-in during the official Friday technical scrutiny. These were: the Wimille car at 1265kg; the Veyron car at 1245kg; and the Benoist car, the lightest, at 1225kg. These weight differences evidently suggest unique build variations for each car, but more of this in a later chapter.

That Sunday, the summer weather was hazy and overcast, with heavy rain forecast for the late afternoon. Whist still hospitalised, Jean's condition had improved, being no longer critical. As a result, Ettore felt he could attend this race, arriving in his Royale, and was observed calmly chatting to friends and officials before the start. The proven performance, reliability and success of Jean's T57G 'Tanks' appear to have somewhat diminished Ettore's previous aversion to the Type, where he demonstrated great pride in the car at last, no-doubt also tempered by the near-loss of its leading visionary.

Honorary starter

Philippe Etancelin, the distinguished former Bugatti driver and three times winner at the circuit attended as honorary

Bugatti Type 57 Grand Prix – *A Celebration*

The other side of Wimille's car showing a similar additional cooling louvre ahead of the rear wheelarch. (Courtesy Bugatti Trust)

Wimille streams down the straight to pass the chequered flag, a minute ahead of Benoist. (Courtesy Bugatti Trust)

starter, where he dropped the flag at 2.00pm. René Dreyfus, in his Talbot 150C, predictably sped off quickly to the front, with Wimille and Benoist chasing his tracks in their Bugattis. Wimille had to work hard to reduce Dreyfus' lead, approaching 225km/h (140mph) in the fastest straight sections. Yet he found the Talbot creeping forward again and again, until, by lap 10, Dreyfus was 26 seconds ahead. Six cars led the field, the order being: Talbot; Bugatti; Bugatti; Talbot; Bugatti; Talbot. Michel Paris, the racing pseudonym of the wealthy Paris businessman Henri Toulouse, was the fastest of the Delahaye drivers. Sadly, on the 21st lap, he spun, cartwheeled and crashed his 135CS, ending his racing career, and leaving him severely disabled. Such were the risks and potential consequences of motor racing. On lap 23, Dreyfus managed to clock the fastest lap speed at 148.17km/h (92mph), increasing his lead over Wimille's Tank by 50 seconds. Fortune, however, chastised Dreyfus for his high revving when his crankshaft broke just two laps later.

Throughout the race the sky was darkening, and around lap 34 the awaited rainstorm broke. Remarkably, Wimille's leading pace was hardly affected, for the Tank's speed and streamlined profile simply coasted its way through the deluge, carrying much of the stinging spray right over his head.

A great victory

After 51 laps and 400km, Wimille in car number 12 was declared the winner as he swept passed the finishing line and, probably, one of the largest chequered flags in racing. Benoist was second, just one minute behind him in car number 14, and Veyron was fourth in car number 44, where the first, second and fourth places amazed everyone. During these two incredible weekends, the new Tanks had enthralled the motoring movement with their astonishing performance. Bizarrely, though, given the different weights of the cars noted at the organiser's technical inspection, the winning Wimille car was actually the heaviest of them all; the significance of which becomes apparent in a later chapter.

5

1936 Class 'C' World Records

THE PHENOMENAL PERFORMANCE OF the new T57G Tanks had firmly consigned them to the annals of motor racing. Given the remarkable unofficial Class 'C' record-breaking speeds at Montlhéry in June, for Jean Bugatti, it was essential that the Tanks' performance should be recognised with a formal record attempt. The Wimille car was thus prepared, being fitted with engine T57G No 4, and was tuned for 163bhp at 5500rpm. This normally-aspirated Tank then achieved 14 Class 'C' World Records at the Montlhéry Autodrome between September and November 1936.

Jean-Pierre Wimille was absent from the September and October record runs because he was in the USA driving the T59/50B 4.7-litre in the Vanderbilt Cup, achieving second place. On Saturday, September 26, Benoist took the 'Hour' in the Tank

Benoist's Tank at the Paris Salon dressed with the Tricolour victory ribbon. Oddly, it was never again seen in public after this. (Courtesy Bugatti Trust)

5   1936 Class 'C' World Records

fitted with oversize rear tyres. This success was also a fantastic opportunity to promote the T57S super sports car. Benoist's very own Tank was placed on the Bugatti stand at the Paris Salon on October 1, draped with a red, white and blue sash. It was later used as a road-going sales demonstrator. Bonnet lip details show this car to have been the former Benoist car, but now with bodywork adapted to accept a passenger, with a second cowl and aero-screen. Perplexingly, whilst being the lightest of all the Tanks, this car was never seen again after the Salon. On October 10 that year, a Tank, also identifiable as the Wimille car, broke six more records. The next challenge was a 24-hour run, held on November 19 and 20. Here, the drive was shared between Wimille, Veyron and Williams, and the Tank broke a further six records and achieved a fastest lap at a speed of 223km/h (138.48mph). This great success for Bugatti was a truly spectacular example of reliable high-speed performance.

The record car has been fitted with 7.00x19in racing tyres, giving a larger rolling radius to increase speed.
(Courtesy Bugatti Trust)

Bugatti Type 57 Grand Prix – *A Celebration*

Note that the engine coolant radiator has been moved slightly to the left (as you sit in the car) to allow cool air to the right side of the engine.
(Courtesy Bugatti Trust)

The Wimille record car at Montlhéry. Note the large driver-side cowl, bigger headlights, and alloy baffles in front of the oil and coolant radiators.
(Courtesy Bugatti Trust)

5   1936 Class 'C' World Records

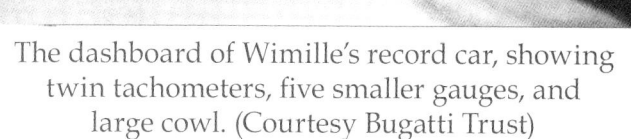

The dashboard of Wimille's record car, showing twin tachometers, five smaller gauges, and large cowl. (Courtesy Bugatti Trust)

Note the headlights and baffles, and, in particular, the offset radiator and its duct. (Courtesy Bugatti Trust)

Bugatti Type 57 Grand Prix – A Celebration

The 24-Hour record car high up on the banking at Montlhéry, with Grover-Williams driving. (Courtesy Bugatti Trust)

Montlhéry, November 1936. Left to right: Grover-Williams, Veyron, Jean Bugatti, and Wimille. (Courtesy Bugatti Trust)

Modifications

Modifications to the Wimille car can be noted from photographs taken during these record runs. The most obvious feature is a higher and cumbersome driver's cowling, combined with a new passenger seat cover that encroached a little further towards the cockpit to narrow it. Despite its unattractiveness, this not only improved streamlining, but importantly, kept the freezing winter air from the drivers during the high-speed endurance runs on the plateau; especially night runs throughout the 24-hour record. Last seen at the Marne, the large cooling louvre on each side of the body just forward of the rear wheelarch had been welded up and levelled. The small ventilation flaps on top of the body each side of the scuttle had gone, too, and the rear axle under-shield was refitted to improve streamlining. Additionally, it may be noted that the original faired-in headlamps were replaced with larger diameter units that now protruded from the bodywork, although as yet without the mesh guards seen the following year. These larger lamps were essential for improved vision at night during the 24-hour record attempt. A small radiator cap access flap was installed to save time lifting the bonnet and subsequently speed up pitstop times. Shortly afterwards, though, the radiator itself was moved slightly to the left, (as you sit in the car), allowing cooler airflow around the carburettor and fuel lines. As a result, the radiator filler cap flap on the bonnet was elongated to the left to compensate.

Curiously, rear wheel covers are observed fitted on some record attempts and removed for others. It was necessary to remove them on runs where the rear wheels were shod with large, 7.00 x 19in tyres, providing a greater rolling circumference, so achieving a higher top speed for the 'Hour.' At that cooler time of year, rear brake overheating would not adversely affect performance on the circuits around the Autodrome, whereas engine over-cooling would. Consequently, light alloy baffles are noted, fitted in front of the coolant and oil radiators in order to maintain higher engine system running temperatures. The engine oil filler was altered, using a winged screw cap almost flush with the bodywork, and the 'token' full width windscreen seen previously was removed. The car's white-coloured gear-change lever knob might have been fitted at this time in preparation for the 24-hour runs to improve visibility during night driving. Photos taken at the Marne Grand Prix show it was black.

The earlier minimal dashboard was completely remade to include twin tachometers, one each side of the steering column, as well as a cluster of five small instrument dials to the left. These comprised: a clock, coolant temperature, fuel, oil pressure and an ammeter. However, it's curious to note that the new dashboard fitted at this time is materially different to that of the surviving Tank, even though externally, both versions are identifiable as the Wimille car. Studies of photos of the two periods show that it has been completely replaced, and I shall discuss the likely significance of this observation in a later chapter.

The 14 Class 'C' records achieved were as follows:

- Saturday, September 26, 1936 – The hour at 217.94km/h (135.34mph) with Robert Benoist driving Wimille's Tank. This exceptional record remained unbroken for almost 20 years.
- Saturday, October 10, 1936 – 200-mile record at an average of 205.55km/h (127.73mph), 500-mile at 204.22km/h (126.9mph), 500km at 201.95km/h (125.49mph), 1000km at 203.25km/h (126.3mph), 3-hour at 202.75km/h (125.99mph) and 6-hour record at 204.38km/h (127mph), shared driving between Benoist and Pierre Veyron in the Wimille Tank.
- Saturday and Sunday, November 19 and 20, 1936 – Following a mid-day false-start due to a fuel pump failure, the car resumed its 24-hour attempt at 8pm, breaking the following records: 1000-mile at 199.07km/h (123.7mph), 2000-mile at 199.23km/h (123.8mph), 2000km at 196.65km/h (122.2mph), 3000km at 199.07km/h (123.7mph), 4000km at 200.52km/h (124.6mph), 12-hour at 198.26km/h (123.2mph), and 24-hour record at 199.44km/h (123.93mph). Wimille, Veyron and Williams took turns to drive the Wimille Tank, although of the three it was Le Mans veteran Pierre Veyron who recorded the fastest speed and covered the greatest accumulated distance, spending a total of eight hours and 36 minutes in the cockpit.

It is interesting to reflect that the 1000km distance record was covered at an average speed of 203.25km/h (126.3mph). This compares with 125.6km/h (77.85mph) achieved during the ACF a few months earlier. This significant contrast clearly illustrates an example of the major difference in overall speed between road circuit racing and flat-out banked oval racing. Furthermore, the highest average speed recorded for the 24-hour was 199.27km/h (123.93mph), giving an average fuel consumption of 21 litres/100km (13.4mpg). This yield was an incredible achievement at the time, clearly demonstrating one of the less obvious benefits of efficient streamlining.

6

1937 Le Mans

THE TOWN OF LE MANS occupies the sandy plains of western France, bordering the Château country, about 190km (120 miles) to the southwest of Paris. Officially known as the Circuit Permanent de la Sarthe, the course is located in the partially forested area south of the town. The Le Mans race is more formally called Le Grand Prix d'Endurance de Vingt-Quatre Heures du Mans. The competition was created by Georges Durand, Charles Faroux, and Emile Coquille when they combined ideas during a meeting at the October 1922 Paris Salon. Durand was the secretary of the Automobile Club de l'Ouest (l'ACO). His aspiration was to found a special 24-hour race that would challenge the reliability of the world's touring cars. Faroux, the editor of *La Vie Automobile,* drafted the regulations, and Coquille, the French Director of Rudge-Whitworth, arranged to put up the purse of 100,000f and the trophy. The mutual outcome was to establish a robust competition that tested production cars and their accessories to their limits, if not often to destruction. Over the years, this leading annual race has contributed significantly to speed with safety and reliability, as well as to technical development and innovation. The course layout has evolved somewhat over the years, although in 1937 the circuit ran 13.5km (8.38 miles). The excellent Class-C records set by the T57G Tank in the winter of 1936 seems to have prompted Jean Bugatti to enter the 24-hour endurance race at Le Mans.

1931 misadventure

WF Bradley suggested that, "Ettore Bugatti never seemed to fully appreciate the prestige of this annual event, or to properly recognize its commercial value to his business." This may have been for several reasons. His 1931 entry, with three, black-painted Type 50s, had disastrous tyre problems which led to treads de-laminating at high speed, and a serious crash. After falling out with Dunlop, it is held that the Michelin tyres chosen by Bugatti were not suitably rated for high-speed racing over long distances. One of Bugatti's drivers, Maurice Rost, lost a tread and crashed into a group of spectators, killing one and seriously injuring several others. Rost was gravely injured in the accident, and left so traumatised he never raced again. The tyre problem clearly affected the other Bugatti team cars, and they all withdrew. As for Ettore, he had always been very pleased with his safety record in racing, so this accident upset him tremendously. It also tormented Jean, for he had just recently taken overall responsibility for the management of the Racing Department. Whilst it is unclear whose decision it was to select inappropriately-rated tyres, the mistake does not appear to have ever been repeated. After this tragedy, Jean Bugatti always favoured Dunlop racing tyres, which were used for his Type 55 entries the following year.

Father-son comparison

Of equal influence to Le Mans entries, Ettore tended to view his competition cars as racing thoroughbreds that should never be hobbled by impractical and heavy detail accessories, such as mudguards, lamps, and self-starters. Conversely, the Le Mans race regulations required that these items should be tested equally for performance. By his nature, Ettore Bugatti seemed inherently unconcerned about such details. The cars of his generation had evolved from horse-drawn carriages, where the fastest were of lightweight construction with the minimum of trimmings. Accessories were merely after-thoughts. With the maxim 'Weight the Enemy,' he simply viewed such items as embellishments, and a needless hindrance to performance, which, in racing, of course, they are. For Ettore Bugatti, there were two distinct breeds: racing cars and luxury touring cars, so it was entirely against his nature to race a touring car.

On the other hand, Jean Bugatti was nurtured with such innovations. From the age of 12 or so, he acquired his practical and technical education in each and every department of the factory, accepting the progressive metamorphosis of automobiles as natural evolution. Jean thought differently, too, being much more meticulous with attention to detail; in fact, he was a counterpart to his father. He had grown up with many of the variously skilled employees, and had observed all aspects of their trades. Perhaps unconsciously, this fostered the mutual respect that would enable him to lead the factory and racing team so effectively in years to come. Moreover, Jean was undoubtedly influenced by some of the most talented people of his time in design and motor racing, such as Felix Kortz, Édouard Bertrand, Noel Domboy, Antonio Pichetto, Robert Benoist, and Meo Costantini, to name just a few. For several years, he worked alongside the brilliant Costantini in the racing team, where he gradually became proficient in every area of tuning and testing, as well as pit-counter planning and management. It was not long before Jean was able to assume total authority for the racing programme, so that by the time Costantini left Bugatti, he was able to take overall responsibility for car preparation, testing and team organisation.

Le Mans Tanks described

Two T57G Tanks from the previous year were entered by Roger Labric for the 24-hour race to be held on June 19 and 20, 1937. The cars are identifiable as noted previously with the ex-1936 Veyron car, race number 1, to be driven by Le Mans veterans and favourites Roger Labric and Pierre Veyron. Robert Benoist and Jean-Pierre Wimille would be driving the former-1936 Wimille car, now race number 2. Wimille was a novice of the Le Mans race, although Benoist had competed in 1928 co-driving an Italia, and in 1929 with a Chrysler.

Several internal and external reforms had been made to the cars since the previous racing season, including weight reduction. When the surviving car was stripped of paint for refurbishment in 2013, it was evident that many single-curvature panels had been replaced using a more rigid and lighter alloy, such as Dural, leaving the more ductile aluminium for double-curvature pieces. Clearly, these changes were too well done to have been truly last-minute alterations.

Interestingly, a factory note for June 2, 1937 records that chassis 57454 and 57455 were marked 'G' and booked to the Paris showroom; denoting that these were the two Le Mans cars. Furthermore, Froude test records show that on June 9, 1937, engines 57G Nos 1 and 3 produced 140bhp at 5000rpm, using 56mm compression height pistons and C2 carburettors choked to 34mm. Markedly, the date sequence suggests these engines were prepared and tested in Paris.

The most visually obvious modification to the cars is that the spare wheel has been recessed into the tail instead of stowed next to the passenger seat. Consequently, this necessitated a re-designed fuel tank providing a 130-litre (28.5-gallon) capacity, giving a range of 490km (300 miles), and was constructed with its twin fuel-filler caps high up on the bodywork just behind the driver's seat. Additionally, two teardrop-shaped blisters are visible in the bodywork on each side of the filler caps, the right-hand one, as you sit in the car, being slightly larger than the left. The re-location of the spare wheel was in response to compliance with the Le Mans regulation driver and passenger door rule, despite the passenger seat being covered. On the Wimille car, the big ugly cowl was replaced with its original one, and the large panel fitted over the passenger seat for the record runs eight months earlier was cut back slightly to provide more cockpit space, and both cars were now fitted with small doors, hinging upwards. The dashboard was revised with new lighting switches, as well as twin tachometers with five smaller instruments spaced differently, otherwise similar to those seen during the record runs.

Experience from the 24-hour endurance world record eight months earlier ensured that both cars had more efficient lighting. The two large diameter main headlamps of the type installed for the record attempts remained, but were now protected with mesh guards. Additionally, the lenses were kept clean with canvas sacking until the pitstop before nightfall. A single large headlamp was mounted inside the inlet duct, just ahead of the radiator, but because this caused a restriction to airflow, the radiator opening in the bonnet was enlarged noticeably in height to compensate. A smaller diameter spotlight was faired into the

Bugatti Type 57 Grand Prix – *A Celebration*

The Bugatti mechanics pose with the Roger Labric/Pierre Veyron car in the town square at La Grand Lucé. Note the temporary passenger-side windscreen. (Courtesy Bugatti Trust)

Benoist poses in his and Wimille's car. (Courtesy Bugatti Trust)

6   1937 Le Mans

A relaxed Wimille poses with the car before the start. (Courtesy Bugatti Trust)

The warmed-up Tanks receive their final fuel top-up before being sealed for the race. Roger Labric, with armband, can be seen on the right. (Courtesy Bugatti Trust)

51

Bugatti Type 57 Grand Prix – A Celebration

right-hand side of the bodywork that some commentators suggested was used for lighting up the side of the road, especially those many right-hand corners of the circuit. Yet curiously, in monochrome photographs the lens appears to be dark, and was reported at the time to be dark red. Other commentators suggested that the amount of angular off-set of the lamp is far too great to serve other than for signalling simple pre-arranged messages to the pit crews, who would also be on this side of the car during the event. This reasoning appears to be plausible, for this would make it easier for the crews to identify their cars at night. Perhaps it was for a little of each, since the later 1939 Le Mans car used a similar lamp mounting, but with a plain lens, which was far more practical for lighting up corner warning markers.

The rear quick-lift jacking bars had acquired 'mushroom' ends in order to prevent the car slipping off its jacks during wheel changes. Additionally, the dry-sump oil tank filler was extended even further for accessibility, with a quick-lift cap protruding just outside the body on the upper left-hand side. The 'token' windscreen was returned to its original position.

The cars initially appeared with rear wheel covers, but these were removed before the race, as, too, was the rear under-shield panel which normally covered the rear axle. This, again, was to enhance cooling of the rear brakes as well as to speed-up wheel changes during pitstops. Whilst it risked a regulation default, happily for Bugatti this was disregarded by officials.

Technical inspection

In accordance with the regulations, the Tanks travelled to the Le Mans circuit from the Paris showrooms driven by their appointed drivers. Race number 1 (previously race numbers 86 and 44 in 1936), was driven by Pierre Veyron, but was noticeably a little late arriving at the Halles des Toiles in Le Mans for technical inspection. The Bugattis were formally entered by journalist and Le Mans veteran, Roger Labric, who had driven in all Le Mans events since 1931, so was familiar with each corner of the circuit, and probably every bump in its surface. The Bugatti racing team stayed at Hotel Moderne in the market town of La Grand-Lucé, just 25km (15.5 miles) southeast of Le Mans, where 'Willy' Grover-Williams attended to provide customary support to the Bugatti team and to manage its general well-being.

Roger Labric

As an aside, Roger Labric was a keen amateur historian of the endurance race. He chronicled the event from its inception, detailing cars, drivers, distances and times into an influential book first published in 1949. The work is highly praised by the ACO as the official history, yet regrettably, this extremely important record never seems to receive the recognition it deserves. Nonetheless, it is always the groundwork upon which later Le Mans writers build their historical references.

The race

Race day weather started bright, though heavy rain was forecast for later. Nevertheless, there was a record-breaking 150,000 spectators through the turnstiles for the event, who would get to see a superb international turnout of 48 cars. The main opposition in the line-up included seven 3.6-litre Delahayes made up of Works cars and private entrants, a single Figoni-bodied 3-litre Delage Coupé, two 150C Talbots, two privately-entered Bugattis, two Chenard et Walckers, three Peugeot 402 Darl'Mat specials, an Alfa Romeo 2.9-litre, and a Lagonda 4.5-litre. The smaller capacity classes consisted of an Aston-Martin, Frazer-Nash BMWs, Riley, Singer, MG, 1.5-litre HRG, and a Ford 10 Special, along with three Adler Triumph Streamliners, a BMW 328, three Simca-Fiats, Austin 7 'Grasshoppers,' and two Gordini Simca 569cc Cinqs. The two privately-entered Bugattis were the skimpy-bodied T57S (57522/18S) of Raymond de Saugé d'Estrez and Génaro Léoz, as well as the rather outdated T44 of René Kippeurt and René Poulain.

The Honorary Starter of the twelfth race was John Cobb, twice holder of the 24-hour world record. There was a little confusion leading up to the 4.00pm deadline when the race commentator's echoing countdown on the public-address system managed to get a second or so ahead of Cobb's official timekeeper. This revealed itself by having some of the drivers sprint off to their respective cars just before Cobb's flag had actually dropped. As this was Wimille's first experience at Le Mans, he clearly did not want anything to go wrong on a technicality, so he held back cautiously until the timekeeper's flag actually went down; otherwise all the cars got away cleanly. The Le Mans event is a long race, so although delayed slightly by the start, Wimille took his time in bringing the car up to working temperature, and was in ninth place at the end of the first lap. However, once warmed-up, he focussed on

6 1937 Le Mans

The first pit stop illustrates an exhausted Wimille, with Benoist changing over as mechanics refuel and check engine oil. (Courtesy Bugatti Trust)

Robert Benoist driving the Tank during the Le Mans race. (Courtesy Bugatti Trust)

Bugatti Type 57 Grand Prix – A Celebration

Benoist in the Tank during the race, the car now becoming stained with oil discharge. (Courtesy Bugatti Trust)

Jean-Pierre Wimille at speed. Note the enlarged radiator opening. (Courtesy Alfa Photo Press Ltd)

increasing the pace, breaking the lap record in the process with a speed of 147.63km/h (91.68mph), whilst also sweeping past Veyron's Tank. The fourth time round, his car broke the lap record again, now with a speed of 148.99km/h (92.58mph), energetically chasing Sommer's Alfa Romeo, so that by the end of lap five he had taken the lead.

Tragedy

Towards the end of the first hour, an horrific tragedy occurred when six cars crashed in quick succession between Maison Blanche and the pits, effectively blocking the whole road. René Kippeurt had rolled his T44 Bugatti, which turned over several times flinging him out hard; tragically, he died instantly. Immediately following Kippeurt, a BMW ran into this wreckage, splitting the Bugatti into two. Pat Fairfield's Frazer-Nash-BMW, impacted an instant later, and then a Delahaye joined this seemingly unstoppable frenzy of destruction, swiftly followed by a Talbot and a Riley. Somehow, Wimille's Tank managed to glide through this carnage by a whisker, miraculously unscathed. Sommer in the Alfa Romeo also scraped through the gap, although he had terminally over-revved his engine whilst urgently changing-down gear, forcing him to retire shortly afterwards. By good fortune, Forestier in the Riley was not badly injured, and in the face of the ensuing kinetic chaos, fearlessly ran back down the track to warn incoming drivers of the dangers ahead. The sheer scale of the disaster soon dawned on officials, who subsequently forced the race to be held up in order to clear the road. This left a long queue of cars forming at the entry to Maison Blanche. Other than Forestier, all the other drivers involved in the tragedy were very seriously injured, and, unhappily, Pat Fairfield died during the night. Kippeurt and Fairfield were the first drivers to die at Le Mans since 1925.

The race went on

This calamity brought an air of bleak sadness to everyone present; yet the race went on. It took over an hour to properly clear the track and get all the contestants up to full speed again. During this time, the big Lagonda had overheated in the bottleneck at Maison Blanche, cracking its cylinder head. When Benoist took over from Wimille, there was a torrential rainstorm that slowed him down to around 130km/h (81mph), but as the road dried he increased his speed, setting yet another lap record of 155.04km/h (96.34mph). By midnight the Bugatti had advanced to a three-lap lead over the second placed Delahaye, with the second Tank running third. The skimpy-bodied Bugatti T57S of Léoz and de Saugé was running in fifth place until on lap 99 it dropped out with a broken gearbox. Shortly after this, the Veyron/Labric Tank began slowing, eventually dropping back to seventh place until, on lap 130, it was forced to retire with what the Bugatti pit claimed was a leaking fuel tank. The *Autocar,* however, reported terminal clutch slip, where the actual symptoms leading to retirement implied the latter. A bitterly disappointed Veyron and Labric had yet again been unable to finish the 24-hour race, and now the Tank's withdrawal allowed another Delahaye to move up into third place.

Throughout Sunday morning the Benoist/Wimille Tank remained in the lead, and even more easily so after the long-term second-placed Delahaye of Schell/Carrière pitted at around 10.00am, with a mortal loss of coolant from its water pump. Whilst continuing optimistically, the Delahaye's engine soon seized-up. Then around noon, with only four hours to go, the Tank, now driven by an exhausted Benoist, hit a bank at Arnage whilst overtaking a backmarker. It slipped off the road and stalled the engine. The car had to be pushed along the track to a 'safe place' by marshals, which was an issue that might have been in contravention of regulations. Fortunately, race director Charles Faroux recognised that the car was in a dangerous position at the time, so the push was allowed; happily, without protest from rival teams. It was also fortunate that the car only damaged a front left-hand wheel, quickly replaced, and so was able to resume the race. The Tank continued progress without further drama in pleasantly glowing sunshine throughout the remaining afternoon, where the closing race sequence was an all-French finish: Bugatti; Delahaye; Delahaye; Delage.

New record and analysis

Race attrition had been particularly high, with only seventeen finishers out of the original 48, but the Wimille/Benoist car, race number 2, completed the 24-hour race covering a distance of 3287.93km (2043.08 miles) at an average speed of 136.99km/h (85.12mph), some seven laps, or 103km (64 miles), ahead of its next rival. This had also extended the record distance, set in 1933 by Raymond Sommer and Tazio Nuvolari driving an Alfa Romeo, by 140km (87 miles), as well as raising the lap record to 155.17km/h (96.42mph). Considering the time lost due to

Bugatti Type 57 Grand Prix – A Celebration

Wimille takes the chequered flag, 103km (64 miles) ahead of his nearest rival. (Courtesy Bugatti Trust)

Wimille stops next to the pits to the awaiting tumult of photographers and spectators. Bugatti's win was a national triumph for France. (Courtesy Bugatti Trust)

6 1937 Le Mans

the tragic multi-car crash, as well as the Bugatti's skid and stall, this outcome was incredible.

Bugatti's great success was due to the outstanding driving skills of Benoist and Wimille, in conjunction with the Tank's overall performance and reliability. Yet this win was also significantly linked to superb fuel economy and race tactics as a direct result of the car's efficient streamlining. In analysis, the astonishing fuel economy of 25-litres/100km, in combination with a 130-litre fuel tank, enabled the car to cover 550km (40-laps) between pitstops. This meant it could race continuously for 3½ hours against its rivals' three, subsequently achieving the 24-hour period with one less pitstop than its competitors, saving both time and fuel for re-acceleration. Moreover, because the car had only six pitstops against its rivals' seven, the keen and youthful Wimille was able to drive the first stage as well as the final. Benoist, of course, had two previous entries in 1928 and 1929, but Wimille's first-attempt success at Le Mans had only been shared up to that time by such greats as Nuvolari and Barnato. Nonetheless, Wimille and Benoist's joint success was a splendid achievement, so it was not surprising that the two drivers received joyful cheers and euphoric applause, for the win was regarded as a national triumph for France, having not been successful for eleven years. L'Ébé Bugatti wrote in her 1966 book, *The Bugatti Story*:

The victorious Robert Benoist and Jean-Pierre Wimille pose for photographers in the winning Tank. (Courtesy Bugatti Trust)

A commemorative postcard celebrating the great success of the Type 57S' 24-Hour records at Montlhéry in 1936, and Le Mans in 1937. (Courtesy Bugatti Trust)

Bugatti Type 57 Grand Prix – *A Celebration*

T57G Le Mans-winning Tank by Spark Models. (Courtesy NMT Collection – photo by D Roberts)

"Then in the almost religious silence which followed the announcement of the result, the Marseillaise was played here for the first time since 1926. The emotion which was felt soon gave way to joyous scenes at the success of the National colours and our regained prestige."

The achievement was a prodigious triumph for the French people and Automobiles Bugatti. This important national success was also noted by Ettore Bugatti's 1948 biographer, WF Bradley, who recalled a story of how this great victory for France and the T57G at Le Mans, might not have happened at all but for the tact and charm of Jean Bugatti and the generous co-operation of the Trades Union during this complicated period of social and political unease in France.

VISIT VELOCE ON THE WEB – WWW.VELOCE.CO.UK
All current books • New book news • Special offers • Gift vouchers • Forum

7

1937 T57S45 Tanks

IN LATE 1936, JEAN Bugatti announced that six of these streamliners were planned for 1937. However, only one car was actually seen by the public, displaying race number 16. It stunned everyone who saw it in practice prior to the ACF at Montlhéry on Saturday July 3, 1937. A second T57S45, noted at the Works with race number 14, was reportedly damaged during transit from Molsheim to Montlhéry that same day. Until relatively recently, the history of the two ultra-streamlined T57S45 racing cars was minimal, frustrating and confusing, often with wheelbase and engine dimensions incorrectly published. The very limited information available about these cars was primarily sourced from news reports and just a few photographs. The cars were reportedly destined for Benoist and Wimille to campaign in the 1937 Le Mans 24-Hour Race, and two weeks after that in the French Grand Prix (ACF) at Montlhéry. However, they never materialised at Le Mans, and just one car had the briefest appearance in practice for the ACF event before seeming to vanish forever.

Erroneous history

A number of modern motoring writers have stated, based upon period publications, that the T57S45 appeared for practice at Le Mans. Yet, it seems these historical news reports were mistaken, and this error was then published in the important 1954 marque compilation *The Bugatti Book* by Barry Eaglesfield and Peter Hampton. Thereafter, it has often been repeated as formal Bugatti 'history,' even though doubt remained amongst some enthusiasts. Compellingly, the official Le Mans organiser, Automobile Club de l'Ouest, has no formal records whatsoever regarding the T57S45 Tanks. Adding to the historical confusion, it seems likely Jean Bugatti and race officials did anticipate that the T57S45 Tanks might run at Le Mans, since it was customary that cars with the largest capacity are allocated the lowest race numbers. Therefore, it seemed credible that, in the 3- to 5-litre class,

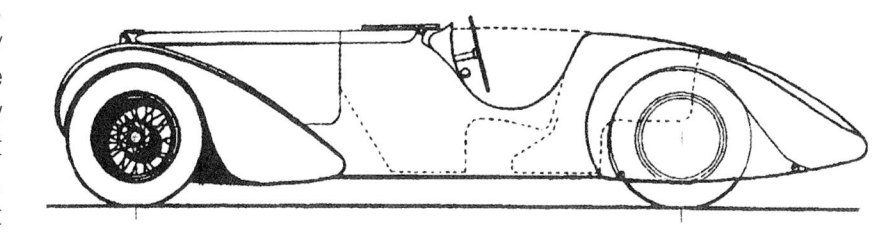

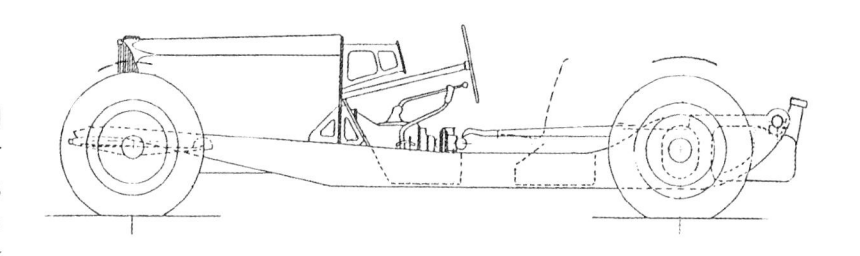

A drawing comparing the T57S45 and T57S chassis, showing their identical proportions.
(Courtesy Bugatti Trust)

Bugatti Type 57 Grand Prix – A Celebration

the allocation of race numbers 1 and 2 to Bugatti for the 3.3-litre T57G Tanks might imply an original Le Mans entry application for cars with larger engines than this. It seemed also that Jean realised they might not be ready in time because of issues with the T50B engine, so two of the 1936 T57G 3.3-litre Tanks were prepared to run in their stead.

Furthermore, studies suggest that the confused technical specification of the T57S45 Tanks originates from formal publicity issued shortly after the Paris Salon, dated November 15, 1935, along with a revised leaflet dated December 1936. These notes illustrate T57S40 and T57S45 road-going sports cars with engine capacities of 3987cc (77mm x 107mm bore and stroke), and 4745cc (84mm x 107mm bore and stroke) respectively. From the published diagram, and comparing scaled ratios of wheelbase and wheel rim diameter, these cars appear to be arranged around a T57S Series 2 surbaissé chassis frame. Oddly, the illustrated rear seating arrangement for passengers appears impossible. Additionally, the T57S45 radiator is 'V' shaped and lowered, as, too, is the body profile, just as the 1936 Series 2 Type 57S, which adopted these features at the same time. Curiously, the 'V' radiator was originally designed for the 1934 T50S Spéciale, later aborted, where it seems Jean Bugatti visualised the T50B-powered T57S45 as a revised version of it. Sadly, the road-going T57S45 never came to fruition as a production car. It might have been prototyped in a T57S frame, but its steering box would have had to have been moved rearwards to clear a T50B supercharger.

Given the leaflets, it would be reasonable for historians to suppose that the racing Tank version would not only have comparable chassis dimensions, but logically, was the next maturation phase of the earlier T57S surbaissé T57G Tanks. For those outside the Works' inner circle, such a conclusion would be encouraged by the fact that one of the earlier streamliners had vanished from active competition not long after the 1936 Paris Salon, as too, the persistent rumour of the existence of a fourth Tank. For that reason, it was entirely rational for historical writers to assume that the two missing T57G Tank chassis had been stripped, re-bodied and powered by the new and much-vaunted T50B engines. Furthermore, bolstered by the erroneous 1937 Le Mans practice reports, a number of prominent Bugatti historians generally upheld this view until the mid-1980s. There was an alternative viewpoint, however.

Revised history

Some years earlier, a number of enthusiasts, including model makers attempting to reproduce a miniature of the car, had difficulty reconciling the endorsed T57S45 dimensions with the well-known photo of the race number 16 car taken at Montlhéry. This is because the published illustrations just did not seem to have the proportions of a T57S chassis. This contention was hampered by the fact that factory documents were not then readily accessible, and very few photos of the T57S45 cars were known to exist. However, having studied the celebrated 1937 Montlhéry photo, some model makers concluded that the wheelbase was closer to 2.6m, effectively that of the Type 59. Besides, such dimensions may be generated using geometry and calculation through projection, in conjunction with the proportions of front and rear wheel diameters, and in relation to the perspective wheelbase. Although not precisely reliable with all photographs such techniques are often used by model makers when the subject prototype, or drawings, no longer exist to measure, especially when wheel rim size or some other dimension is known. This technique can work very well.

Alternatively, a more pragmatic, direct comparison test is also possible by superimposing a photocopied transparency of a T59 over a print of the T57S45, providing the overlay has been suitably adjusted for scale and selected with a closely equivalent perspective angle. In fact, the precise difference in wheelbase between the T59 and the T57S is 380mm (15in), being even more conspicuous to the eye than the 320mm (12.5in) notable variance between the T57S and T57, especially when viewed from the side. Unfortunately, when viewed in perspective, the eye's interpretation of wheelbase proportion is complicated by the distinct difference in track between the T57 and T59 at 1350mm (53in) and 1250mm (49in) respectively. However, with some encouragement for new research, and the committed studies of Hugh G Conway (Senior), by 1987 and Edition four of his book *le pur sang*, it was formally confirmed, as long-suspected by some, that the T57S45 Tank was in fact constructed using Type 59 chassis side frames. The rather confused knowledge about the T57S45 is reflected in the small quantity of production scale models made of the car, every one of which is incorrect to some degree or other.

With the establishment of The Bugatti Trust, copies of factory records are now more accessible than they were, although, unfortunately, the Trust archive does not have either a complete set of engineering drawings of the T57S45 or adequate photographic records that show the precise layout and composition of all components. Accordingly some informed guesswork has been applied. Nonetheless, with the research of Bugatti Trust photographer and archivist David Morys, along with period material compiled by the late Anthony Blight, American Bugatti specialist Ray Jones has obtained enough information to construct a replica of the super-streamlined T57S45 Tank. The re-creation itself has shed new light on these enigmatic and apparently transient racing cars. The project build sheets for the T57S45 are headed 'Voiture de Course ACF 1937,' and these clearly specify T59 chassis side frames, yet they do not appear to have been pierced with holes as per the 1934 standard T59.

Jean Bugatti's commitment to build light alloy T50B-powered racing cars stems from October 20, 1935. This followed the receipt of Fonds des Course funding of 100,000f "… for machine tools" towards the development of a new racing engine that might be capable of competing against the state-sponsored German and Italian teams. It is interesting to note that the first T50B MOT.1 engine drawings are dated July 1935, suggesting Jean's anticipation of financial assistance, and there is a letter, dated December 13, 1935, ordering three pairs of T59 side frames with a resistance of 55-65kg. Evidently, these particular frames were especially-designed for the T50B cars, modified on the right-hand rail to clear the large supercharger. Additionally, they were not pierced, and had a large tubular crossmember at the rear chassis up-sweep. This brings the total number of Type 59 frames manufactured to fifteen.

T57S45 Tank described

The T57S45 Tank seems to have evolved as one of Jean Bugatti's 'ultimate' super-sports car prototypes, constructed around the obsolete Grand Prix Type 59 chassis. The appellation T57S45 is a paradox, though, being not as described, since it used a T59 chassis instead of T57S. A more accurate title might have been T59/50B, yet this would be more appropriate for a single-seater Grand Prix car. Sceptics suggest the title T57S45 was simply to insinuate itself as a T57S, in order to defeat the AIACR requirement that a minimum of 20 of the type had to be built. On the other hand, this same fact evidently illustrates Jean Bugatti's perspective that the T59 was always a T57 variant from its inception, and, as the creative influence behind their respective designs, such a conclusion can only be correct. As previously discussed, the T57 and T59 projects were studied and developed concurrently during 1932, and, technically, the T59 was always deemed to be a racing version of the T57. As a result, if Jean Bugatti considered it to be a T57 Grand Prix car, then it qualifies for this book.

The two chassis side rails were separated using far more robust spacer beams than used on the original T59. In particular, the one just behind the cockpit was a straight alloy tube with a diameter of 100mm, and the rearmost 'C' section strut has similar dimensions. An undated drawing exists, curiously titled 'Chassis 50B,' which appears to be a draft General Arrangement showing the position of components in the chassis, with an impression of bodywork in section. It illustrates the relative position of engine, gearbox, transmission, bulkhead, fuel and oil tanks, electric battery and spare wheel stowage. The T57S45 used a standard T59 split front axle and slide-block spring bearings, utilising a track of 1250mm rather than the 1350mm of the T57S, just as the T59-framed 'T57 Sport' – 57248. The De Ram dampers were standard units, but used special brackets at the front, with conventional T59 side-frame mountings at the rear. A standard T59 steering box was used, too.

This chassis was combined with a T50BII, normally-aspirated engine, using high strength, Rolls-Royce RR50 aluminium casting alloy, although without the additional lightened features found with the Grand Prix single-seat prototype known as the T50B (50180) in its earlier guise. The bore is detailed as 84mm, which, combined with an assumed crankshaft stroke of 100mm, provided a capacity of 4432cc. It has been declared that this engine produced around 400bhp, but at this stage of development, 300bhp was probably more realistic. Froude test house records note MOT.1 and MOT.2, described as '50B 4.500 ACF,' and are dated June 24, 1937. This clearly suggests the two engines for the T57S45 streamliners. The power units used a special light alloy, two-piece flywheel cover, not a conventional bellhousing, with a Bendix double-reduction starter motor arranged centrally above it.

Mounted on cross-tubes, the EB inspired transmission used a strong, four-speed, all-synchromesh gearbox, designated 57S.45.CV.ENS.3 in a drawing dated October 20, 1936. It was similar to the T50B single-seat version, but used a central gear change top cover. The gearbox employed straight-cut constant

Bugatti Type 57 Grand Prix – A Celebration

mesh gears, pressurised lubrication using jets and dry-sump scavenge to a reservoir mounted on the outside left of the frame just ahead of the rear wheel. Power was transmitted through a large diameter prop-shaft to a T59-like double-reduction rear axle fitted with a ZF limited-slip differential. This, with the T57S45 gearbox arrangement, necessitated revised rear suspension geometry that incorporated long radius arms. Since the gearbox used straight-cut gears, the shafts were not usually subject to significant end-thrust; so none of the bearings were designed for such loading, many using large diameter rollers.

Unfortunately, the original Type 59 rear suspension geometry, in conjunction with prop-shaft spline grab under torque loading, could sometimes place extreme fore and aft axial thrust on the gearbox output shaft and its simple roller bearings; leading to wear, damage and jumping out of gear. The more powerful T50B engine installation simply exacerbated this defect, where the issue was resolved by completely isolating these parasitic loads. The revised design to better control rear suspension geometry, used new quarter elliptic rear springs with slide-block bearings; similar to those on the front; a shorter prop-shaft, an amended rear axle torque beam along with its forward link mounting, as well as 950mm long external radius rods. These components were developed for the T50B single-seaters, between August and September 1936; too late for the Swiss Grand Prix, but ready in time for the Vanderbilt Cup race.

7   1937 T57S45 Tanks

Left: Car number 16 at Montlhéry. Note the additional fuel filler cap recessed into the bodywork just ahead of the driver's door. (Courtesy Bugatti Trust)

Above: Car number 16 at Montlhéry. In this photo, the proportions of design better illustrate its derivation from the Type 59 chassis. (Courtesy Bugatti Trust)

Right: Note that the fuel filler cap is almost identical to that of the 1939 Luxembourg Grand Prix T57S45 in the National Museum, Mulhouse. (Courtesy Bugatti Trust)

Bugatti Type 57 Grand Prix – A Celebration

Jean-Pierre Wimille at speed, although a shortfall in race preparation is suggested by the engine cover lifting in the airstream. (Courtesy Bugatti Trust)

Body details

To date, no final body drawings have been discovered for the T57S45 Tank, although a provisional GA drawing indicates a width of 2200mm. Unfortunately, the overall body length is not detailed. This super-streamlined body was less Tank-like than the previous cars, where the body sides swept down below the level of the wings, giving a much smaller frontal area. Nevertheless, the car retained the Grand Prix Bugatti shape in its raised portions, as well as the two-tone blue 'arrow-head' flash. A photograph of the elevated engine cover shows it was made up from several different panels.

The dark tarnish of some panels suggests rigid sections of Dural or magnesium, combined with the more malleable aluminium used for compound curvatures. Aeronautical ram-air technology is clearly apparent, using tubular intakes at the front to duct cool air to the front brakes, and large vertical openings on each side of the radiator duct cool air to the carburettor on the right, and to the exhaust side of the engine on the left. A small, outward opening driver's door reflects the passenger side, but is covered with a panel. Engine and gearbox reservoir oil fillers were accessible with the passenger door open. Dashboard detail consisted of a large tachometer, set to the left side of the steering column, with four smaller dials arranged on each side of it in pairs; these being ammeter, water temperature, oil pressure and fuel, respectively. To the far left is the lighting switch, and to the right the advance and throttle levers.

The primary fuel tank illustrated in the GA drawing suggests it had a capacity of 120 litres (26 gallons). A photo of the tail end shows a single large central fuel filler cap protruding just behind the rear suspension crossbeam. It also shows another filler cap, recessed into the top of the bodywork, just ahead of the driver's door. The provisional GA drawing suggests this to be an additional, flattened, L-shaped fuel tank, ahead of and below the door opening, having an estimated capacity of 65 litres (14 gallons). It is mounted on a subframe that extends the full width of the bodywork, counterpoised on the other side by what appear to be engine and gearbox oil reservoirs, as well as an electric battery.

If correct, the unbalanced, changing fuel load would have had unpredictable effects on car stability under racing conditions. Whilst not detailed, the gearbox oil tank capacity appears to be enough to make an oil-cooler unnecessary. At the rear, generous crescent-shaped scoops in the leading edges of the rear wings ducted air to the rear brakes. The spare wheel was recessed into the bodywork directly behind the cockpit. The design utilised mushroom-headed, quick-lift jacking beams, as seen on the 1937 Le Mans Tanks; these being mounted on bracketed extensions from the rearmost chassis rails.

Disqualification

The story of the T57S45's first appearance for the French Grand Prix (ACF), held on July 4, 1937, and its subsequent withdrawal, was reported in the July issue of *Motor Sport*:

"Benoist insisted on showing off the paces of a private Bugatti to a prospective customer during a practice period, in the face of a direct warning of the officials. For this he was disqualified from taking part in the race, and as the cars were late anyway Bugatti withdrew both his cars."

This report was a bizarre, if not shameful, situation for Robert Benoist. After sixteen years in the motor racing arena, and having been honoured by France as a champion, Benoist was highly respected amongst his peers for his courtesy and generous nature. He had never before been known to deliberately defy track officials like this. Sadly too, this was his final appearance as a Grand Prix racing driver, having announced just two weeks earlier his imminent retirement during the post-Le Mans celebration dinner. Nevertheless, there are other versions of this drama told by Bugatti historians, each of which has a similar and more considered theme.

The formal practice sessions and technical scrutiny of the cars were held on the Friday and Saturday before the race proper, the Saturday deadline being 7.00pm. In addition, the protocols of the ACF allowed informal practice opportunities on the Thursday, but no later than this. However, with their cars having failed to turn up, Benoist and Wimille were growing progressively frustrated throughout that Thursday. By Friday, Benoist was becoming extremely restless and agitated. Following anxious telephone calls to the Works, it was eventually confirmed that Wimille's car was in transit and would be arriving with Robert Aumaître the following morning. Alas, Benoist's car was still being assembled, so if it could be completed in time Jean Bugatti would drive it directly to the circuit. With this strong hint that his car might not be ready, Benoist considered that it would be sensible to have another entry in lieu of the T57S45. This option took the form of the T57S showroom demonstrator, which had a much higher level of performance than the standard model. Having informally discussed this with race officials, he wrongly believed he had permission to proceed with a practice. So he took the T57S out on to the Autodrome from the road circuit access behind the western banking, completing several circuits with a best

Bugatti Type 57 Grand Prix – A Celebration

time of 6min 4sec. This easily qualified for the race; in fact, some 15 seconds faster than Fretet's Delage – not bad really for a road car. However, the fact that officials had recorded Benoist's circuit times seems to undermine their next decision; whereupon concluding his run was told he would be excluded for practising an unauthorised car.

The following day, upon hearing of this in Paris, an angry Ettore Bugatti insisted on withdrawing both T57S45s, but Benoist and Jean appealed to him to wait until Wimille's car arrived so that they might at least evaluate its still untested performance on the track. The car arrived as promised on the Saturday morning, but late, after practice had already started. All the same, Wimille took the T57S45 Tank out around the circuit, and to the astonishment of the ACF officials, and Bugatti's rivals, set the fastest practice lap in a time of 5min 33sec, with an average speed of 135.91km/h (84.14mph). This beat Sommer's Talbot by 0.4 seconds. The astounded and embarrassed race organisers quickly offered to overturn Benoist's exclusion in lieu of a 1000f fine, whilst urgently securing the agreement of the other racing teams, and even extending the arrival deadline for the other car to midnight. However, when the second car failed to arrive, Ettore Bugatti

Jean Bugatti at Molsheim sat in race number 14, road registered 2103-W5. Note the recessed fuel filler cap ahead of the driver's door. (Courtesy Bugatti Trust)

7   1937 T57S45 Tanks

The second T57S45 Tank, number 14, at Molsheim prior to transit to Montlhéry. (Courtesy Bugatti Trust)

Another photo of number 14 at Molsheim. Note that the engine cover is made up from different alloy panels. (Courtesy Bugatti Trust)

Bugatti Type 57 Grand Prix – A Celebration

declared that both cars would be withdrawn anyway, because they were " ... still not yet ready to race." Later, it was clarified that the second car, whilst still not fully fit, did actually start out from Molsheim, but was involved in a minor traffic accident during the journey: a delay that needed time to sort out, and so the car later returned to the factory.

Mystery

Archive photographs exist showing two essentially identical cars, as well as a good rear view of car number 16. The Montlhéry ACF practice car has the registration 1202-W5, and race number 16, whereas the other is registered 2103-W5 with race number 14. At that time, 'W' registration plates were issued and used as the French equivalent of a 'trade plate,' so it may be taken that they represent a range of plates issued to the Bugatti works for transient use only. Curiously, the T57S45 Tanks were never seen again, and the factory records contain few clues as to their fate. Moreover, it is a mystery as to why they both disappeared, or what subsequently happened to them. Nevertheless, Bugatti wasted very little, so it must be accepted that most parts were recycled back into the Racing Department.

Fate

Some members of the Bugatti Owners Club and Bugatti Trust have been permitted to briefly examine the T50B single-seater Grand Prix car, and the T59/50B sports car, held in the National Museum at Mulhouse. Their observations allude to the fate of the two T57S45 Tanks. The T59/50B sports car shows a close similarity to the rear fuel tank noted on the T57S45 Tank, and both cars use practically identical chassis elements. Furthermore, holes noted in their respective un-perforated chassis frames show comparable positions for T57S45 Tank body mountings and subframes. It is possible that, when examined more closely at some future date during conservation, their respective T59 frame numbers might be revealed, and the redundant component mounting holes better evaluated.

T57S45 models from Michael Ottenwalder's Vroom and Knopp Hynek's Bohemia series.
(Courtesy NMT Collection – photo by D Roberts)

Vroom T57S45 model narrowed, shortened, and extensively modified; still not quite right, though.
(Courtesy NMT Collection – Author photo)

Another view of the modified T57S45 model.
(Courtesy NMT Collection – Author photo)

1937 T57 'Sport'

AS DISCUSSED IN THE previous chapter, it seems Jean Bugatti sincerely considered the Type 59 to be a variant of the Type 57. This mind-set can be traced to its inception, and was evident in early 1935 when he announced the development of a super sports car to replace the outmoded Type 55. Whilst we can be fairly certain that his Type 57S, which clearly combined attributes of the outmoded GP Type 59, was the intended outcome for a production car, there are also indicators to suggest that the T59 would be destined to become a competition sports car very early on. The T57 'Sport' was always raced with an un-supercharged T59/57G engine, whereas, from April 1935, the supercharged T59/57G always formally appeared as a GP Type 59. Nevertheless, both versions were technically similar, using many otherwise identical parts (the exceptions being the supercharger, piston compression height, and a few material details).

57248

Chassis number 57248 was allocated, and a plate fitted to T59 chassis, engine number 5, which was the only one of the five active 1934 Team cars not sold off in 1935. The car appears to have been newly built in April 1934, with T57 2-4-2 crank timing in its T59 crankcase, rather than the usual 4-4 of the T59. While the Factory Register allocation of 57428 is not dated, it falls sequentially, between December 1934 and May 1935. This period coincides with Jean's formal departure from Grand Prix racing, and his publicised 'ultimate' T57 super sports model.

It seems the earlier 4-4 crank T59 engines were sold off to private owners in March and April 1935. During 1935, all Works 3.3-litre T59 cars were developed into 2-4-2 T57G-powered racers, in both supercharged and un-supercharged form. Transformed along with three other T59 engines in April 1935, chassis 57248 was fitted with a special T57 large valve engine block developed under the appellation 'G.' This car appears to have been the same one, arranged without supercharger, entered as a Type 57 into the BARC 500 Mile Race at Brooklands in September 1935, looking just like a Type 59. In August 1936, it, and another chassis were completely refurbished to un-supercharged Type 59/57G engine specification for entry into the Comminges Grand Prix; both still looking just like Type 59s. This is their story.

1935 Brooklands 500-Mile Race

On September 21, 1935, Jean Bugatti entered a T59 into the BARC Brooklands 500-Mile Race, bearing race number 35; a drive shared by the Earl Howe and the Hon Brian Lewis. The 1935 British Automobile Racing Club handicap regulations favoured un-supercharged cars, so Howe asked Bugatti for one of the new T57GR models he had driven two weeks before in the Ulster TT. However, to Howe and Lewis' utter dismay, the Works sent what was declared to be a T57S, yet superficially appeared to be no more than an unblown version of the Grand Prix Type 59 fitted with a Brooklands silencer. This interesting car has created a lot of discussion amongst Bugatti scholars over the years. However, one thing is certain, the T59 was neither Howe nor Lewis' own. The British motoring press at that time reported it to be a Works car, and this has also been

Bugatti Type 57 Grand Prix – *A Celebration*

The T59/57G on the banking during the 1935 Brooklands 500-Mile Race. (Courtesy Bugatti Trust)

Opposite top: Howe and Lewis change places during the 1935 Brooklands 500-Mile Race pit stop. (Courtesy Bugatti Trust)

Opposite left: 1935 BARC 500-Mile model based on a 1/24 scale Wills' Finecast kit.
(Courtesy NMT Collection – photo by D Roberts)

Far right: 1/24 scale 1935 BARC 500-Mile Race car model.
(Courtesy NMT Collection – photo by D Roberts)

8   1937 T57 'Sport'

71

Bugatti Type 57 Grand Prix – A Celebration

confirmed by Howe's former chief mechanic, Percy 'Tommy' Thomas. The BARC annals record it as a T57S, and the press also declared the car to be fitted with a normally-aspirated Type 57 engine.

Earlier in the year, Jean publicly confirmed his commitment to the development of the 'ultimate' super sports car, where the T59/57G cylinder block was revised with larger valves and ports, including a special normally-aspirated manifold and Stromberg 29mm choke UUR2 carburettor, arranged to fit into the frame of either a Type 59 or Type 57. A T59 mechanic's notebook records:

"19th September 1935, number 5 engine rebuilt without supercharger. Inlet manifold Type 57 new model (Tourist Trophy); Pistons 53.5 (crown height) and new con rods and piston rings."

The TT manifold used larger conduits to suit the 45mm valve ports of the revised cylinder block, so it follows that engine number 5 already had the 'G' block. Also, since chassis, engine number 5 was designated 57248, this would have verified documentation when processed at borders. A photo of the car's rear in the pits shows only the final part

Wimille's car, 8265-NV2, accompanied by mechanics Joseph Spiesser and Robert Aumaître at the 1936 Comminges Grand Prix. Note the tail spine. (Courtesy Bugatti Trust)

8   1937 T57 'Sport'

1936 Comminges Grand Prix. Benoist's car, accompanied by mechanic Lucian Wurmser. Note the fabricated tail.
(Courtesy Bugatti Trust)

of a Bas-Rhin registration number: *unreadable*-NV2. Fifteen months later, this car was more formally known as a T59/57G; the T57 'Sport.' Since the TT engines delivered 158bhp at 5250rpm, it's rational to assume this one produced similarly at that time, but the smaller T59 car also had a favourably lower aerodynamic impact and weight than the T57GR(TT).

During the race itself, the car was going well, and Howe attained second place, averaging a speed of over 118mph when he came to the pit counter to refuel and hand over to Lewis. Recorded on film by a Pathé newsreel team, the changeover was very fast; the pit crew replaced four wheels and replenished 90 litres (20 gallons) of fuel in 1min 40sec. Second place was held, but, 15 minutes later, Lewis made two brief pit stops for a misfiring engine, where, initially, the sparkplugs were changed. On the second stop, however, the crew realised the engine-driven fuel pump was over-pressurising, and flooding the carburettor. The car had arrived so late before the race that neither driver had the chance to test-drive it, or to use the unfamiliar compound fuel tap, so Lewis was uncertain how to release the over-pressure. By now the car had dropped back to third place, although at the end of the race, the Bugatti was only one minute behind the first-placed Napier-Railton, and just eight seconds behind the Riley that was second. Conspicuously, however, this car was something rather special, for had Lewis

Bugatti Type 57 Grand Prix – A Celebration

not made those ill-fated pit stops, the car might have won easily. The tale of the unfamiliar fuel tap indicates it was not just an un-supercharged T59 engine, for Lewis was an experienced T59 driver, with his own car. As discussed, the engine was entirely that of a Type 57 in a Type 59 crankcase, and used a revised T57 fuel feed system.

1936 Comminges Grand Prix

A year later, two un-supercharged Type 59/57Gs were entered for the Comminges GP held on August 9, 1936 at St Gaudens. It was a race for unblown sports cars, where the rules allowed them to be stripped of mudguards, lighting equipment, and spare wheel. Furthermore, the rules did not even require the cars to be production models, or to have electric starters. This race gave Jean Bugatti the chance to prepare two specially-revised T59 chassis fitted with the most advanced and proven T57G elements available at that time. Here, some of the chassis crossbeams were made in Dural to reduce weight. Froude records show 'Preparation Comminges' for engines 59/57G No 0 and No 8. Also, their engine sumps were modified with a copper basin, 517mm x 112mm, 22mm deep, protruding from a cut-out in the original aluminium casting, and held in place with multiple copper rivets. These cars used T57G engine parts within a T59 crankcase, employing the latest normally-aspirated manifold used by the 'Tanks,' as well as the Bugatti C2 updraught carburettor attached with six mounting screws. They also included magnesium pistons, as well as the T57G 'Y' camshaft tower that drove a Bosch J08 magneto from the second intermediate idler at engine speed, mounted centrally in a brand new bulkhead, drawing 59.CH.440 dated July 17, 1936.

A photo on page 145 of Robert Jarraud's superb book *Bugatti doubles arbres* shows Benoist's car with its centrally-mounted magneto, normally-aspirated manifold, and Bugatti C2 carburettor; also shown is its T57 fuel pump. Additionally, the cars utilised an aircraft type, seven-layer oil cooler stack between the front dumb-irons. This was protected from stone damage by a grille in a frame below the coolant radiator. The cars were fitted with an external change lever version of the T57S45 gearbox, too, but pre-dated the revised rear suspension geometry associated with this unit. Without blower, the cars were lighter than a supercharged T59, yet with 9:1 compression ratios these engines could still develop 170bhp at 5600rpm. Pierre Veyron informed reporters that the two cars were " ... tremendously fast," and had reached 230km/h (143mph) on test. He also said their engines were identical to those used at Montlhéry and Reims, and would be arriving in the morning.

However, when the cars appeared, there was disbelief from Bugatti's rivals, followed by disappointment, then outrage, especially since they had anticipated T57G Tanks with non-removable mudguards. Despite impassioned complaint and fist waving, it was confirmed that the cars did not break any of the rules laid down by Automobile Club du Midi. Threats to leave in dissent were simply countered by warnings to financially penalize anyone who did. Peace eventually prevailed. Car race number 14, registered 8265-NV2, was driven by Wimille, whereas the second car, race number 16, was driven by Benoist. Just as with the BARC 500, they were not simply Type 59s with their superchargers removed. They were true Type 57 Grand Prix sports cars, just as asserted by Veyron. Clearly, the engine internals were otherwise identical to those fitted in the Tanks at the ACF and Marne, but in a T59 crankcase.

As a result of the earlier dispute, during practice the Bugatti drivers exercised a little discretion by ensuring they did not both get pole position on the grid. However, once they were away, the Bugattis made rapid progress; after the first lap, Wimille was 200m ahead, and then, by lap two, 300m. By the third lap, Wimille was 600m ahead of the pack, with Benoist in second place only 15 seconds behind. Halfway, the end of the tenth lap, Wimille was a full minute ahead of Dreyfus in his Talbot. At the finish of the first heat, the Bugattis were placed first and second. After a short break, allowing mechanics to service the cars, the second heat began. Now both in pole position, the two Bugattis quickly took the lead again and held it, although on lap 11, Benoist's car began to trail smoke that steadily worsened until he was forced to retire on lap 14 with a cracked piston. Wimille, however, maintained his blistering pace and won easily. His race average between the two heats was 152.58km/h (95.36mph), demonstrating that this normally-aspirated T59/57G's performance was actually little different to that of the supercharged T59 two years earlier.

Criticism and overhaul

Several historians have strongly criticised Jean Bugatti for passing off a Grand Prix T59 as a T57 sports car, but as we have seen in this analysis, from Jean's point of view, it was a

8   1937 T57 'Sport'

T57 Grand Prix. The original T59 evolved alongside the T57 in 1932 with distinctive and different engine applications, yet mechanically, it began to merge with the T57 throughout 1933 and 1934, until, by 1935, it became a T57 engine in a T59 crankcase. At least one car obtained a T57 chassis number. By 1936 the engines were refined T57Gs in T59 crankcases, and the un-supercharged Works cars had faster lap times than the blown T59s the year before. Despite losing 50bhp, this increased performance was due to several factors; a higher-revving T57G engine, new all-synchromesh gearbox allowing faster changes, a wider range of axle ratios, and newly developed Dunlop '5-Stud' tyres, first trialled by Bugatti at Turin in April 1936. These tyres may be identified by their five parallel rows of disjointed rectangular blocks. In retrospective analysis, the new Dunlop tyres alone probably improved circuit times by as much as two seconds per lap, and had outstanding grip in the wet.

During the winter of 1936-37, the two cars were completely overhauled, with their right-hand chassis rail specially modified to accept the projected, but problematic, T50B supercharged engine. As discussed earlier, in late 1936, Jean announced that six T57S45 streamliners were planned for 1937, where the revised chassis arrangements reflect this undertaking. The six may have comprised the two, as mentioned; two 1933 spare frames; as well as two chassis frame sets from the three ordered in December 1935.

Stripped chassis of 57248, engine number 5. Note the cutaway prepared in the frame for the T50B unit. Note the special dynamo mounting, too. (Courtesy Bugatti Trust)

75

Bear in mind that some chassis had been badly damaged in crashes, but it would appear that 15 frames were constructed in total. Subsequently, the T57S45 venture was abandoned, yet Benoist and Wimille's cars were clearly prepared with a modified frame, revised rear suspension geometry, and long external radius rods. Both were also fitted with a twin-pump, dry-sump version of the T57S45 all-synchromesh gearbox, installed slightly further back in the chassis to allow room for the T50B engine, although the frame was never actually drilled for its mountings. In due course, one of the cars was rebuilt with skimpy bodywork in preparation for Pau in February. The ex-Benoist Comminges car was rebuilt with a supercharged version of the T59/57G 3.3-litre engine for the 400,000f prize trials to be held at Montlhéry in April.

1937 Pau Grand Prix

The car prepared for Pau retained several features from the Comminges GP version, although its rear bulkhead plate was replaced with one 50mm wider. This enabled widened bodywork from the scuttle back, and the car was given two token opening doors to comply with the AIACR sports car regulations. Dated February 4, 1937, a drawing 59/57G.MOT.156, for the car 'Competition (Pau)', illustrates the new rear bulkhead plate, detailing the opening for an electric battery cradle mounting. Here on this document, the car is formally recognised by the factory as 59/57G. The Pau car had its fully developed, normally-aspirated T57G engine in a T59 crankcase. This was modified to take a dynamo support bracket, 59.MOT.219 – January 26, 1937, attached with four screws from the inside; it was driven by the water-pump shaft just as the T57. Froude test records dated February 12, 1937 shows that this engine developed 175bhp at 5500rpm, using 'Elektron' (magnesium) pistons with a 56mm compression height, and a Bugatti C2-34mm choke carburettor. The car used a central gearchange cover version of the T57S45 all-synchromesh gearbox, 57S45.CV.ENS.3 – October 20, 1936. It also utilised the fully-revised rear suspension for this gearbox, although the long radius rods were hidden beneath bodywork panels. A swept-down exhaust system ran the whole length of the left-hand chassis sideframe, tucked just below it. The car's rear axle was fitted with a ZF limited-slip differential, which essentially upgraded its specification to that of the T50B single seaters.

The car was now an authentic Type 57GP, and no longer looked like a GP Type 59. The dashboard was made from wood, hinged in the centre to allow the left-hand side to open, granting access to the fuses and magneto. On the right half, to the left of the steering column, was a Jaeger 8000rpm tachometer and horn. To the right of the column were oil pressure and coolant temperature gauges, magneto kill button, as well as the original hand-throttle and advance/retard levers. On the left-hand dashboard were the ignition/lighting switch, fuel and ammeter gauges, starter button, and Ki-gas pump.

The car employed an electric self-starter, lighting equipment, and mudguards. A 15-litre (3.3-gallon) engine oil tank, 59.CH.475 – February 16, 1937, was arranged below the rather thin passenger seat. The rules demanded this detail, but not that the passenger should have any sense of pain. The car was installed with an 85-litre (18.5-gallon) fuel tank, 59.CH. 470, February 4, 1937, mounted behind the cockpit, and featuring a single filler cap. Beneath this, at the rear of the frame, a long, narrow, 10-litre (2.2-gallon) gearbox oil tank, 59.CH.469, February 17, 1937, was mounted transversely between the rear crossmember and suspension spring mounting tube. An enclosed spare wheel was arranged above a rounded tail, complete with a detachable alloy cover. Weighing in at 960kg (2112lb), the car looked more like a sports model, and was registered with a Bas-Rhin 'Works' number, 344-NV3. For the event it carried race number 16.

The race

The race was held on Sunday, February 21, 1937, where the Spanish/French border Auto Club de Basco-Bearnais promoted an 80-lap, 220km sports car race in and around the city of Pau, with a purse of 30,000f for the victor. Set against the backdrop of the Pyrenees Mountains, the 2.76km (1.715-mile) circuit arose and fell through 30m (100ft), meandering its way through many twists and turns. Six of the tight bends snaking through the city itself changed direction by almost 180°. Wimille had injured his thumb whilst skiing in the mountains prior to the race, which caused him a lot of discomfort and threatened his performance on this twisting circuit. The 'one-off' T57 'Sport' was allowed to compete under the provisions of the ACBB rules, since they acknowledged 'Specials' and 'Prototype' cars in this event. Wimille's main rivals consisted of two works T150C Talbots, three works T135CS Delahayes, seven privately-entered T135CSs, and the skimpy-bodied

8 1937 T57 'Sport'

1937 400,000f prize at Montlhéry, where Wimille drives the former Benoist car, now supercharged. Note the fabricated tail. (Courtesy Bugatti Trust)

Bugatti T57S driven by Raymond de Saugé (57522/185) registered 1041RK8, and carrying race number 22. During Friday practice, Wimille was fastest, lapping in 1min 56sec, averaging a speed of 86.7km/h (53.84mph), two seconds faster than Sommer's Talbot, and despite gaining 100kg and losing 50bhp, was as fast as his time the year before in a supercharged T59. During the second practice on Saturday, Wimille improved his time further by lapping in 1min 53sec, at a speed of 88.23km/h (54.79mph).

Race day was sunless and wet – a fine drizzle throughout made the streets especially slippery – yet there was a total of 14 starters, with Dreyfus in pole position alongside Wimille.

Bugatti Type 57 Grand Prix – A Celebration

At the 2.00pm 'Run-Start,' the car was in perfect tune, and a class apart from the rest. Wimille took the lead straight away, with Dreyfus and Sommer in second and third, respectively. With the excellent-in-the-wet Dunlop racing tyres and well-chosen axle ratios, Wimille was able to gain 3-4 seconds per lap over his rivals.

As the track dried, Wimille went even faster, and, after 20 laps, was 1min 34sec ahead; after 29 laps he had lapped everyone. He then relaxed a little to remain a safe lap ahead for the rest of the race.

Surviving attrition, and finishing 11 laps behind Wimille, the T57S of de Saugé finished last, having been fitted with an unsuitable axle ratio. However, the motoring press did not fail to emphasize the discrepancy between the two Bugatti cars, one of which purported to be the same as the other: T57 'Sport' and T57S; the former placed first and the latter absolute last. The combination of Wimille's driving skill, a high-revving T57G engine, all-synchromesh gearbox, improved suspension, a good permutation of axle ratios, and '5-Stud' Dunlop tyres, seem to have contributed to his car's performance and great success.

1937 Montlhéry 400,000f prize

The 1936 ex-Benoist Comminges car was rebuilt with a supercharged version of the 3.3-litre T59/57G engine for the 400,000f prize trials to be held at Montlhéry on Tuesday, March 23, 1937. It retained the same Grand Prix T59 body, with a plain tail riveted at the flanks. Froude Test House records show that engine 59/57G No 8 was tested on March 19, 1937. Whilst otherwise similar to the Comminges car, with external right-hand gearchange lever, it was now fitted with a dry-sump, twin-pump version of the T57S45 all-synchromesh gearbox. It also used revised rear suspension, sliding blocks, and long external radius rods to control axle movement. The aircraft-style oil radiator between the front dumb-irons was discarded, the copper sump-tray being effective at maintaining the oil at an efficient running temperature. However, the car retained the Comminges bulkhead and centrally-mounted, high-performance Bosch J08 magneto, driven at engine speed. The Comminges bonnet was replaced with one having an air scoop for the intake, as seen at Deauville in 1936.

The prize event itself was created by the Fond des Course Committee to encourage French racing car makers to build a more competitive Grand Prix entrant, compliant with 1938

1937 Tunis Grand Prix: 57248, 344-NV3, accompanied by mechanic Lucien Wurmser. Note the single fuel filler. (Courtesy Bugatti Trust)

AIACR specification that could challenge the main opposition. It involved a timed trial covering 16 laps (200km) of the Montlhéry circuit at an average speed better than 146.508km/h (91.04mph). The supercharged T59/57G Bugatti was first trialled there by Wimille on March 23, but did not run well. The following day, the best run achieved an average speed of only 144km/h (89.48mph).

The weather worsened with two days of rain, but cleared for Saturday the 27th. The car started well, averaging a speed of 149km/h (92.59mph) until the fuel pump failed, and night fell before it was corrected. On Sunday the 28th, after just a few laps, disastrously, the final drive failed so badly it could not be repaired, requiring a new axle assembly. The range of available T59 gear ratios was wide, but the correct combination crucial for the Montlhéry circuit and this event was unique. Accordingly, the car was returned to Molsheim, presumably to have these exclusive components re-manufactured. Even so, it was still under repair when the midnight, March 31 deadline expired.

Following discussions, the Committee and the AIACR agreed to extend the attempt deadline to Sunday, April 18. So after a relaxed Easter break on the Côte d'Azur, Wimille returned to Montlhéry with the car on Monday, April 12. Now, the car's performance in Wimille's skilful hands was outstanding, with an average lap speed of 146.807km/h (91.224mph) after just four circuits of the track, and by lap ten, his margin was 19 seconds ahead of schedule. Journalist Maurice Henry noted that Wimille just brushed the apex of every curve on the road circuit. On lap 16 he took the prize with the tiniest margin of just 4.9 seconds, or about 200m. His overall average speed was 146.654km/h (91.072mph), and Bugatti received a very welcome Fonds des Course cheque for 320,000f, the remainder being held back.

1937 Tunis Grand Prix

The T57 Sport was entered for the Tunis GP held on Sunday, May 16, 1937 with a new radiator cowl and race number 8. Froude records note engine "57x59 No 5 prep Tunis/Bône." The roughly triangular Carthage circuit was flat, covering a distance of 12.6km (7.8 miles), and employed a chicane on the primary straight just before the pits. The event used the Le Mans-type run-start becoming favoured for sports cars, and consisted of three, eight-lap sprints covering 302.4km in total. There would be a 45-minute break between heats, but refuelling was disallowed.

In heat one, starting at 1.30pm, amongst 13 starters Wimille led all the way, making the fastest lap of the day by lap three, in 4min 50sec, averaging 156.4km/h (97.2mph). At the end of the eighth lap he had a 35sec lead, yet, instead of a chequered flag, he was black-flagged, obliging him to continue an additional 12.6km lap. In heat two at 3.00pm, Sommer's Talbot led the first few laps, shortly after which Wimille took the lead. In the final heat at 4.30pm, the field was reduced to ten cars. On the seventh lap, Wimille was running well, and 60 seconds ahead of his second-placed rival, when the car ran out of fuel. The 85-litre (18.5-gallon) fuel tank had the capacity to cover the total distance, but was surely under-filled. Wimille's biography blames the additional lap distance in heat one, whereas Wurmser's biography suggested there was an issue with incorrect filling of the fuel tank. Both versions are probably correct if someone calculated the fill without allowing leeway for an emergency lap.

1937 Bône (Annaba) Grand Prix

The Bône Grand Prix was held on May 23, 1937, on the 1.9km (1.18-mile) circuit; nick-named 'La Grenouillère,' because of its relatively slow and fairly unexciting course. The track consisted of local pavé roads, most of which were uneven and heavily worn in places, making it practically impossible to achieve top speeds. The agile little T57 Sport used axle ratios which were better suited to the slower road circuit around the old town and harbour quay.

During Friday practice, Wimille set a fairly quick time, so, with self-assurance, did not bother with a Saturday second run. The T57 Sport was running beautifully, and in heat one Wimille lapped everyone. In heat two, he led the race initially, but then developed a slight misfire, which permitted René Carrière to take the chequered flag in his Delahaye. Nonetheless, this made no difference to Wimille's first place on aggregate, with an average speed of 100km/h (62.13mph). Following the race, the Team got wind of an escalating dockworker's strike so escaped quickly, departing from the port of Bizerta, Tunis, and returning to France on the ship *La Chanzi*.

1937 Marseille 3-Hour Race

The Grand Prix de Marseille was held on the flat, 5km oval Miramas Autodrome on Sunday June 6, 1937. The Auto Club du Marseille rules divided the three-hour race into three, one-hour heats using chicanes; each effectively a different circuit. The first heat used two chicanes, each in the middle of the two straights. For the second heat, only one chicane was used, and there was none for the third and final heat, making for a flat-out, high-speed race to the finish. Refuelling was permitted only during the heats, not in-between them. These rules demanded clever tactics for team managers, who had to select a suitably-compromised axle ratio, given the maximum

Bugatti Type 57 Grand Prix – *A Celebration*

top speed restrictions in each heat, which rose throughout the day. The Bugatti T57 Sport was now fitted with two fuel filler caps, and an alloy passenger seat cover to assist in the high-speed section of the race. The car had race number 14, and was otherwise physically as seen at Bône, although, after its sand-blasting in North Africa, the little car had been given a fresh coat of paint. Froude records show the car again used un-supercharged T59/57G engine number 5; tested on May 28, 1937. Given the date sequence, these revisions and Froude tests were undoubtedly carried out at the Bugatti workshops in Nice, rather than the car having to travel all the way back to Molsheim.

For Bugatti, the nimble little car with its high-revving engine had the potential to succeed well, given a suitable axle ratio, but would have to build up as much of a lead as possible in the first heat. Since the T57 'Sport' had only an 85-litre tank, the 500km event required a fuel stop, so tactics would dictate as to when this would be best executed.

Each heat began with drivers sitting in their respective cars with the ignition off. This increased complications for entrants with more temperamental engines when the flag dropped. Heat one began at 2.00pm, with 25 cars on the grid. Sommer's Talbot got away first, with Wimille hot on his tail, 25 seconds behind. For two laps, Sommer got to the chicanes first, only to have the agile T57 'Sport' catch up through them. By lap three, however, Wimille took the lead, stayed there, and won the first heat. In heat two, Sommer's Talbot was reluctant to start, delaying him by 30 seconds. This allowed Wimille to lead, but Comotti's Talbot passed and re-passed him several times during the following 15 laps. When Wimille went in to refuel, he lost his 25-second advantage, where Sommer promptly caught up and passed them both, 54 seconds ahead of the 'Sport,' so that Wimille finished third. Léoz's T57S, 57522/185, retired with a failed rear axle during this heat. In heat three, Sommer led straight away, where Wimille's T57 'Sport' was clearly feeling the strain, and, within minutes, Comotti passed him, shortly after which Wimille retired with failed big-end bearings. Nevertheless, even before its first, and last, mechanical catastrophe, the T57 'Sport' was unquestionably defeated on merit by the Talbots.

8   1937 T57 'Sport'

1937 Marne Grand Prix: Wimille in 57248, race number 2, speeds past the grandstands. (Courtesy Bugatti Trust)

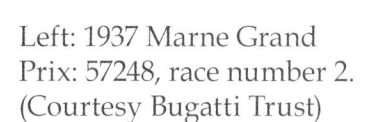

Left: 1937 Marne Grand Prix: 57248, race number 2. (Courtesy Bugatti Trust)

1937 Marne Grand Prix: 57248 race number 2 in the pits. Note the exhaust tail pipes and twin fuel fillers. (Courtesy Bugatti Trust)

Bugatti Type 57 Grand Prix – A Celebration

1937 Marne Grand Prix

The Grand Prix de la Marne was held on July 18, 1937, at the 7.8km (4.85-mile) Reims-Gueux triangular circuit, and would run a total of 492km (305 miles) over 63 laps. This would be the very last race held under the 1936-37 sports car regulations, and final of the season, especially since the projected Comminges Grand Prix on August 1 had been cancelled due to a shortage of entrants. The on-going Depression episode had gradually depleted the number of entries for sports car events throughout the season, and despite the organizers massaging the rules to maximize potential competitors, many could barely afford the fees. After their first appearance at Montlhéry, T57S45 Tanks were anticipated, but instead Wimille turned up with the T57 Sport. Jean Bugatti must have realised that the demise of the sports car formula also ended the career and further development of the T57S45 Tanks. The race was fast and ran on normal roads, with very few opportunities to overtake, yet the agile little T57 Sport had an obvious tactical advantage over the larger and wider T57G Tanks used the year before. The car appeared to be similar in form to that seen at Marseille, including the cockpit fairing, but wearing race number 2. Froude records show "57x59 No 5 (Voiture Wimille) Marne" tested on July 9 and 13, 1937. The main rivals were two V12 T145 Delahayes, seven T135C Delahayes, and five T150C Talbots.

Friday practice was wet all day. Saturday was dry, however, whereupon, with a minimum fuel load, Wimille set the fastest time at 151.90km/h (94.33mph) for pole position alongside Dreyfus in a T145 Delahaye, and Sommer in a T150C Talbot. The T57 Sport already had a fuel tank capacity around 100-litre less than its challengers, but Wimille's strategy this season was to compute precise volumes and distances for refuelling and tyre checks, allowing him to exploit the reduced weight in order to get as far ahead of his rivals as possible. There is some evidence on the surviving car that it had once been fitted with a precision fuel level gauge, such as the Hobson KS fluid Telegage. Whilst he would have to refuel more frequently, the combination of a narrow and nimble little car with lower overall weight would allow him to accelerate past most of the backmarkers more readily than the bigger cars on this very narrow circuit. Race day was hot, with blazing sunshine so bright that Wimille wore tinted goggles, and there was a superb turnout of 40,000 spectators to enjoy the fine weather and performance of the competitors.

The race

Wimille took the lead immediately, with Dreyfus close on his tail and Sommer a few seconds behind him; with no change by the end of the first lap. On the second, Wimille set a record at 149.54km/h (92.86mph), although with Dreyfus still close behind him until his Delahaye burst a front right tyre and spun off at La Garenne corner. This allowed Carrière to move up past Sommer into second place, 12 seconds behind the 'Sport,' until on lap 22 his Delahaye also lost a tyre. It was quickly obvious that the Goodrich-Colombes tyres were not entirely suitable for these racing conditions and the high ambient temperatures. The T57 'Sport' was gaining around two-three seconds per lap on its '5-stud' Dunlop tyres, and, by lap 30, Wimille had a lead of 70 seconds over Sommer in the Talbot. On lap 32 the Bugatti pitted for a refuelling stop.

With the gruelling heat, the race was hard going for the cars and their drivers, who took on plenty of water, too. When Wimille returned to the race his lead was reduced to 31 seconds over Sommer. Chiron's Talbot overtook Sommer on lap 42, but just three laps later he dropped out with a blown head gasket. On lap 52, now with a two-minute lead, Wimille went in again for another quick fuel top-up and tyre check, taking just 45 seconds. In the final remaining laps, Wimille lapped second placed Sommer, and then eased off on the throttle to win the race in 3h 23min 49sec, at an average speed of 145km/h (90.12mph). The three pit stops led some dissenters to accuse Bugatti of using alcohol fuel, but clearly, Wimille was exploiting his tiny car and minimising its weight, thus giving him a greater chance to overtake backmarkers with ease on the fast but narrow Reims road circuit.

Criticism, revision and disposal

Bugatti's critics have dismissed the T57 'Sport' as a thinly-disguised T59 Grand Prix racing car, yet overlook the great advances made in the development of its unblown T57G engine throughout 1935, 1936 and 1937, as a result of the AIACR's Sports Car formula. These same critics also overlook the fact that the V12 T145 Delahaye sports cars were specialised racing cars, and that the works T150C Talbots were equally far-removed from their production brothers. The T57 'Sport' formally retired from racing at the same time as the French Sports Car formula ended.

Eventually superseded by the T59/50B sports car in 1938, 57248 was never fitted with the long-promised T50B engine,

8   1937 T57 'Sport'

Side view of 57248 in recent times. (Courtesy NMT Collection)

where the frame was not even drilled for its mountings despite having the right-hand chassis rail modified to clear its large blower. Still, it obtained a similarly-revised lamp pod and radiator cowl as the sister car. The T57 Sport's engine was revised with lower compression height pistons, and fitted with a blower, supercharger number SP2, but was detuned for road sensibility, with just one Zenith 52 K1-type carburettor. The Bosch J08 magneto was exchanged for an easy-care Scintilla MN8D, mounted horizontally in the centre of the bulkhead with a new advance/retard lever. This important historical T57 'Sport' racing car was sold to King Leopold of Belgium. Its subsequent owners should be highly praised for maintaining this rare and unique T57G sports racing car in original condition; always sympathetically conserved. Whilst usually referred to as a Grand Prix Type 59, we should now all recognize that it is really a supercharged Type 57 Grand Prix car.

Bugatti Type 57 Grand Prix – A Celebration

Left: The dashboard of 57248.

Lower left: View of 57248's T57S45 gearbox with central change. Also note the pipework to the under-seat oil reservoir.

Lower right: Note the bolted top-plate and castellated sparkplug cups.

8   1937 T57 'Sport'

Right: 57248's chassis plate and number. (Courtesy NMT Collection)

Lower left: 57248's exhaust manifold.

Lower right: 57248's drag link cutout in the body, showing the specially modified chassis side with external flange. (Courtesy NMT Collection)

85

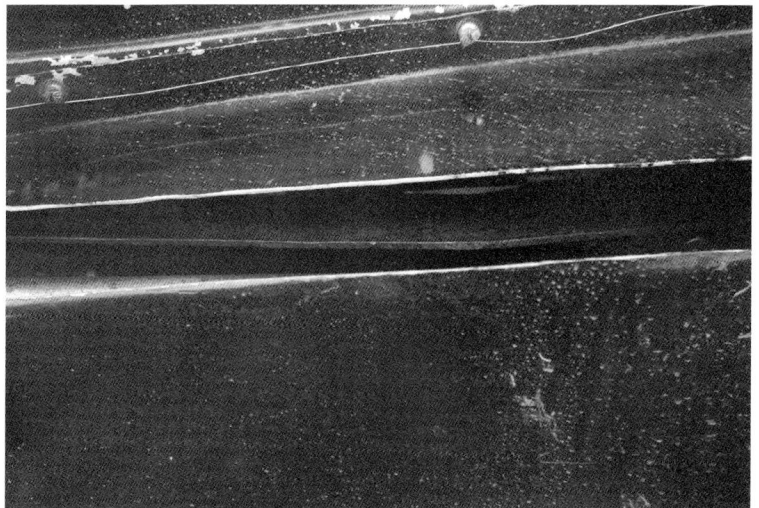

1939 Le Mans

FOLLOWING THE INCREDIBLE ACHIEVEMENT of the T57G Tank at Le Mans in 1937, the Bugatti standard of sports car performance was elevated far higher than its rivals. As a result, and much to Jean's displeasure, Ettore declined to support an entry for 1938. In reality, the firm was financially stretched to its limit, and Automobiles Bugatti bankers were practically living on-site in order to increase pressure and maintain rigid budgets throughout 1938. For this very same reason, the racing department was no longer a high priority in the company's overall business strategy. Driven by Eugene Chaboud and Jean Trémoulet, the 1938 Le Mans-winning Delahaye's distance of 3180.94km (1976.59 miles) had failed to increase that attained by Bugatti in 1937. Consequently, Ettore took the view that it was unnecessary to enter in 1939 either. However, for that year, there was a conspicuous threat to Bugatti's record from the latest Alfa Romeo 2900B and Delahaye V12 Type 145. So, following months of badgering by Jean, and with promises to keep to a very strict fiscal plan, his father eventually conceded to permit just one car for the great 24-hour race. Ettore is said to have settled terms with: "Only one car can win, so only one car will be entered."

Only one car

On January 5, 1939, senior mechanic Robert Aumaître was instructed to select a chassis from the production line and to begin modifying it for the great competition.

Historians have not yet formally identified its chassis number, but its road registration was 1244-W5. Interestingly, wartime French government travel documents show that this trade plate was associated with chassis number 57454, when used in 1940 for the Works Atlantic Coupé demonstrator during relocation to Bordeaux. In turn, it was also one of three numbers allocated to T57Gs in 1936-1937. I believe it was common practice at the Works that only specific chassis numbers and road plates were formally registered with the district authorities, to limit costs. That is, they were used as the equivalent of 'trade plates' for insurance and legal purposes.

Intriguingly, Bugatti publicity promoted an impression that the new Tank was merely one taken from the production line and fitted with a streamlined body. Yet, this was massaging the truth. Like many motor makers of the period who also raced their cars, very few parts used from the production line ever remained un-modified, and many others were special-material items or unique, one-offs. Likewise, as we shall see, it is apparent that most of the more specialised components used for this car were already available to Jean's team from stock. Furthermore, if absolutely vital to save costs, some components could even be refurbished from secondhand items. Clearly, some of the more expensive parts could have been cannibalised from the 1937 ex-Labric/Veyron Le Mans car, which has otherwise never been properly accounted for in the records. In practice, it was not difficult to build a highly-competitive car using the minimum of new parts. This is to suggest that the over-hyped publicity promoting the car as a barely-modified standard model, was perhaps for the benefit of accountants rather than others, in order to insinuate a very limited build budget when this was not the case.

1939 Tank described

The 1939 Le Mans car is no longer accessible for any sort of detailed internal examination, so we only have known Works drawings, specification records, and formal factory statements to go on. Additionally, a number of photos exist of the wreckage following the fatal crash that so sadly ended Jean Bugatti's life. We must assume, too, that the special drawings produced for this 1939 car were actual elements of its construction. Publicly, the chassis was declared to be a standard Type 57C from the production line, yet with frame sections 5mm thick in stock form, these were around 25 per cent heavier than the T57S surbaissé of 1937 that used 3.5mm sheet steel. Therefore, the chassis had a massive potential for weight saving. Drawing number 57G.CH.ENS.1, titled 'ALLEGEMENT CHASSIS 57 T. 24 HEURES 39' dated March 17, 1939, illustrates a long T57 Series 2 frame with its sides lightened with holes throughout its length. Curiously, the drawing detail indicates that these holes were not merely pierced, as with the 1937 car, but had specially-flared edges for added strength, as used in aeronautic design practice. Internal chassis plating and some brackets were already lightened with holes as standard, but to what further degree the chassis was modified for competition is unclear. It does not seem unreasonable to suppose that, in line with previous racing practice, it may have had other reinforcing pieces and crossmembers lightened or pierced with holes, too. As an example found in the records, the tubular bracing strut above the rear axle was unique, having its own drawing dated February 17, 1939; using slightly lighter gauge tubing.

Curiously, the chassis drawing title '57T' hints that it employed a lowered body profile akin to the 1935 T57GR and T57T competition cars. However, it otherwise appears to illustrate a complete Series 2, semi-cruciform rigid chassis for a flexibly-mounted engine. The Series 1 T57GR and T57T chassis versions in 1935, with a solidly-mounted engine, had

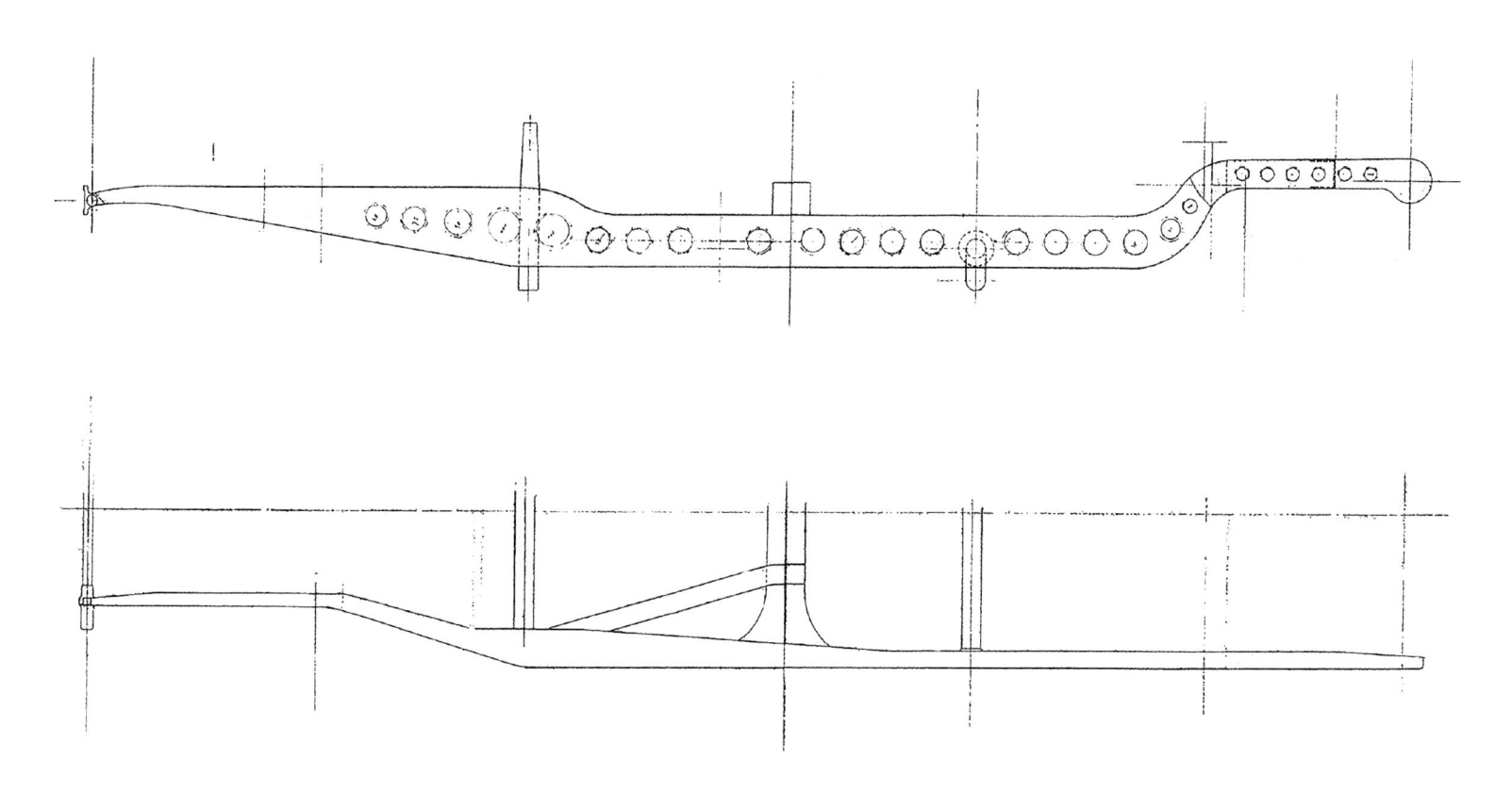

Chassis drawing of the 1939 Le Mans T57C. Note it is a Series 2 version that has been extensively lightened with holes. (Courtesy Bugatti Trust)

seats, steering column and bonnet lowered by 80mm. The un-braced Series 1 frame allowed the driver's footwell to be positioned between the chassis sideframe and the gearbox, making for a more comfortable, lowered driving position. The lowered clutch linkage arrangement for the T57S originates from this time. If a Series 2 frame was used with a body profile 80mm lower, the driver's legs would be above the chassis sides, as well as almost straight out in front. However, a factory drawing 57G.CH.72, dated April 6, 1939, illustrates the 1939 Le Mans car bulkhead assembly, clearly designed for a 'G' specification, centrally-mounted Bosch J08 magneto. It also shows that the upper profile is 615mm above the top of the chassis sides, instead of the usual 650mm. Consequently, it is clear that the body was, in fact, lowered, but by only 35mm from standard. Such a compromise permitted a semi-lowered bodywork profile in union with a 1939, Series 2 chassis frame, yet still retained a comfortable lowered position for the driver.

Being a lighter car than normal, the special suspension detail reflects this by having fewer spring leaves; seven for the front and nine at the rear; although tempered to be slightly stiffer like those of the 1936 Tank. The front axle was adapted for T59 stub-axles, brakes and racing wheels, but should have been a standard 1939 T57C solid item rather than hollow. It is, of course, possible that the specially-modified T57S hollow front axle assembly was cannibalised from the 1937 Veyron Le Mans car.

Specification changes to the rear axle provided three final-drive sets: 14:42-3:1, 13:43-3.3:1 and 12:42-3.5:1, where the Le Mans circuit choice was 14:42, housed in a standard T57S lightweight ribbed casing. This strong 3:1 ratio better suited the rolling circumference of the racing wheels, and increased engine torque, providing 230km/h (143mph) at 5000rpm. The rear axle trumpets were uniquely modified, and special half-shafts made to accept the very latest T59/50B brakes, backplates, hubs, racing wheels and locknuts. This item, too, could have been adapted from one cannibalised from the 1937 Veyron car.

The new brakes incorporated hydraulic actuators, with special 400mm diameter brake drums that were 10mm wider than those fitted to the 1937 Le Mans cars. The 1939 production T57C was fitted with French Lockheed twin master cylinders which, when combined with the latest Grand Prix brakes, provided the car with remarkable braking potential. Also, new Grand Prix hub locknuts, with 70° flared ears, ensured the mallet would be further away from those precious and expensive radial wires during rapid wheel changes in the pits. We may perhaps assume that the frantic hammering off of the wheel nuts in 1936 had damaged wheel spokes, and this simple change to the hub nuts was in response to this particular issue. Predictably, these were designed for the T59/50B single-seat cars, as drawing 59.EA.74, dated May 12, 1939.

By 1939, the exotically expensive De Ram dampers were beyond the very limited budget of the racing department. Consequently, Jean returned to a T57 scheme first studied in February 1934, before committing himself to De Rams. Le Mans car drawing number 57G.EA.ENS.3, dated February 2, 1939, illustrates a special T57 vertical mounting strut modified to accept two types of damper concurrently: Lovejoy-Delco hydraulic telescopic units, as well as André Telecontrol Hartford friction disc items. A number of other drawings from this period relate to rear axle and chassis bracket fittings for these same dampers. What is particularly significant about them is that they are clearly intended to accept both types of damper, not either/or, where in unison, perhaps Jean Bugatti hoped they performed as well as De Rams. The new design had to be adjusted manually, though, using a small hand wheel on the dashboard, instead of being automatic to road conditions. The more complicated and hugely expensive De Ram dampers were 'wet' friction discs, adjusted automatically through hydraulic action and the rate of suspension movement. Jean's version, which combined the two, was heavier, but clearly the best solution he could afford at that time. Both of these units were essentially stock Bugatti T57 parts, except never previously used together.

Special engine

The factory drawings show that the 1939 Le Mans car was designated Type 57G. For publicity purposes, though, Jean Bugatti formally declared its engine to be a standard supercharged T57C unit except for an alternative carburettor; in this case a Bugatti C2 unit with a 34mm choke. A standard T57C yielded 160bhp at 5000rpm. Even so, dynamometer test records for this engine show it produced 200bhp at 5000rpm, clearly suggesting power, endurance and reliability tuning to at least T57SC specification. T57C engines were always dry sump lubricated, and there is a May 1939 T57G drawing for a 30-litre engine oil tank. As implied, the more expensive parts of this build could potentially have been sourced from the fairly low-mileage earlier racing Tanks. Even one of the ex-1937 Le Mans T57G power units could have been renovated and rebuilt with a supercharger to limit costs. Jean Bugatti did this previously with his T59/57G engines in their racing days, converting from normally-aspirated to supercharged during rebuilds, revising piston height, engine timing and carburettor settings.

The crankshaft was a specially-lightened 57G item, where the removable 27-tooth camshaft drive gear used straight-cut teeth and was case-hardened. The main bearing caps were made in high-strength forged Rolls-Royce RR56 alloy, and special material (AD3) con-rods were used, being heat-treated, stronger and lighter. The pistons were machined from Elektron magnesium forgings, with a relatively modest crown height of 46.5mm. Used by Bugatti since 1936, Elektron alloys are just 60 per cent of the weight of aluminium, greatly reducing inertia and enabling higher engine revolutions. The cylinder block was 'G' specification, as drawing number 57G.MOT.ENS.1, dated January 11, 1939. It was identical to the T57G 45mm valve engine block used in all competition T57, and in T59s as 59.MOT.195, dated March 12, 1935, always using a bolted top-plate.

The engine also utilised the 'Y' camshaft tower of the sports-racing T57Gs of 1936, with a centrally-mounted Bosch J08 magneto, driven at engine speed through a 27-tooth Celeron (fibre) gear. The first intermediate camshaft drivetrain gear was made from steel, the second intermediate gear from cast iron, and both camshaft gears from steel. Idler and camshaft wheels were lightened with holes, and all had narrow, 14mm wide, straight-cut teeth. The 'G' engine modifications included the usual enlarged ports, 45mm valves, special valve guides, triple valve springs and retainers, a higher specification ignition system, as well as improved cylinder head cooling with a bolted top-plate. The supercharger was a standard T57C twin-lobe Roots type, driven through a 23-tooth gear, rotating at 1.17 times engine speed. Drawings show that the supercharger used special pressure relief valve components to better balance the increased engine performance and output needs. In Grand Prix supercharged form these engines were much higher-revving than production versions. I believe this engine was easily capable of generating reliable surges of 240bhp at 6000rpm.

Since the standard T57C used a single-plate clutch, Pichetto sent a note to Jean Bugatti asking whether to fit a single- or a twin-plate clutch. Other than "See me," Jean's reply remains unknown. However, a twin-plate clutch had been specified for the long-wheelbase TT cars in 1935, and had worked successfully for the Le Mans car in 1937. What's more, a twin-plate clutch was standard specification for the T57SC engine anyway, so the parts required were available off-the-shelf. Consequently, it is rational that the more durable T57SC twin-plate clutch was used to match the more powerful T57SC engine, especially in the longer and relatively heavier chassis.

Gearbox

It has been reported by some historians that the 1939 Le Mans car used a bellhousing version of the T57S45 all-synchromesh gearbox. Jean Bugatti may have intended such usage, because the pierced chassis drawing shows a space in the sequence of holes where a forward radius rod ball-joint housing would attach. Such revisions of the rear suspension were required with this gearbox. Conversely, I believe this report is an error, since I was unable to find drawings of either a suitable bellhousing, mounting parts, gearbox front cover converter, or an appropriate clutch shaft that would adapt to the T57SC engine. Additionally, there are no special components that would suitably revise the rear suspension geometry of the T57C. What does exist in the records, though, is a sequence of drawings (57G.CV.1 to 57G.CV.8), dated between March 16 and 20, 1939, relating to the special parts needed to convert a standard T57 gearbox to synchromesh; as used for the 1936 and 1937 Tanks. From these records, therefore, it is clear that the 1939 Le Mans car also adopted the special 1936-37 T57G gearbox; with synchromesh on second, third and top. Additionally, a 1939 drawing shows the same triple oil tank top-up system that was used for the 1937 Le Mans cars. For economy, it is feasible that one of the ex-1937 Le Mans, low-mileage, synchromesh gearboxes was refurbished using these special parts, all others being stock T57 items.

Advanced streamlining

Externally, like the 1937 car, the body was 'Tank-like,' but aerodynamically far more refined and developed. It was aesthetically much more elegant on the longer 3.3m wheelbase chassis, where the body profile was clearly lower than the production model. Lessons had been learned from experience with the earlier Tanks, where the new design vastly improved the airflow rate through the engine compartment. This significantly reduced issues with vapour-locks in the fuel lines due to high under-bonnet temperatures and hard working front brakes. As a result, hot air from the radiator and front brakes could now escape easily from two massive exits, one on each side of the cockpit scuttle, completely avoiding the need for multiple rows of louvres. This clever arrangement was assisted using a specially-profiled firewall, although the bulkhead assembly to which it was attached was otherwise similar in design to the 1937 car. All oil and fuel filler caps, whilst remaining easily accessible, were now recessed into the bodywork, giving a much cleaner line. A 155-litre fuel tank was placed behind the cockpit in a cradle, where the longer wheelbase meant it no longer encroached over the rear axle. This allowed the spare wheel to be stowed above the rear chassis rails, and inside the bodywork beneath a tail panel. The car used a pair of Lucas-made electric accumulators, mounted in a cradle attached to the chassis frame below the driver's seat. Collectively, these detail changes provided a vastly improved overall aerodynamic efficiency.

The bodywork clearly exhibited innovative elements and extremely advanced knowledge of streamlining, although brake and tyre cooling employed even more cutting-edge aeronautic ram-air technology. This was undoubtedly influenced by expertise acquired from the on-going Louis de Monge/Bugatti P100 airspeed record aircraft project. In principle, this technology took advantage of aerodynamic surface pressure differences, both high and low, to provide balanced, ducted airflow characteristics that would not detract from overall streamlining efficiency. These typically applied carefully managed calculations, the laws of fluid dynamics, as well as taking into account ambient air temperatures, heat expansion and pressure differentials; technology scarcely ever seen again in Grand Prix cars until the 1970s.

Two long rectangular ducts (one each side) jutted out from the radiator air intake. They projected ahead of the bodywork so as to avoid any influence of air resistance and pressure change caused by the car's movement through the ambience. The right-hand duct (as you sit in the car) directed cool air to the supercharger inlet, whereas the left-hand duct directly cooled the dynamo, which was otherwise very close to the exhaust manifold. Similarly, tubular ducts protrude from the top of each wheelarch to direct cool air to the brake drums. On top of the scuttle, a rectangular air intake picked up cool air for the driver's feet, and a relatively small diameter ram-air tube fed cool air directly to the bulkhead centre-mounted Bosch magneto. A large diameter oval hole in the left-hand lower side of the bodywork appears to be the low-pressure exit for the magneto ram-air cooling system. These carefully considered individual cooling systems would help to maintain the reliability and efficiency of these important elements without compromising the overall aerodynamic effectiveness of the car.

The front and rear quick-lift jacking points of the 1937 cars were replicated, with distinctive 'mushroom' heads on the rear to prevent the car slipping off its jack. However, rather than being mounted on heavy chassis extension plates, these tubular light-alloy bars were simply anchored into the hollow rear spring hanger crossbeam, as extensions of it. Also, instead of the massive 'gaping alligator' engine cover of the 1937 cars, under-bonnet access was now in two separate areas. The engine cover now hinged forward, toward the radiator, and the radiator air-inlet cover hinged likewise, averting problems if inadvertently released at speed. The driver and passenger doors hinged outwards on this car in a more conventional manner than the 1937 cars. Plain-sided rear wheel spats were fitted initially, but these were discarded before the race itself, perhaps this time simply to speed wheel and brake shoe change times.

The car was properly equipped for the road, and registered

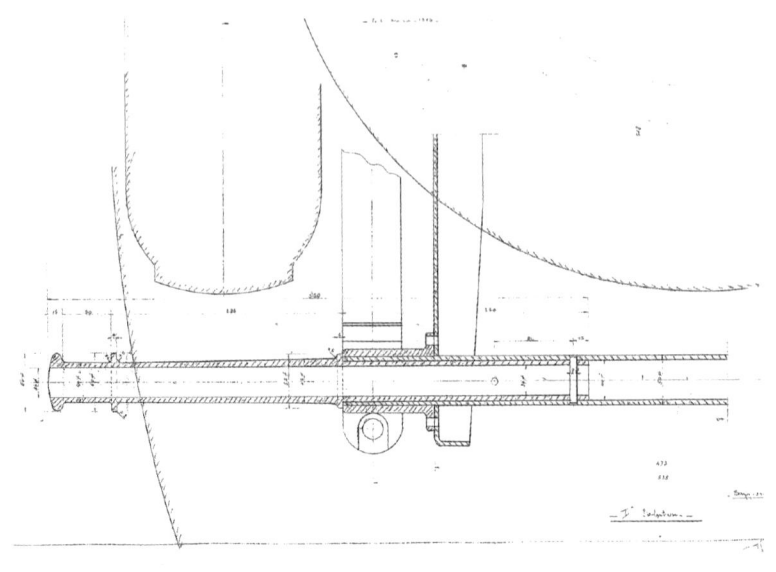

The 1939 Le Mans T57C jacking bar is arranged directly into the rear suspension crossbeam and pinned. (Courtesy Bugatti Trust)

A smartly-suited Jean-Pierre Wimille presented the T57C for technical scrutiny, with Pierre Veyron driving, accompanied by mechanic Lucian Wurmser. (Courtesy Bugatti Trust)

1244-W5 with a factory 'Trade' plate. Electric horns were mounted inside the bodywork just above the front jacking points, behind a pair of star-pattern holes drilled into the bodywork. The 1939 T57C 'Tank' reproduced the lighting array used in 1937, except that the angled spotlight set in the right-hand bodywork was now fully-recessed behind lightweight avant-garde 'Perspex,' and fitted with a clear lens. Perspex also replaced the glass in the driver's windscreen. The two main driving lamps now had streamlined cones to blend them into the bodywork. Dashboard details are unknown since photos are not clear enough, but a note exists from Jean to Pichetto, affirming 'No' to mounting twin tachometers. Otherwise, it was probably very similar in layout to the 1937 Le Mans car.

Jean Bugatti declared a top speed of 255km/h (158mph) for this car, although a more realistic 230km/h (143mph) was plausible at an engine speed of 5000rpm with this permutation of engine, gearbox, rear axle and grand prix wheels, in conjunction with its highly efficient bodywork. Bear in mind that the 'G' engine was capable of 6000rpm in lower gears. The former contention appears to be a purely calculated one from engine speed and

Bugatti Type 57 Grand Prix – A Celebration

gearing, without taking high-speed aerodynamic resistance into account on the power range. Alternatively, this speed may have been attained on the rolling-road Ranzi brake; again, without taking practical aerodynamics into account.

Star driver

As in 1937, the Bugatti team stayed at the Hotel Moderne in Le Grand-Lucé, although this time accompanied by the Delahaye team. On this occasion, at last, Jean-Pierre Wimille was acknowledged as the star driver who formally entered the car with Pierre Veyron as co-driver. The car was presented just in time for technical inspection at 4.00pm Wednesday, June 14, where Robert Benoist, now formally retired from racing, was delighted to escort the car and to speak to the awaiting motoring press. He was thoroughly positive about the Bugatti's technical superiority over its competitors who had failed to beat the Tanks' 1937 record in 1938, and, whilst extremely confident, he added the usual Grand Prix driver's proviso: "But racing is ... racing, with many risks." How very true that is, and how very close the car came to not running at all.

The Thursday practice period at the Circuit went according to plan until midnight, when, during the second test-run, the car stopped suddenly at Maison Blanche. The supercharged T57G engine, so carefully run-in for hours on the test-bed, had seized and brought the car to a stop. Magnesium pistons were very light and strong, but had crucial expansion tolerances, being susceptible to seizing. Wimille walked back to the pits in despair, as if in the firm belief that the Bugatti was well and truly out of the race. Jean Bugatti, too, seemed defeated, and began packing up for return to Molsheim. However, the resourceful senior mechanic, Robert Aumaître, sincerely believed there was sufficient time to repair the damaged engine. Wimille and Veyron might have been some of the best drivers in the world, and Jean Bugatti one of the most talented car creators and organisers, but that night, Robert Aumaître was to become a true hero of Le Mans. The story of how the seemingly hopeless T57C was salvaged from this calamity reads like high-adventure fiction. However, it is best left to the great man himself, who recorded this memoir on tape for *Bugantics*, repeated here:

The 1939 Le Mans Story by Robert Aumaître

(Edited and transcribed by NMT from the original taped interview translated by René Rieger, previously published in *Bugantics* Volume 48, Issue 1, 1985.)

"In 1936, the Le Mans race was cancelled due to widespread strikes, but for 1937, Jean persuaded his father to run two cars; and we won! These cars had the famous wire wheels with bicycle spokes, serving only to carry the rim. The Rudge hub had a disc secured to the brake drum, and had teeth, like a large gear pinion, where the rim had internal teeth, so the driving force was taken by these in mesh; the advantage being that the drive was taken directly to the hub.

"In 1938, Jean approached his father again, who said, 'No, no, we will leave it to another make, although if the winner extends the 24-hour distance further than we did, we can come back in 1939 and try to beat it.' In 1938, our record distance was not extended; yet for 1939, Jean went to his father again, but the answer was 'No; we are not beaten.' Jean persisted, and Ettore eventually changed his decision, but on one condition: in 1937 there had been two cars; but for 1939, he would sanction only one!

"So, on January 5, 1939, I was given a factory order to go to the assembly hall and select a T57C chassis from the production line, take it to the racing shop, and prepare it for Le Mans. Therefore, I collected a chassis to prepare, and put an engine on the test-bed, running it in for 36 hours non-stop. Lydia (Bugatti) arrived during the evening with the electric vehicle (T56) bringing food and drink. In the engine test bay we had a table upon which we set clean paper for the food and red wine, around which Jean, Lucien Wurmser (mechanic) and I dined whilst the engine ran at around 5000-5200rpm – rr – rr – rr (Robert imitates the sound of the engine on test). Subsequently, we went to Le Mans with this single car.

"All went well in the first practice on the Thursday, but on the second practice, at 12.30am during the night, Wimille, who had been driving, returned to the pits on foot; the car had broken down. Jean asked 'What's up?' Wimille made the sound of an engine seizing solid. I asked, 'Where is it?' 'At Maison Blanche,' Wimille replied. At that time, Maison Blanche was still there after Arnage. Now, I called our truck driver over and told him to collect the loading ramps and take the truck to the escape road near the Dunlop corner; I would leave on foot to collect the Tank. Wimille said it would be useless, but I advised that the engine would have now cooled down. I got to the car and put it straight into bottom gear so I could start off immediately; first, second, third, the engine made a terrible noise! I got to the pits and cut the engine.

"We loaded the car onto the truck and took it to a large workshop, by now, 1.00 or 1.30am on Friday morning. Jean said, 'Our carrots are cooked' (as the English say, 'Our goose is cooked'), There are no miracles for machines; we shall abandon and come back next year.' I reasoned, 'Monsieur Jean, our carrots are not cooked, we have one or two seized pistons and we have spare ones at the Works already inspected but oversize. What we have to do is telephone Molsheim, ask (Pierre) Marco to get a mechanic to put on a clean overall, pack a small overnight bag, give him the eight new pistons and put him on the Railcar for Paris. Robert Benoist, Veyron or Wimille can take the T57 to the Gare de l'Est (in Paris) to meet him, and bring them here. I will take the cylinder block into Le Mans to get it re-ground.' Jean looked at me and said, 'You have no car.' I said, 'I can take the truck.' Jean affirmed, 'Alright, full authority.' I said, 'I will not leave until I've cleaned up and changed.' Meanwhile, the mechanics began removing the cylinder block.

"It was 10.00am on Friday morning when I arrived at a cylinder grinding shop near the station. The start of the race was 4.00pm the next day. I asked the manager of the shop to grind the block, but he said, 'Too difficult, we have never done an eight cylinder block.' Meanwhile, I noticed the grinding machine operator who was listening, his eyes popping out of his head when he heard the name Bugatti. So I said to the Manager, 'If you won't take the responsibility, will you hire me the machine so I can grind the cylinder myself? Your grinder can lend me a hand.' So he rented me the machine and the grinder operator. At that time one charged so much per cylinder, 40 or 50 francs, I don't remember.

"We got the block on to the machine by 10.30 or 11.00am when Veyron arrived to see how we were progressing. So I asked him, 'Be a good chap, as we are not stopping for lunch, go and get us some food; cold chicken or lamb, spinach, strawberries and so on for my friend the grinder and me.' But the grinder said, 'My wife is expecting me at home.' So I said, 'Don't worry about your wife, you'll both have seats in the stand like you never dreamed of; Veyron will warn her.' So Veyron got the address and went off to tell her that her husband could not return for lunch; meanwhile we went on grinding.

We worked on until about 11pm that evening. Meanwhile, everything had gone smoothly; Marco found the pistons, the lad took them to Paris where Benoist collected them, and the engine was prepared for refitting the block. Veyron returned about 10.00pm where I told him to tell the chaps that I would be there by midnight. I got it back about then and went off to get some sleep, telling them to wake me when the engine was ready to start. Exhausted, I went to bed without undressing.

"At 7.00am Saturday morning, I was on the road to Tours with the car running fine, no problems. I returned about 8.30am, and we brought Veyron to drive 100-200km, but to be back by 11.00am. At 11.00am, Veyron was there and we got the car prepared, so by midday the car was on the track. At 1.00pm, we checked in, we started at 4.00pm, and by 4.00pm on Sunday afternoon we had won the Le Mans; Wimille and Veyron achieved a record distance!"

The race
Bugatti's 1937 Le Mans record distance remained unbeaten in 1938, yet, for the 1939 race, the main challengers were essentially 1937 and 1938 Le Mans cars. Of the 42 starters,

The T57C in front of the pits with its bonnet open, receiving a lot of attention from onlookers as well as mechanics. (Courtesy Bugatti Trust)

Bugatti Type 57 Grand Prix – A Celebration

The 1939 Le Mans T57C with Pierre Veyron cornering at speed. (Courtesy Bugatti Trust)

only a few new cars had the performance to compete effectively against Wimille and Veyron in the 200bhp supercharged T57C Bugatti 'Tank'. 25 of the entries were French, which included eight 3.6-litre Delahaye-Delages, two normal Delages, three 4-litre Lagonda-Talbots, three 4.5-litre Lagonda-Talbots, and eight Simca variants. The German entries consisted of three BMW 2-litre 328s, one of which had futuristic coupé bodywork, along with a streamlined 'Rennlimousinen' Adler. A new Alfa-Romeo 2.9-litre was rumoured entered for Italy, shared by Bira (Prince Birabongse Bhanubandh of Thailand) and Raymond Sommer, but lamentably, they arrived with an outmoded 6C-2500SS coupé instead. Nonetheless, it seems that the car had been heroically driven by the pair through snow-covered Alpine passes on its way to Le Mans.

Britain entered 12 cars consisting, in the main, of small-capacity Aston-Martin, HRG, MG, Morgan, Riley and Singer models, as well as two new WO Bentley-designed, 4.5-litre V12 Lagondas.

The weather was bright, sunny and dry for the 4.00pm start, and, fortunately, remained dry for the entire race. Nevertheless,

9   1939 Le Mans

The 1939 Le Mans T57C with Jean-Pierre Wimille cornering at speed. (Courtesy Bugatti Trust)

Jean-Pierre Wimille about to pass a group of back-markers. (Courtesy Bugatti Trust)

Bugatti Type 57 Grand Prix – A Celebration

for the Bugatti team, the physical and mental strain of the overnight engine rebuild had taken its toll on everyone, including Jean-Pierre Wimille. Observers remarked that he was unusually quiet and appeared ashen and unwell. When the flag dropped, the Talbot of Luigi Chinetti quickly went into the lead, and almost immediately, the Alfa-Romeo of Sommer and Bira began misfiring, caused by a leaking cylinder-head gasket. Four hours into the race, Mazaud's Delahaye and Louis Gerard's Delage challenged each other for the lead, although Chinetti's Talbot seemed happy to remain third. Bugatti's strategy was intelligent and cautious, especially since the Tank's new pistons and rings were still technically 'running in,' maintaining a steady fourth. The Delage-Delahaye-Talbot fight for the lead went on until 2.00am, when the Delahaye broke the lap record, but it then caught fire and burned out within sight of everyone in the grandstands.

Shortly after this misadventure, the Talbot, now driven by Mathieson, left the road at Tertre Rouge having lost a tyre. Around 4.00am, the Bugatti was just one lap behind the Delage when it also lost a tyre, damaging both the wheel and telescopic damper. Veyron stopped briefly on the Mulsanne Straight to assess the situation before carefully driving into the pits for repairs. This task took longer than expected, so, when he finally got away from the pit-counter, the Bugatti was five laps behind the leader, having dropped back to sixth place. When Wimille took over, he steadily increased the pace so that by 10.00am, he was in second position and just three laps behind the Delage. The Bugatti continued toward a close finish, but then around 1.00pm, the Delage began misfiring, forcing Gerard into the pits for a plug change. He was quickly out again, but still misfiring. Upon returning to the pits the mechanics found that a valve-spring had broken. Nevertheless, Gerard continued, his Delage still misfiring but with very little chance of getting ahead unless the Bugatti broke down, too. However, as optimistically asserted in racing circles, 'No race is lost or won until the chequered flag has fallen.'

By 4.00pm, it was clear that race attrition had been considerable; there were only fifteen finishers from the original 42 starters. The Bugatti was three laps ahead of the Delage, exceeding its own 1937 record distance by 66km (41 miles), completing 3354.65km (2084.54 miles), averaging a speed of 139.78km/h (96.74mph). Jean Bugatti declared that the engine cover was never opened during the race. The fuel consumption had averaged 26 litres/100km (10.8mpg) on pump-standard 80-octane 'ESSO' (Ethyl), and the distance record set in 24 hours remained unbroken until 1950. Wimille had, yet again,

Postcard showing two 'Tanks' at the 1939 Le Mans. (Courtesy NMT Collection)

9 1939 Le Mans

2003 Riesling label from the Molsheim vintner Antoine Klingenfus, celebrating the 1939 Le Mans-winning Bugatti T57C. (Courtesy NMT Collection)

A fine 1/18-scale model by Spark, the master pattern having been created by Benoît Moro. (Courtesy NMT Collection – photo by D Roberts)

demonstrated that he had the ability to succeed in the 24-hour race, and Veyron, who had failed to finish previously in three of the events, had triumphed at long last.

Controversy

As an aside, a popular postcard photograph exists showing the 1937 Le Mans-winning Tank at the 1939 Le Mans circuit, just ahead of the long-wheelbase Tank entry. Here, both cars carry the racing number 1 roundel. Curiously, this has led to a belief that the 1937 car must have attended as a spare, modified with a supercharger. This notion is completely incorrect, for it may be noted that the roundels on the 1937 car have a white numeral on a black background, whereas the 1939 car has a black numeral on a white background. Given that photos of the line-up at the start of the race show that all the competitors that year in the 3- to 5-litre capacity class, have black on white racing numerals on their sides, it follows that a white on black layout would be wholly inappropriate for an entrant; even as a spare car. The 1937 Le Mans- winning car won the event in that year carrying a white on black race number 2. Therefore, it is clear that the car's refurbishment, with Benoist and Wimille's stylised signatures on the car's flanks, with race number 1, represented an historical exhibit, flaunting Bugatti's success in the race two years earlier. In addition, it is likely that the 1937 car was, by then, fitted with a standard T57S engine and horizontally-mounted Scintilla Vertex magneto, driven from the left-hand camshaft, making it both road-friendly and practical. Plated-over bulkhead details suggest these changes were carried out before the 1939 24-hour race. Given these considerations, it follows that the postcard simply shows the 1937 winning car preceding the 1939 entry as part of the usual Le Mans Endurance Race cavalcade. The 1937 Le Mans-winning car was still carrying this racing number 1 roundel after the war, following its storage at Bordeaux.

97

10

1939 – Friday, August 11

ON THIS DAY IN August 1939, the Bugatti dynasty was about to receive a devastating blow. The successful 1939 Le Mans 'Tank' was being prepared for the annual handicap race held at the fashionable seaside resort of La Baule, near St Nazaire, on September 3, 1939. Here, the event was run along the 8km (5 mile) stretch of curving beach in front of the Casino. Car handicapping was based on the results of the Le Mans race, and utilised a staggered start, with all entrants covering 23 laps of the hard sand circuit. Jean-Pierre Wimille was appointed to drive the car, and it would have been customary practice that he should conduct the final functional and performance tests to his personal satisfaction. However, on this occasion, he declined to travel to Molsheim, perhaps because he was content with the car's control settings and efficiency; being more than confident to allow the Works to complete this task in his absence.

Tragedy

By the late afternoon of Friday, August 11, senior mechanic Robert Aumaître had finished most of the adjustments and tests on the car, ready for the final high-speed tests. These were carried out quite close to the factory on a stretch of the Route Nationale N420, Molsheim to Strasbourg road, which had previously formed a part of the 10km straight in the 1922 Strasbourg Grand Prix race circuit. Bugatti had used this section of tree-lined public road between Dorlisheim and Entzheim for many years when verifying high-speed performance. It is understood that the district authorities and local residents were quite favourably disposed to this practice, since the factory employed many local people. There were two significant junctions where cars could join the route, so, for safety, factory employees were posted as watchmen to prevent inadvertent entry during testing. Aumaître and Jean Bugatti made a number of runs together, but for the final high-speed test of around 230km/h (143mph), Jean took the car alone. Upon his return, unexpectedly, a cyclist rode along his path from a minor lane. Both took evasive action, but the car clipped the cyclist from behind, whom, providentially, received only relatively minor injuries. Regrettably, however, the Tank swerved at such high speed it glanced off two pear trees before colliding head-on with a third, effectively cutting the car in two – a third part of the left-hand side was entirely torn away. This instantly split open the fuel tank and set fire to the tree and a nearby corn mill. Tragically, Jean died instantly when his neck was broken by the final impact that catapulted his body 20m into a field. He was just 30 years old.

Debate

Ettore Bugatti was in Belgium when Jean died. He was with his friend, King Leopold, discussing a proposal to relocate the Bugatti factory to the old Invicta Works in Laeken, near Brussels. Just two weeks beforehand, Bugatti's financiers had warned of impending liquidation, so there is an opinion that Bugatti was planning to dodge his creditors by moving out of France. Additionally, Jean Bugatti was very heavily insured, so there has also been an incessant rumour that the cyclist was a pretext, and that Jean deliberately killed himself in order to save the factory. This suggestion was touted again when it

10   1939 – Friday 11 August

the inclined-valve cylinder heads for the Types 50 and 51 in 1930. Moreover, Jean took overall responsibility for the Types 57 and 59 projects, as well as the Racing Department from autumn 1934 when Costantini left Bugatti; and the whole of the Molsheim factory from 1936 onward after his father went into unhappy pseudo-exile to his Paris office following the industrial unrest of that disorderly summer. Given Jean's vital status, it would have been extremely wise business acumen for him to be heavily insured, yet this same status made him more valuable to the company alive, rather than dead.

Historical facts

Historically, of course, some facts speak for themselves. The cyclist implicated in the crash was a real person, and was not part of a conspiracy made up to conceal anything. On Sunday, August 13, 1939, a Strasbourg newspaper reported that the cyclist involved was 19-year-old Joseph Metz, a telegraph operator who worked at the nearby Entzheim airport. It gave an account that he suffered two broken fingers and other minor injuries; his bicycle was crushed. Additionally, there are other factors to consider. Just eight months earlier, Jean's passionate and sometimes indefensible driving actually killed a cyclist, Alfred Rudloff, at a junction in the village of Lingolsheim on the outskirts of Strasbourg. This surely must have influenced Jean's reaction to this incident. In fact, it had only been a matter of weeks since the Court found Jean four-fifths guilty of excessive speeding, and of 'ignoring the most elementary principles of prudence.' He was sentenced to three months in prison (suspended), with damages totalling 56,000f going to the Rudloff family. Whilst Jean's shortcomings included egocentric driving, they did not embrace melancholia. Consequently, it cannot be realistically suggested that the conditions surrounding Jean's death were deliberately staged; in fact, the idea is totally absurd.

Although no one has yet written a full financial history of the Bugatti Company, it is clear from many of its undertakings since 1909 that the business was no stranger to cash-flow complexities and fiscal embarrassment. Several times during the firm's history it had hovered on the brink, and threats of insolvency were nothing new to the Bugattis. Moreover, the family and business possessed quite a number of substantial properties upon which collateral could be drawn if the need arose. In and around Paris were showrooms; several workshops and offices; a boat yard; and Bugatti's Ermenonville

The sad remains of the crashed 1939 car.
(Courtesy Bugatti Trust)

appeared in the French journal *l'Express* during the Bugatti Centenary Rally in September 1981; it has been repeated since. This assertion has caused great distress to Jean's friends and colleagues.

Contrary to the *l'Express* article, however, whilst Ettore Bugatti was always the official head of Automobiles Bugatti, it should be remembered that Jean Bugatti was, without any doubt, the dynamic influence behind the company at that time. Jean was entirely responsible for the automobile side of the business, and had been for many years, even before 1932 when Ettore first took on the Railcar project. From 1927 onward, at just 18 years of age, Jean was formally inputting ideas to the design team, and then led the development of

Bugatti Type 57 Grand Prix – A Celebration

The sad remains of the 1939 car. (Courtesy Bugatti Trust)

Estate. In Alsace, there was the factory at Molsheim, as well as several other significant properties nearby. Bugatti also owned Villa Tunis, in Beaulieu-sur-Mer, on the Mediterranean coast near Nice. Many of these properties remained on the books until 1963. Whilst sales were not good at that time, the T57C Tank had just achieved an incredible win at Le Mans, this being a fantastic publicity exercise for the astonishing performance, reliability and success of the Bugatti Type 57 model.

Reconsideration

Significantly, WF Bradley made a salient observation in his 1948 biography of Bugatti that seems to have been overlooked by later historians. He wrote:

"During 1938 and 1939, fears of war and hopes of peace alternated in every country in Europe. But to the Bugatti family the threat was greater than to most. They had fled, homeless, at the outbreak of the First World War, and by reason of their position they would feel the first brunt, if the armies were again unleashed. Living within half an hour's ride of the German border, and ahead of the Maginot line, they knew exactly what was happening on the hills to the east of the Rhine. There could be no secret of the fortifications which were being erected, of the vast military manoeuvres, of the growing arrogance of the Nazi party."

As a result, it should be seriously considered that Bugatti's negotiations to re-locate his factory to Belgium, and the complete lack of confidence shown by his creditors, was not an attempt to escape his financial responsibilities. It was surely driven by the overtly strident ambitions and actions of the Third Reich to annex German historical lands. These, of course, included Alsace and Lorraine, lost to France as a result of the 1914-18 conflict. Here, the Bugatti factory nestled between the German border and the Maginot line; a territory extremely rich in coal mines. On March 7, 1936, the German military entered the Rhineland in direct contravention of the treaties of Versailles and Locano. Moreover, in the year leading-up to Jean's death, Germany annexed Austria, and appropriated the Czech Sudetenland through belligerent intercession, before ruthlessly seizing the remainder of Czechoslovakia in March 1939. Soon after this the Nazis intensified pressure on Poland to hand over the port of Danzig, and for some time it was obvious to France that Alsace and Lorraine were under close scrutiny. Just across the Rhine, Germany was quite systematically preparing fortifications and declaring its hostile intentions towards this border area.

Under these increasingly darkening clouds of overt intimidation and imminent war, both Ettore and Jean Bugatti must have realised they would soon have to abandon Molsheim, just as they had done 25 years earlier; hence the attempt to negotiate a move to Belgium. Bugatti's financiers, too, must have speculated on their investment risk and the penalties of such a loss of French territory to the Germans, including many of Bugatti's properties – and their surety. Clearly, they were all making preparations to escape the conspicuous menace of Germany's machinations, and it is surely this that motivated their decision to call-in loans in the face of other options. Of course, when the storm broke, Nazi forces ruthlessly seized the whole of Poland by force, and later all of Western Europe, including Belgium. No one had accurately predicted the extent of Hitler's ambitions at the time. Nevertheless, I think these were the real reasons why Bugatti was planning to leave Molsheim, and why his creditors were losing their nerve. As a result, it may be seen that Jean's death was, in truth, a most terrible and tragic accident. Sadly, Automobiles Bugatti never really recovered from the dual calamities of Jean's death and the Second World War.

Robert Aumaître's response
Reproduced from page 524 of Hugh Conway and Maurice Sauzay's book *Bugatti Magnum*, courtesy of HRG Conway.

"In October 1981, in response to the l'Express article and the increasing speculation surrounding Jean's death, Robert Aumaître felt it was necessary to express his story of the night of August 11, 1939. He was, after all, a first-hand witness to the events.

"The sad souvenir of the day and night of August 11, 1939: the Bugatti factory closed for the annual holiday except for essential services kept going with skeleton staff. This was the case also for the Racing Department where there were two of us, Lucien Wurmser and myself. We were preparing (for the La Baule GP) the T57C Tank, which had won at the 24-Hour race at Le Mans in June 1939 with Wimille and Veyron as drivers. I had taken the car out twice in the afternoon to test it on the straight between Duttlenheim and Entzheim. Each time I had to pass through the main entrance of the villa as the Works gate was closed. On my second return at about 5pm, Mr Jean came over to the shop to ask if all was well and if it was easy to reach 200kp/h, I replied that all was well but it was too dangerous to try and reach 200kp/h due to the traffic.

"The farmers were harvesting and there were many farm carts on the road. Moreover we could still hear the creaking of the brake drums as they cooled down in the shop. It was then that Mr Jean decided to continue the tests that evening after 9pm. He asked me to have dinner and to return at 9pm, taking out the car on to the straight road to warm it up, and said he would follow me out in his own 57. After dinner, once again to the shop and the car through the villa entrance, and while passing, Mlle Lidia called out through a first floor window, 'Is that you Jean? and I replied 'No, it's Robert,' she adding that she hoped he wouldn't be foolish. I reassured her and took the road, meeting Mr Jean who had deposited his brother Roland at Duttlenheim, the stable lad at the Duppigheim road, and Lucien Wurmser at the ESSO Station at Entzheim. Their job was to stop road users and ask them to be so kind as to wait for the test of a racing car.

"We met Mr Jean between Duppigheim and Entzheim. He had parked his 57 between two trees, and took the wheel of the Tank in the direction of Duttlenheim, where he turned round and, coming back, stopped in front of me, who had remained alongside his car. The dashboard lights were not connected and he could not read the revolution counter. Having tested the car in daylight I had not noticed this problem. He asked me to sit on the floor beside him, there being only a single seat for the driver, and to use a glowing cigarette end to indicate 5000rpm on the rev counter, and to tap his left leg each time we reached 5000rpm on 1st gear, then 2nd gear, 3rd gear, 4th gear, and then 5200 and 5500rpm (235kph). We made at least four double runs, that is eight or nine straight runs, and on the return to Entzheim a brake application made me stub out my cigarette on the rev counter. We stopped beside his car, the engine of the Tank switched off, and we both got down; he offered me a cigarette from his packet and lighted one himself. I took the wheel again of the Tank to take it back to the factory, and then he, almost at his car, suddenly made a sign to let him once more take the wheel, as he wanted to do one more test alone, and to tell him how it rode in passing. At this point there was a small hump and at 200kph the car left the ground a bit. He went off turning in front of his brother Roland at Duttlenheim, and on the way back passed in front of me flat out, to crash into a tree 200m further on. The fuel tank, having exploded, set fire to a corn mill and a tree; jumping in the car I arrived on the scene, searching for Mr Jean whom I found in a field on the left 20m from the roadway, and used the car to drive him immediately to the hospital in Strasbourg, where Sister Angelique and I got him to an operating theatre. It was here that an intern told me Mr Jean was dead – it was explained to me that Mr Jean had been killed instantly on the impact with the tree. Professor Fontaine asked me to telephone to the villa where I had Mlle Lidia on the line. She said she would come at once with Roland, but asked me to telephone immediately to the Patron at the Château de Laeken, Belgium. I had the Patron on the line at 1am in the morning, and about 6.30–7am he was at the hospital with Toussaint (chauffeur) and the Royale.

"I went home in the afternoon of August 12 after recovering the remains of the Tank 57 with some workmen from the factory and the head of the ESSO Station at Entzheim. It was the end of Bugatti. Mr Jean had never thought of suicide, he was not a man to do such a thing. He was a fighter, courageous, I loved him very much."

Interment and memorial

The morning after the tragic crash, Robert Aumaître organised workmen from the factory, along with a local breakdown truck, to recover the wreckage of the T57C Tank. The car's remains were taken to the Molsheim Estate and buried privately somewhere in the grounds. Only a few days after Jean's death, the Nazis forced their way into Poland, and the World was at War. These two misfortunes set in motion the imminent demise of the company, effectively sealing the fate of the Bugatti Works from which it would never again recover. Following the German invasion of France and subsequent occupation of the factory by Hans Trippel's Machinenfabrik, several attempts were made to locate the remains of Jean's car, especially its engine. So far as can be ascertained, they found nothing; it is still there.

Jean was buried in the Bugatti family plot at the local cemetery, east of the village of Dorlisheim. On August 11, 1999, 'Enthousiastes Bugatti,' an Alsatian club based in the Hostellerie St Jean in Molsheim, where Bugatti used to entertain his clients, placed a memorial stone by the side of the section of unpaved road near the site of Jean Bugatti's fatal accident. The anniversary and their commemoration coincided with the sixtieth anniversary of Jean's death, as well as the striking solar eclipse that passed over northern Europe that day. Called 'The Rock of the Eclipse,' the memorial stone poignantly marked the anniversary of the eclipse of Jean Bugatti on the day when the sky went dark around noon ...

VISIT VELOCE ON THE WEB – WWW.VELOCE.CO.UK
All current books • New book news • Special offers • Gift vouchers • Forum

11

The surviving Tank

UPON THE OUTBREAK OF World War II, the French Ministry of Air Defence directed Bugatti's factory to move to Bordeaux in the southwest of the country, the operation being completed by the end of January 1940. Transportation orders required that many of the cars held as museum pieces were to be placed into storage, including the ex-1937 Le Mans winning T57G Tank. Most of the factory equipment was transferred using special trains, but because the car would have to make the journey by road, driven by one of Bugatti's employees, the expensive and fragile Grand Prix wheels were removed and replaced with Rudge wire-spoke versions from a Type 46. Such practice seems to have been used previously since 1936, as well as when the car took part in the 1939 Le Mans cavalcade, evident from a photo used as a popular postcard. Additionally, a photo shows the 1937 and 1939 Tanks together behind the Hotel Moderne in Le Grand-Lucé. Here, the 1937 car's spare is noticeably a Type 46 wire wheel. Clearly, these racing cars travelled to the circuit by road, as was sometimes required by racing regulations, using these Rudge wire wheels in order to save wear and tear on the exotically expensive radial-spoke versions.

The victorious 1939 car and mechanics at the back of Hotel Moderne, Le Grand Lucé, alongside the 1937 car fitted with Rudge wire wheels. (Courtesy Bugatti Trust)

Bugatti Type 57 Grand Prix – *A Celebration*

This post-war photo shows how the Wimille Tank suffered distress during storage at Bordeaux. Note the Rudge wire wheels. (Courtesy Bugatti Trust)

A post-war photo of the car's dashboard shows that this version is different to that seen during the record runs at Montlhéry in November 1936. (Courtesy Bugatti Trust)

11 The surviving Tank

The car at de Dobbeleer's c.1969. Note the pre-existing bulkhead panel changes converting the engine bay from T57G to a T57S power unit ... (Courtesy Bugatti Trust)

... and at de Dobbeleer's c.1969. Note the pre-existing bulkhead panel modification to accept a horizontal, camshaft-driven Scintilla Vertex. (Courtesy Bugatti Trust)

Bugatti Type 57 Grand Prix – A Celebration

Patch panels

Interestingly, examination of the surviving car shows large patch panels on the crescent-shaped bulkhead. These indicate modifications to horizontally mount a Scintilla Vertex magneto, driven from the left-hand camshaft; so the car has clearly been altered to take a normal T57S engine. This suggests that the car was legitimately modified to accept a road-friendly engine at some time, as yet unknown. The precious T57G racing engine may very well have been removed prior to evacuation in favour of a T57S version, yet the changes appear complex and thorough, seemingly too well done to be a last-minute job. As a result, it appears more likely that this modification was carried out prior to the 1939 Le Mans historical spectacle, to which it would have driven. Hence, its valuable and refined engine had already been removed and preserved immediately after the 1937 endurance race; soon replaced by a normal T57S unit.

Damage

Nonetheless, during the course of its journey to Bordeaux, the car suffered some damage to the front left-hand wing. When put into storage, its engine was removed and boxed up, along with several other 'attractive' items, including fuel filler caps and instruments. The tachometers were expensive and fragile, so may have been removed after the 1937 Le Mans race. Despite these well-meaning attempts to protect the car from the ravages of conflict, the car's bodywork was further badly damaged by falling debris during an air raid by the Royal Air Force in late October 1940. After the war, the now un-drivable car was returned to Molsheim, still on its T46 wheels, somewhat distressed, battered and bruised.

Sold

In 1959, the well-known Belgian Bugatti dealer Jean De Dobbeleer chanced upon the car in this sad condition on the Bugatti estate, and, in 1961, purchased it for American Gene Cesari, whereupon it was subsequently shipped to the United States in 1962. Since the car had never been taxed for the road in France, it probably did not have any formal documentation for export, so there is a view that the car may have been smuggled out of the country. However, when it reached the United States, the car was stored in a barn owned by Jerry Sherman, a close friend of Cesari, at Willow Pond Farm, Malvern, just outside Philadelphia, Pennsylvania. Fervent collector Fritz Schlumpf was apparently interested in the car, writing to Cesari in August 1963, but was not prepared to agree to the terms. In 1965, Cesari offered this historically valuable car to the Automobile Club de l'Ouest, organiser of the Le Mans race, for the relatively small sum he had originally paid for it. The response was that the Club would be pleased to accept the car, but only as a gift, providing Cesari paid all the return transportation costs. It seems the Club was of the opinion that he should never have had possession of the car in the first place, so should return it free of charge. Needless to say, Cesari declined the offer.

Retired US Air Force Colonel and Bugattiste Eri H Richardson had purchased a number of Bugatti T57G Tank parts from several sources during the 1960s, including newly-discovered components at the factory. These items comprised the original revolution counter and other instruments removed before the war. Subsequently, Richardson and John Truslow purchased the Tank in 1968. During negotiations, it is reported that Richardson frequently complained that the car was 'not original' and 'not in running order.' For example, one of the camshaft covers was chamfered rather than square.

Ex-Bugatti mechanic André Blanchard at work restoring the non-original Tank engine. Note the massive Bugatti C2 carburettor. (Courtesy Bugatti Trust)

11 The surviving Tank

Note that this engine lacks the special 'G' cylinder block with bolted top-plate and bronze castellated sparkplug cups. (Courtesy Bugatti Trust)

The Tank chassis during restoration: note its lightened frame pierced with holes, Dural crossbeams, and Type 59 stub-axles. (Courtesy Bugatti Trust)

Rear view of the Tank frame: note the Type 59 hubs and the additional bracket on the frame to accept the rear jacking bars. (Courtesy Bugatti Trust)

Rear of the Tank frame showing a Dural crossbeam: note the reinforced differential housing, T59 drive coupling, De Ram mounting, and lightened frame. (Courtesy Bugatti Trust)

The non-running T57G at Essen, c1975. (Courtesy NMT Collection – photo by Pim Faber)

This indicates that some original parts of the car had been misplaced whilst stored in Bordeaux, although it's not really surprising. The modification to its bulkheads also suggested 'non-original' condition, although, as discussed, this was probably done in 1939 before Le Mans anyway. Photos of the car during its initial restoration show a standard T57S engine and incorrect radiator. Nonetheless, the car did just about run; though misfiring. The paintwork was original, at least from its 1939 refurbishment when it paraded in front of the winning T57C Tank at Le Mans. It still carried the number 1 racing roundels applied at the time, as well as the two stylised signatures of Benoist and Wimille picked out in white paint on its cockpit sides. Richardson carried out quite a lot of work on the car, re-building its inherited engine with a lightened 'Le Mans' (T57G) crankshaft, and installing the distinctive T57G 'Y' camshaft tower, as well as bringing it closely back to 1937 Le Mans specification.

Restoration

In 1974, Richardson sold the car to Bugatti collector Uwe Hucke, who was then living in Germany, where for the first time since the 1939 Le Mans it was presented for public scrutiny

The nicely-restored T57G at Goodwood 1999. (Courtesy NMT Collection – photo by Barry Lloyd)

at the 1975 Essen Motor Show. It looked a little distressed, and was displayed as a non-runner, but was admired by many. Hucke had a number of important Bugatti projects in hand, so the car remained essentially untouched for several years. However, in 1981, Hucke moved to Roquebrune, Cap Martin, just east of Monaco on the Cote d'Azur in the south of France. There he contacted former Bugatti mechanic, André Blanchard, who sympathetically stripped and rebuilt the Tank. However, the engine remained without a true 'G' engine block. The car has rear axle number 4, with a 12:44, 3.67:1, final drive. Its gearbox number is 486.

Hucke also purchased a firewall and identification plate carrying the serial number 57335 that George Beer had discovered in a Dorlisheim scrapyard (near Molsheim) in 1975. It had a T57G-like central magneto mounting that both he and HG Conway Senior believed, at the time, were from the original Tank, so the plate was fitted to the car in good faith. However, modern research has shown that the plate was also used for a 3.3m wheelbase T57GR (TT) Works car, so was probably only a temporary 'Works' issue. Registration numbers and chassis plates were often swapped about. The T57TT was the one driven by Yves Giraud–Cabantous at Spa, Belgium, in the

Bugatti Type 57 Grand Prix – *A Celebration*

1936, July 11-12, 24-Hour Francorchamps, where it crashed after four hours.

Exhibited

In 1987, during Hucke's stewardship, the Tank came to Britain for the very first time, where it was displayed at the Earls Court Motorfair in London during October that year. Upon its return to France it resided in the Musee d L'Automobiliste, just off the Cannes to Nice A8 Autoroute, not very far from the Hucke residence. Uwe Hucke sold the car in 1989 to Klaus Werner, a German collector, after which it went to Edgar Bensoussan for Nicholas Seydoux, who sold it in 1998 to Fred Simeone. In 1999, the famous Tank was again in Britain, displayed and paraded running well at the Goodwood Festival of Speed. Back in the United States the car was presented at the 2003 Pebble Beach Concours d'Elegance simply as an exhibit; yet it still managed to win a prize.

During the ex-Wimille Tank's restoration in 2013, all paint was stripped from its body, having persistently peeled from the sides. Interestingly, this not only revealed details of the body fabrication process, but that two types of light alloy were used in its construction. It was noted that the side panels and scuttle show a dark tarnish. The Simeone Foundation tested one of the dark panels and found it to be an alloy of magnesium, suggesting a material invented in 1930s Germany known as 'Elektron.' This material's actual composition is currently unknown, although a book published in 1939 does have some information about comparable British magnesium alloys. Titled *Metallurgy for Engineers* by EC Rollason, Edward Arnold Ltd, whilst emphasising magnesium's low weight and 1.74 specific gravity, it suggests that the material's pure state has very little use in engineering unless alloyed with aluminium and zinc. The published equivalent specification of 1939 magnesium alloy, in rolled sheet form, contained just 3 per cent of it. Wrought alloy used 8 per cent magnesium, and casting alloy, 9 per cent. In each variant, it seems strength and ductility could be improved with heat-treatment.

Automobiles Bugatti publicly extolled the use of 'Elektron' alloy for the bodywork of its Type 57S models. The 'Aérolithe,' seen at the Paris Salon in October 1935, was sometimes referred to as the 'Elektron Coupé.' Nonetheless, historians have generally discounted this public claim for many years, suggesting it was unlikely that the Germans would have allowed this material to be exported abroad. Other historians suggest the material used may have been Duralumin, which contains only 0.3 per cent magnesium. Whether the material was Dural or Elektron, both of these materials are more rigid and stronger than aluminium, allowing the use of thinner, and therefore relatively low-weight panels. The compound-curvature bonnet, wings and tail employed the more ductile aluminium, and the lightweight, more rigid magnesium alloys were used for the single curvature side panels and scuttle top.

These particular light-alloy side panels appear to have been included in its assembly only during the 1936-37 winter rebuild in preparation for the Le Mans race. This is because they are pristine. Recalling Chapter 4, an extra rear-brake cooling slot was cut into the side panels of all three cars for the July 1936 Marne Grand Prix. These slots had disappeared by the Class 'C' World Record runs in September, presumably welded up.

Given that neither the slot, nor its scar is visible in the pristine panel, it follows that these were new and added between the Marne Grand Prix and Le Mans. In addition, recall that the Wimille car was the heaviest of the three weighed-in at the Marne Grand Prix during technical scrutiny. Therefore, it is clear that its existing weight-reduction modifications were not acquired until its preparation for Le Mans.

This historically important car is now a principal exhibit in the Simeone Foundation Automotive Museum in Philadelphia, Pennsylvania.

VISIT VELOCE ON THE WEB – WWW.VELOCE.CO.UK
All current books • New book news • Special offers • Gift vouchers • Forum

The Type 57G engine

12

AT THE TIME OF writing, the Type 57G engine was designed almost 80 years ago, so for a description that details the elements of a T57G power unit nearly at its development and performance peak, what could be better evidence than a time capsule? In 1965, the late TA (Bob) Roberts purchased a T57S engine from the Belgian dealer Jean de Dobbeleer, as a spare power unit for his Vanvooren Cabriolet, chassis 57513. When it arrived, however, it turned out to be a run-in but otherwise pristine T57G unit. Former Bugatti engineer François Seyfried believed it was created as a spare for the 1937 Le Mans race, although no markings to verify this were found anywhere on it. Presumably, this was because it was never allocated to a particular car, and following the race, was returned to store unused. However, before fitting it to his Cabriolet in 1967, Bob decided to have the engine completely dismantled and examined in detail by engineer Robert Patrick, who meticulously recorded its details before re-assembly. Happily for historians, he noted down all the differences in design and specification of this time capsule as compared with the standard T57S engine. His fascinating findings were published in *Bugantics* Vol 33/4 winter 1970, although additional details have been noted since, so are included in this section with commentary.

Special cylinder block

Externally, the main T57G recognition features include the distinctive 'Y' camshaft tower with a central magneto drive, only ever found in association with 'G' engines. Curiously, this component is found in the factory drawings as 57S.MOT.51, dated May 1, 1936, not as a 'G' related item. The special layout drives a 27-tooth 'Celeron' pinion at engine speed in the cleavage between the camshafts. Celeron is a hard resin-reinforced fabric that, via a driveshaft, rotated a Bosch J08 magneto mounted horizontally behind the firewall bulkhead

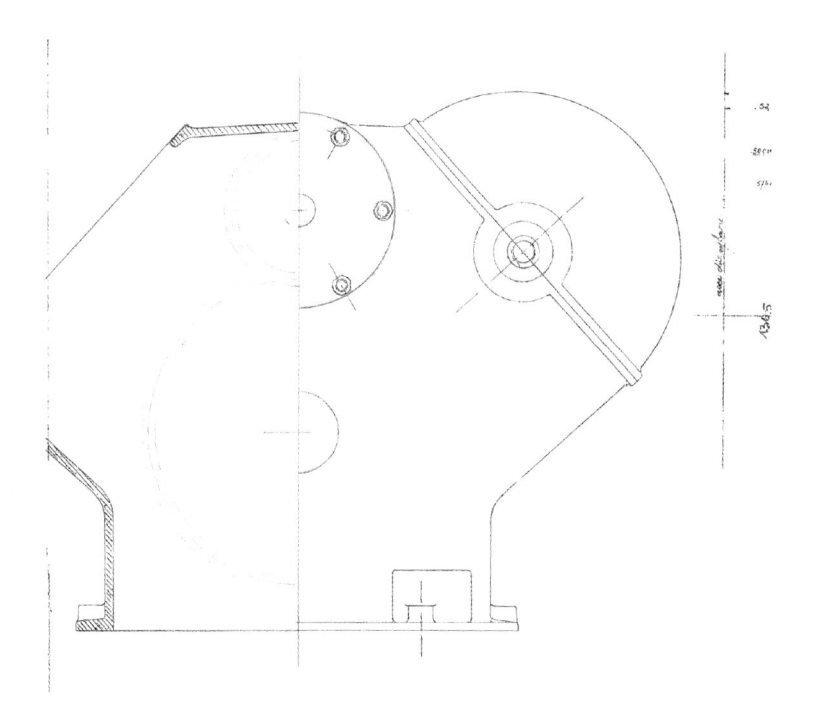

Drawing of the special 'Y' camshaft tower with a central magneto drive. (Courtesy Bugatti Trust)

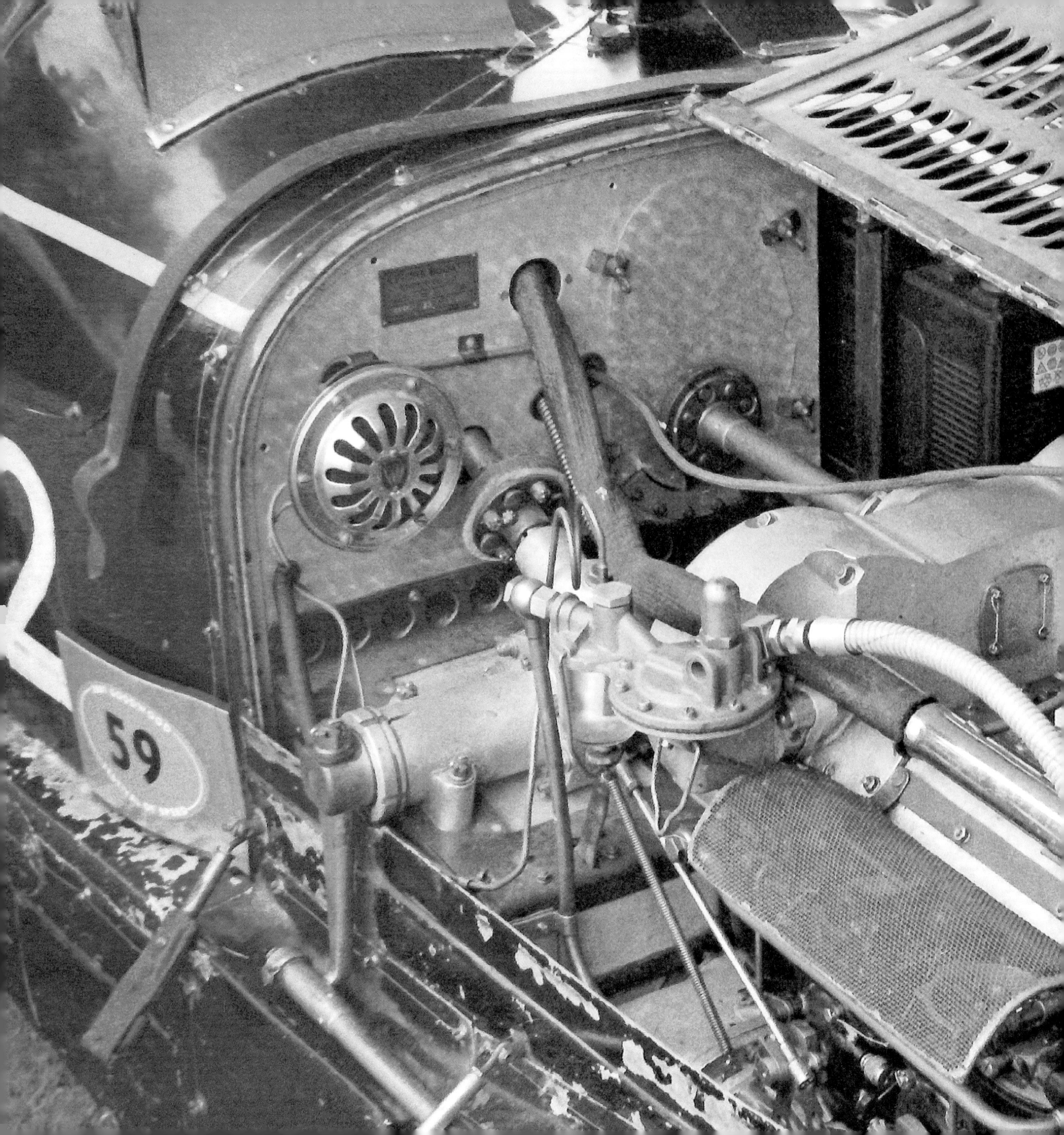
59

12 The Type 57G engine

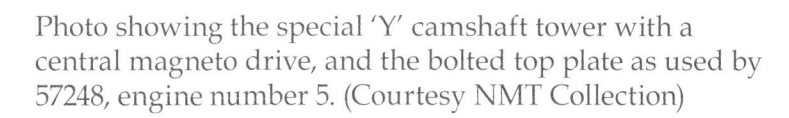

Photo showing the special 'Y' camshaft tower with a central magneto drive, and the bolted top plate as used by 57248, engine number 5. (Courtesy NMT Collection)

on the 'Tank.' The special T57G cylinder block features a detachable top plate. Here, the bulk of its crown has been omitted in order to precisely locate the core elements in the casting. It also provides good access to the cooling surfaces, especially around the valves and combustion chambers, enabling the close visual inspection of the casting's internals for any imperfections or obstructions.

This March 1935 design, 57G.MOT.1 (also 59.MOT.195), was produced from a T57 cylinder block casting whose cores had been modified to allow 45mm valves and ports. It used cast sparkplug cups, and was fitted with 14mm sparkplugs; probably one of the very first engines outside the USA to be specifically designed for these new, more compact, versions following the development of superior Alumina ceramics in 1933, invented by Helen Blair Bartlett. Smaller sparkplugs significantly reduced the risk of cracking between the larger diameter valve seats. In addition, the upper-section of the cylinder bore was increased in thickness for strength. These special blocks were identical to all Works 3.3-litre competition 'G' engine Types – T57GR, TT and T59 from March 1935 onwards, including the 1939 T57C Le Mans car. The top opening was sealed with a 5mm thick 'Dural' alloy plate, secured using 34 Bugatti 5mm, square-headed screws, as well as eight special castellated screw-in bronze nuts.

Furthermore, since the top plate was bolted above the head casing, it provided around 700cc of additional coolant volume above the cylinders. Comparable work on the core side of the lower portion of the casting around the cylinders was already accessible beneath their existing covers. This arrangement ensured a more precise and reliable flow of coolant around each cylinder pair, valve, combustion chamber and sparkplug cup. Such improvements to endurance performance were essential for a high-speed, high-compression Bugatti competition engine, especially in order to avoid valve and piston overheating. It is notable that similar bolted top-plates are found on T59 engines photographed during the Monaco and Deauville Grands Prix in April and July 1936; although that particular version trialled an experimental seven-branch riser manifold to the radiator (59.MOT.207).

Bugatti Type 57 Grand Prix – A Celebration

Top end

Both the inlet and exhaust valves of the T57G engine were 45mm diameter, their operation being enhanced using triple valve springs, with stronger and specially-designed valve caps, domed on top. These T57G items were also used for the Type 59 engine version from March 1935. The camshafts of the 'G' engine were machined from standard T57S billets, inlet and exhaust shafts being identical, but were specially-ground to give a longer opening period. One shaft of the Roberts' engine was stamped P109, whilst the other was unmarked. Undoubtedly denoting dwell and lift properties, factory records do not define what the codes meant. Articulated fingers operated the valves, the reciprocating inertia being far less than the inverted bucket type used for the T50B; both have two rubbing actions. The camshaft drive used narrow, 14mm wide spur-cut steel gears, identical to those of the Type 59 engine, secured using the three and four keyway system cut for precision adjustment of the timing. Standard T57 wheels are helical-cut and 34mm wide, but for a racing engine, noise is not an issue, where narrow spur-cut gearwheels are lighter and have less acceleration inertia; they were also lightened with holes. A revised inlet manifold, 57G.MOT.ENS.6, dated May 5, 1936, with enlarged conduits and its own heating jacket was used, accepting an updraught Bugatti C2 carburettor, choked to 34mm.

Bottom end

At the bottom end, the 2-4-2-throw crankshaft was machined from a T57 forged billet, but had its webs reduced for lightness and acceleration like the T59. It was more economical for Bugatti to machine them from solid, because the special tooling necessary to forge eight-throw crankshafts required very large volumes to justify costs. The crankshaft was fitted with a T59-like removable rear section, providing an appropriate, narrow, spur-cut camshaft drive gear, with a 140mm flange to fit a T57S flywheel and twin-plate clutch. The crankshaft was secured into the block using high-strength and heat-treated main bearing caps, manufactured from RR56 Hi-Duty Aluminium wrought alloy. The special material, AD3 60 ton/sq in nickel-chrome connecting rods were found to be 24gm lighter than standard, with all edges rounded and polished. The pistons were made from forged Elektron magnesium alloy with a crown height of 56mm, giving a compression ratio of 8.95:1. This is quite high when compared with the 8.5:1 ratio of the production T57S.

The compound oil pump was identical to the T57S, although its scavenge-feed pipe ran forward to a gauze filter pick-up about 25mm above a copper trough. This shaped tray was riveted into a cutout in the sump, and arranged to assist with oil cooling. These special troughs were a common feature of all 'G' engines from July 1936 onwards, becoming universal in all competition Types 57 and 59 crankcases.

Performance

Developed from a standard T57 crankcase engine, a prototype 'SG' (238) tested prior to the 1936 ACF, recorded an incredible 182bhp at 5500rpm using special fuel mixes. Nevertheless, the normally-aspirated T57G engine had a maximum power output of almost 170bhp. This is superb considering that the standard T57S produced 135bhp. A Froude dynamometer test sheet presents the following results:

64.5bhp at 2000rpm
84bhp at 2500rpm
107bhp at 3000rpm
123bhp at 3500rpm
139bhp at 4000rpm
151bhp at 4500rpm
161bhp at 5000rpm
166bhp at 5500rpm

Froude records

For the 1937 Le Mans race the 'G' power units were tuned for endurance where, during test on January 22, 1937, engine 57G number 4 recorded 150bhp at 5500rpm. Engine 57G number 1 (Wimille) tested similarly on June 9, 1937, noted with 56mm compression height pistons. Engine number 3 was also fitted with 56mm pistons and tested prior to Le Mans. There were at least four 'G' engines suitable for T57GR and T57S chassis, as well as at least four versions built within T59 crankcases. It would appear that, other than T59/57G number 5, the 'G' engines specifically intended for T57GR and T57S chassis were not stamped on their casings, but used tag plates for individual identification. An engine identified only as, '57G Mulet Banc' was tested on February 10, 1937, producing 168bhp at 5800rpm, fitted with RR56 alloy pistons with a compression height of 54mm. Given the power output in relation to the piston height, this engine must have been a supercharged T59/57G unit, and therefore likely to be that under development for the Benoist car and the 400,000f prize. Later noted as T59/57G number 8, it was tested again on March 19, 1937. Since the Roberts engine used 56mm compression height pistons, it would appear that his was one of only three normally-aspirated 'G' engines prepared to Le Mans specification. It would appear Nos 1 and 3 were used for the two cars actually entered, which might suggest that number 4 was reserved. Engine 57G number 2 disappeared from the record by June 1937, so may have been converted into a more road-friendly version for use in a Works demonstrator, becoming number 2SG, but retained its 45mm valve engine block.

Summary

In summary, the spare Le Mans T57G engine is based upon a T57S power unit that has been modified with a special large-port cylinder block, unique valve and camshaft drive, as well as a lightened crankshaft, special con-rods and pistons. It is analogous to a modern mass-produced engine that has been systematically modified for competition, representing the zenith of the development of the T57S power unit by 1937. It should be borne in mind that the various modifications highlighted would have evolved incrementally during the previous two years through Bugatti's T57 and T59 competition entries. These changes are discussed in a later chapter.

Bob Roberts' T57G engine spent several years in chassis 57513, but when it finally needed a major overhaul, the car's original power unit was refurbished and refitted by Henri Novo, with whom the T57G engine remained as payment in-lieu of the work done. It has since been sold through the dealer, Monsieur Ariztegui.

13

T57G Tank chassis detail

THE 1936-37 T57G TANK utilised the production T57S surbaissé or 'lowered' chassis. This was arranged much lower than the T57, with very deep sections and large openings at the rear through which the back axle passed. The frames were made by the Brunon-Vallette forge, at Rive-de-Gier, in the Rhone valley between Lyon and St Etienne, 500km (310-mile) southwest of Molsheim. The rear crossmembers of these frames are usually stamped BV. The frame sections were not pressed out, but skilfully and labour-intensively hand-forged from 3.5mm high quality mild steel sheet. Its ingenious design offered a strong yet relatively lightweight frame, closer to the road thus reducing the car's overall centre of gravity. Curiously, there are two versions of this chassis.

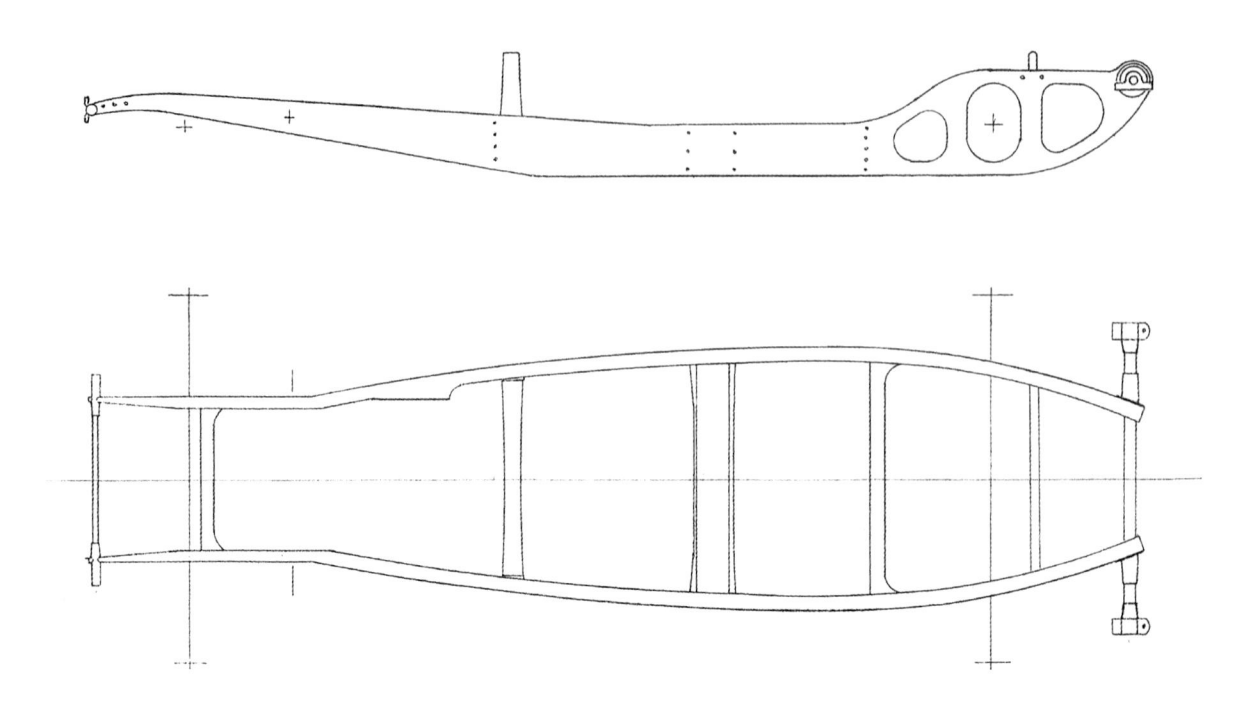

The 1935 Series 1 'Gondola' T57S frame. (Courtesy Bugatti Trust)

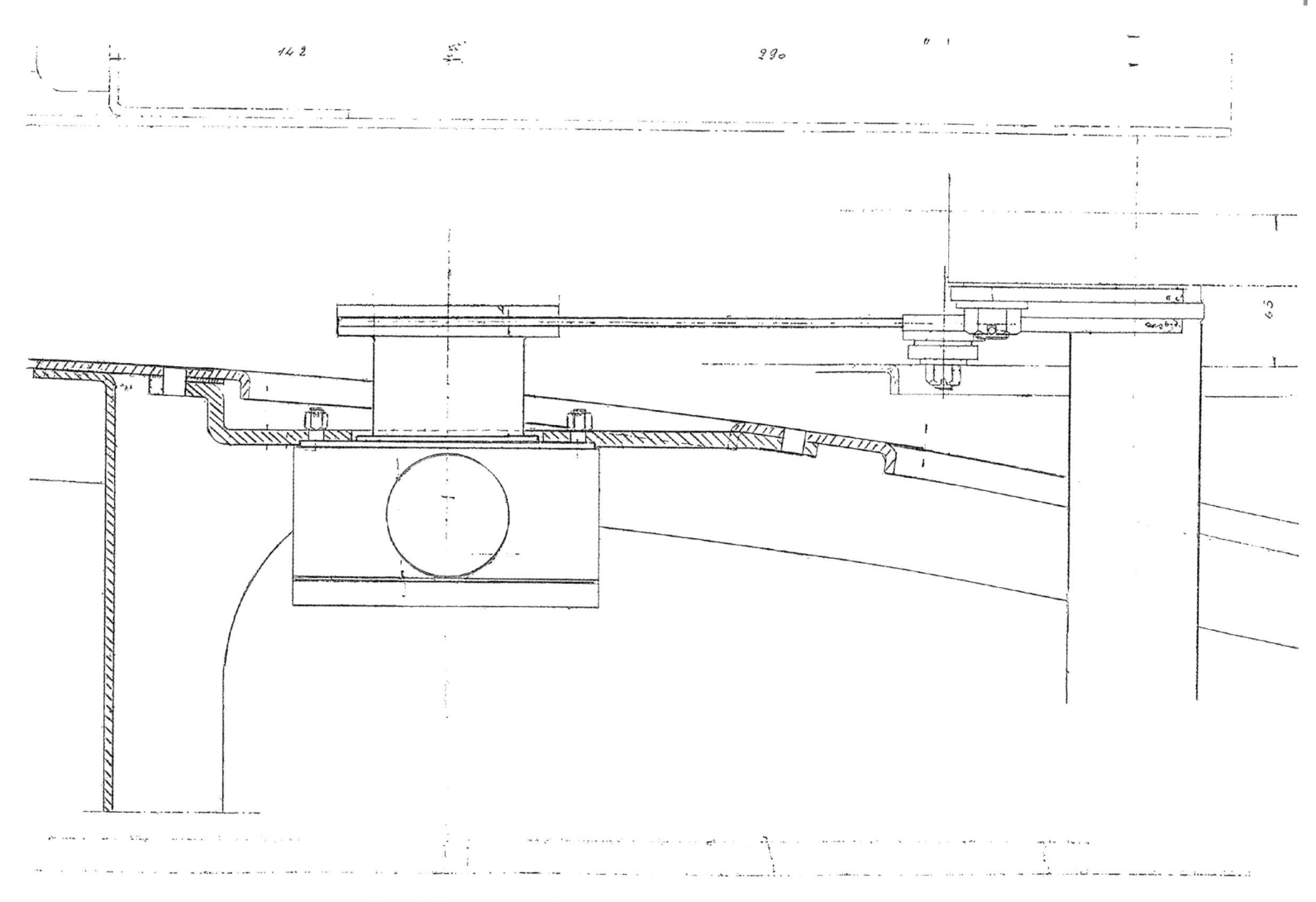

13 T57G Tank chassis detail

Gondola De Ram bracket detail. (Courtesy Bugatti Trust)

Series 1 T57S frame – gondola

The very first T57S 'surbaissé' chassis drawings were detailed in July 1935, with the first General Arrangement diagrams completed by August 7. This version is variously known as the 'waisted,' 'boat-tailed' or 'gondola' chassis. Here the side frames curved inward toward the rear, invoking the famous T35 racing cars. Yet, by the beginning of 1936, the original gondola T57S chassis design was completely revised to a form with parallel sides. At the time of the original design, it was still quite fashionable to have a chassis frame that closely followed the streamlined teardrop shape of the body. The gondola chassis had a rear engine mounting plate width of only 705mm, so, with the gearbox in unit with it, made the control pedal area around the feet quite cramped. Moreover, by curving inward at the rear, the chassis needed a heavy-duty rear spring hanger beam to take both twist and bending forces when cornering. Additionally, special inboard rear mounting brackets for De Ram dampers were also necessary to compensate for the curvature.

This extra weight was theoretically surplus if the rear of the chassis could have been designed parallel in the first place. Besides, fabricating a complex curve in a chassis frame required high levels of skill to shrink the ripples from the curved folded flange, and was very labour intensive. Monthly

Bugatti Type 57 Grand Prix – A Celebration

factory records indicate issues raised over the extent of re-work required to get these frames to an acceptable standard of precision. As a result, these all appear to be sound reasons why the design was reviewed, in order to simplify labour, cost, and to reduce weight. Early frames were narrower at the rear engine bulkhead, and four narrow firewalls are noted to exist. As a result, it is assumed that four gondola chassis were manufactured before revision, although these may not have been made by Brunon-Vallette, since the Bugatti Works did have some limited facilities and expertise for prototyping chassis frames.

It has been suggested that the reason for re-design was because the original gondola chassis was in some way defective in strength and structure. On the other hand, even with the relatively heavier Aérolithe coachwork, this seems unlikely. It is notable that, in late January 1936, even before the new frame was ready, this ex-Paris Salon car was tuned for 167bhp at 5500rpm, and driven relentlessly around the Montlhéry road circuit by Robert Benoist. Following many laps and a change of tyres, it eventually achieved a record speed of 193.53km/h (120.25mph). These results were reported by the motoring press to be the fastest for any un-supercharged production car. Later, during a trip to London, the car was demonstrated to BOC Chairman, Colonel GM Giles and CWP Hampton, for the May 1936 issue of *Bugantics*, being driven hard by William Grover-Williams. With three in the car, it is not recorded who was left cramped behind the seats. Public road speeds of 115mph were reported, with only praise for its structural integrity and cornering performance. So, as suggested, the change in design was more likely intended to ease manufacture, cost and weight.

Series 2 T57S frame

The Series 2 T57S chassis was detailed between November 1935 and late January 1936. The new design was closely similar to look at from the side, but had altered significantly in plan. The width at the engine rear mounting plate was enlarged to 780mm, providing additional room in the footwell. The peripheral length of the frame remained the same, equalised with the now parallel rear section, and by halving the

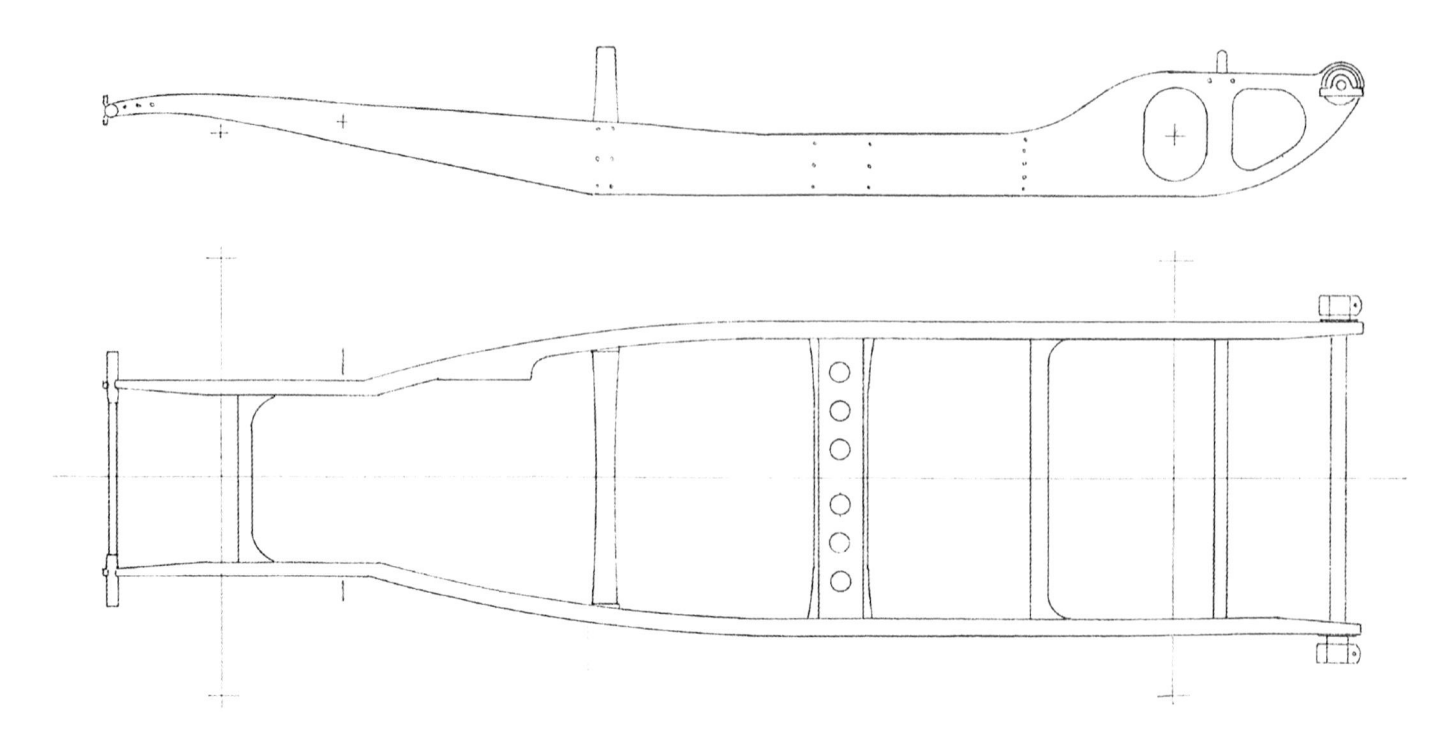

The 1936 Series 2 T57S frame. (Courtesy Bugatti Trust)

13   T57G Tank chassis detail

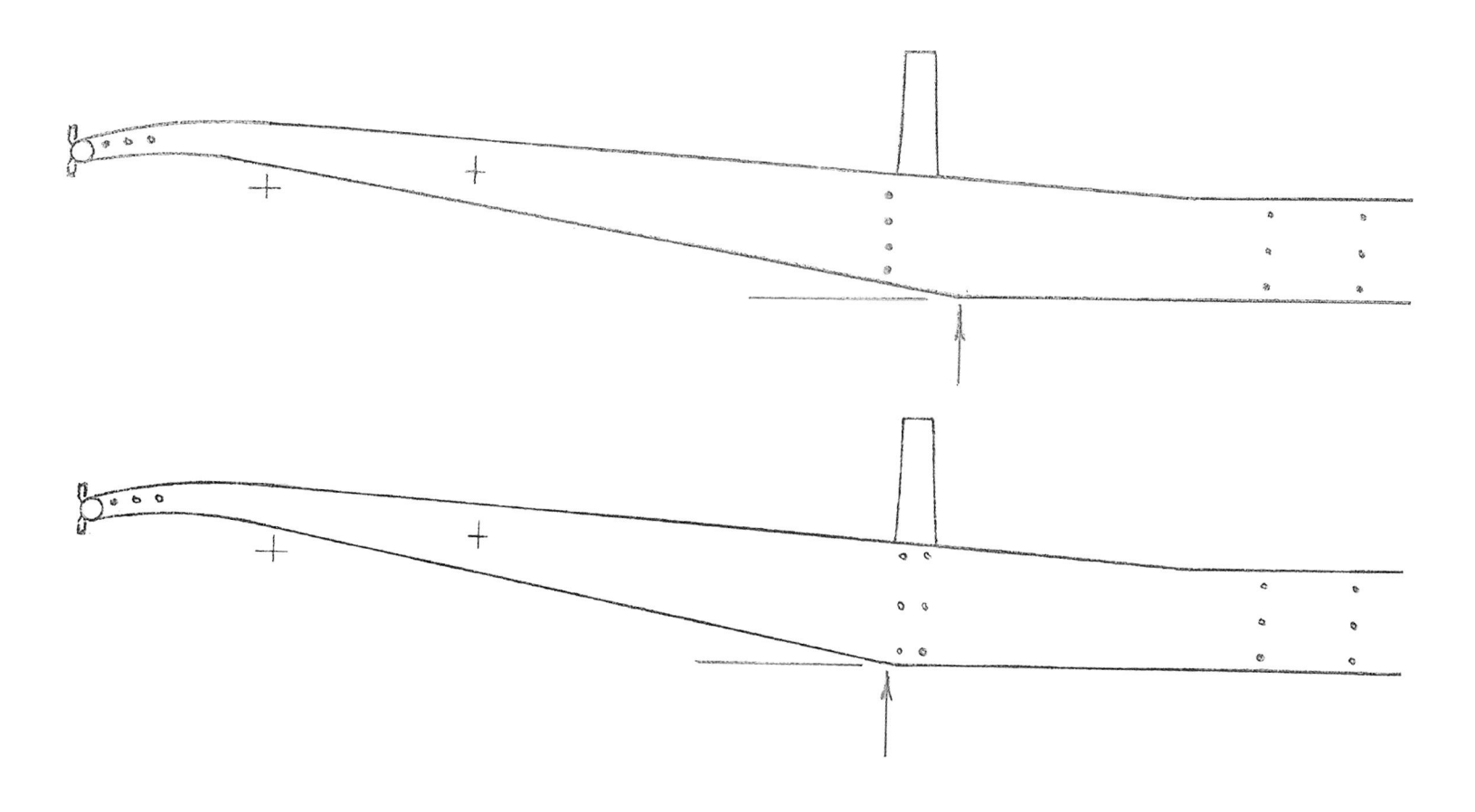

T57S Series 1 and 2 frames compared. (Bugatti Trust)

10m original curve radius of the chassis in plan to 5m. Hence, it seems that most of the dimensions of the blank-former could remain unaltered, and, as a result, it may be possible that early frames were retrospectively worked to the revised design, rather than being scrapped. The special De Ram rear mounting brackets were discarded, and the Bugatti-designed damper casings were now bolted directly inside the parallel chassis frames. The rear spring hanger crossbeam could now be made lighter, because all suspension forces fed into the frame more directly.

Other than the front spring bar, every one of the original frame crossmembers was re-designed to compensate for the change. In addition, the new chassis was increased in depth by 25mm at the rear engine mounting, where the down-sweep of the new frame lower edge ceased 200mm before that of the Series 1 version.

Narrow firewall
The change in form, with a 75mm increase in width of the engine rear mounting plate, naturally increased the width and shape of the chassis in plan, and, as a result, affected all earlier coachwork designs. This would explain conclusively why the original closed Coupé Spéciale coachwork of the Paris Salon car could never easily be re-worked to fit the new chassis shape. The body was now simply too narrow at the bulkhead, being extremely difficult to enlarge it to fit the wider chassis, especially a closed coupé with all that glazing. Hence, the Aérolithe body was scrapped, as confirmed by chief mechanic Robert Aumaître. By contrast, the simpler Torpédo body probably had sufficient material, when lowered by 32mm, to adapt to the wider bulkhead frame design.

Given the financial difficulties at that time, it is possible that earlier frames, made before revision, might have been

Bugatti Type 57 Grand Prix – A Celebration

The T59/50S seen at the ACF in June 1935. (Courtesy Bugatti Trust)

retrospectively 're-worked' to the new parallel design, rather than scrapped. Four narrow firewalls are known to exist amongst the surviving T57S cars, these being: 57373, 57374, 57375 and 57384. However, it is not established whether there is any evidence that these particular frames themselves have been altered; besides, the narrow firewalls would not necessarily have remained with their original chassis. Nevertheless, if any frames were reworked, there should be clues to be found: (1) The frames will be about 25mm shallower at the rear engine mounting; (2) Assuming some original frame side rivet holes were re-used, all the new crossmembers, between the engine and rear suspension tube, might be about 20mm further forward than they should be, which will mean that the rear spring or propeller shaft length might be unique to the car; (3) The hole at the rear of the frame, where the suspension spring hanger is mounted, is certain to show signs of modification or repair; (4) There may be signs of repair plating, just forward of the oval opening for the rear axle where the earlier De Rams once passed through the frame. On the other hand, I have not discovered one yet, although this does not mean that none survived.

Cut-down long frame

Some historians suppose prototype Tanks used a cut-down, long-wheelbase, Type 57 chassis frame. Froude dynamometer engine tests record one of several T57G power units prepared for the 1936 ACF. '57SG No 238 Prep Montlhéry,' was possibly a four bearer-arm crankcase type, plainly insinuating a 1935 prototypical origin. On the basis of this thought-provoking fact, some enthusiasts have suggested that a prototype Tank must have utilised a cut-down, long T57 Series 1 touring frame. This is unlikely, though, since an engine from this early period could also have been one of several experimental T57S/G power units used in T57GR chassis, where, with the rear mounting arms cut and ground away to clear the steering box, would have adapted easily to the engine rear mounting plate of a prototype T57S surbaissé chassis. With a solid front mounting, De Ram dampers could be mounted using a tubular crossbeam, just as the Types 59 and 59/50S. Furthermore, number 238 was clearly a special engine that Froude tested for 182bhp at 5500rpm on April 23, 1936. As a result, engine number 238 appears to be a 1935 prototype T57G power unit, so, logically, would have been fitted into the 1935 T57S gondola chassis that existed at the time.

Clutch

The T57G's twin-plate clutch was initially developed for the 1935 T57GR long-frame models, in particular the Ulster TT cars, after which it became standard to T57S specification. Curiously, formal drawings of the T57S twin-plate, Ferodo lined dry-clutch date from early 1936, yet they were reported in the motoring press for the 1935 Ulster TT cars, as well as in the Paris Salon and Olympia Catalogue Sheets dated October 1, 1935. The December 1935 issue of *Motor Sport* also described the T57S Torpedo in some detail, including its double-disc dry-plate clutch. Consequently, the prototype clutch may have been quite different to that we know today, so original drawings may have been scrapped or lost after the 1936 revision. There were certainly notable clutch issues with the two T57GR Ulster TT cars in September 1935, which sufficiently impaired Howe's original leading placement to third,

and was terminal for Lewis. In addition, for the T57S surbaissé chassis, arranged with a low seating position, the pedal cross-shaft axis was set lower into the frame, where, instead of the clutch pedal acting directly on the clutch-operating shaft, its lowered cross-shaft used a linkage. Otherwise, the position of the clutch, brake and accelerator pedals were conventional by modern standards, although were closer together in order to fit between the gearbox and chassis sideframe. This lowered pedal arrangement seems to have been developed from the long-framed Series 1 T57GRs.

T57G synchromesh gearbox

Externally, the T57G Tank's four-speed and reverse gearbox was identical to the standard T57S, which, in turn, differed only slightly from the T57 Touring unit. The T57S casing was derived very simply from the T57 original by modifying the patterns with relocated bosses to reposition the handbrake. The gearbox was mounted in unit with the engine using a standard Type 57 clutch-to-gearbox housing. The Type 57 and 57S gearboxes both employed identical bearings, gear ratios, and dog-clutches. They also used helical constant mesh, 19:29 primary to secondary shaft pinions, giving reduction ratios of: 0.774 for third, 0.554 second, with spur-cut 0.296 first and 0.359 for reverse. Nevertheless, for the very first time on a Bugatti, the prototype T57S gearbox used 'silent' synchronising dog clutches on second, third and top gears. In this case, it was not practical to synchronize first gear, because the first to second sliding dog clutch carried a straight-cut first gearwheel that passed the reverse pinion on its travel, limiting the speed of change anyway. The device was initially revealed with the prototype Competition models seen at the 1935 Paris Salon. It was described in the Paris Salon catalogue as: "3 vitesses silencieuses"; and the 1935 Olympia Exhibition catalogue: "Silent second, third and top gears." Given this, it follows that the prototype synchromesh gearbox must have been developed through the 1935 T57GR models. Regrettably, synchromesh was never extended to the production versions, but was only ever employed for the T57G Tanks.

The racing Tanks used closer ratios, with 17:19 primary to secondary shaft pinions, providing ratios of: 0.800 for third, 0.639 for second, with a spur-cut 0.490 first and 0.404 reverse. A general arrangement drawing illustrating the T57G gearbox, No 57G.CV.ENS.1, was finalised on June 17, 1936, yet a rough

Bugatti Type 57 Grand Prix – A Celebration

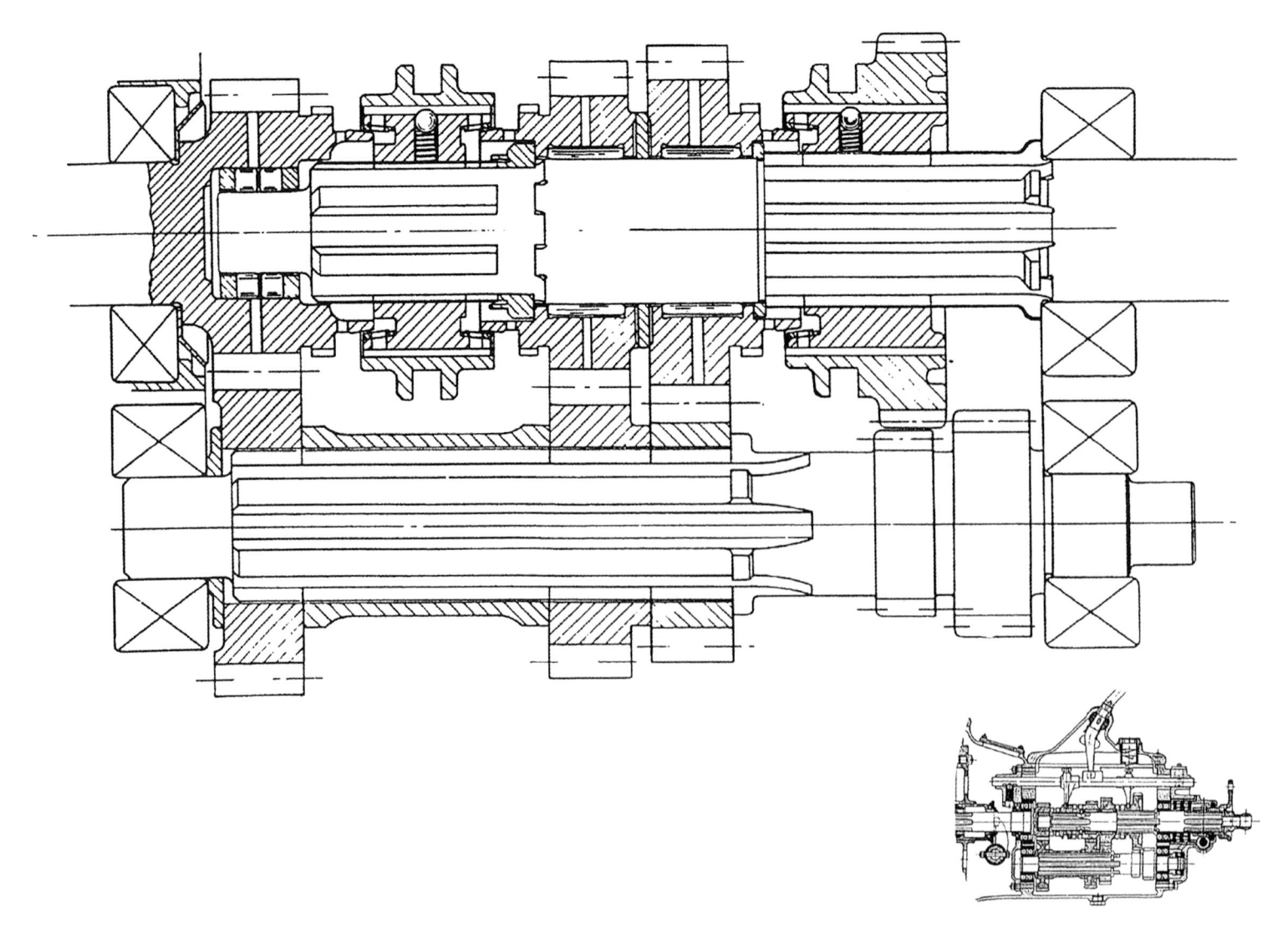

The 1936-37 T57G synchromesh gearbox. (Courtesy Bugatti Trust)

draft, 57S.CV.ENS.1, dates from April 29, 1936, showing detailed manufacturing tolerances. Clearly, even earlier drawings must have once existed, showing the necessary dimensions of the revised components. All the original, 1935, T57S synchromesh drafts seem to be lost.

The Bugatti 'silent' synchronising dog clutch utilised a single-pair cone design, without a baulking mechanism. Designed by Antonio Pitchetto, this clever device allowed it to be compact enough to fit into the same space as the original T57 dog clutch, where, ingeniously, this avoided having to modify the casing or to narrow the width of the gear wheels and bearings. When the clutch disengages the drive from the engine to the gearbox, the synchronizer mechanism allows gears to be changed faster and more silently than the standard gearbox. A 'male' cone, cut into where the original dog clutch would have been on the constant mesh gear, corresponds with a 'female' cone, cut into the sliding splined dog selector sleeve. This has a thin bronze liner riveted to it. As the gearchange sleeve is

122

13 T57G Tank chassis detail

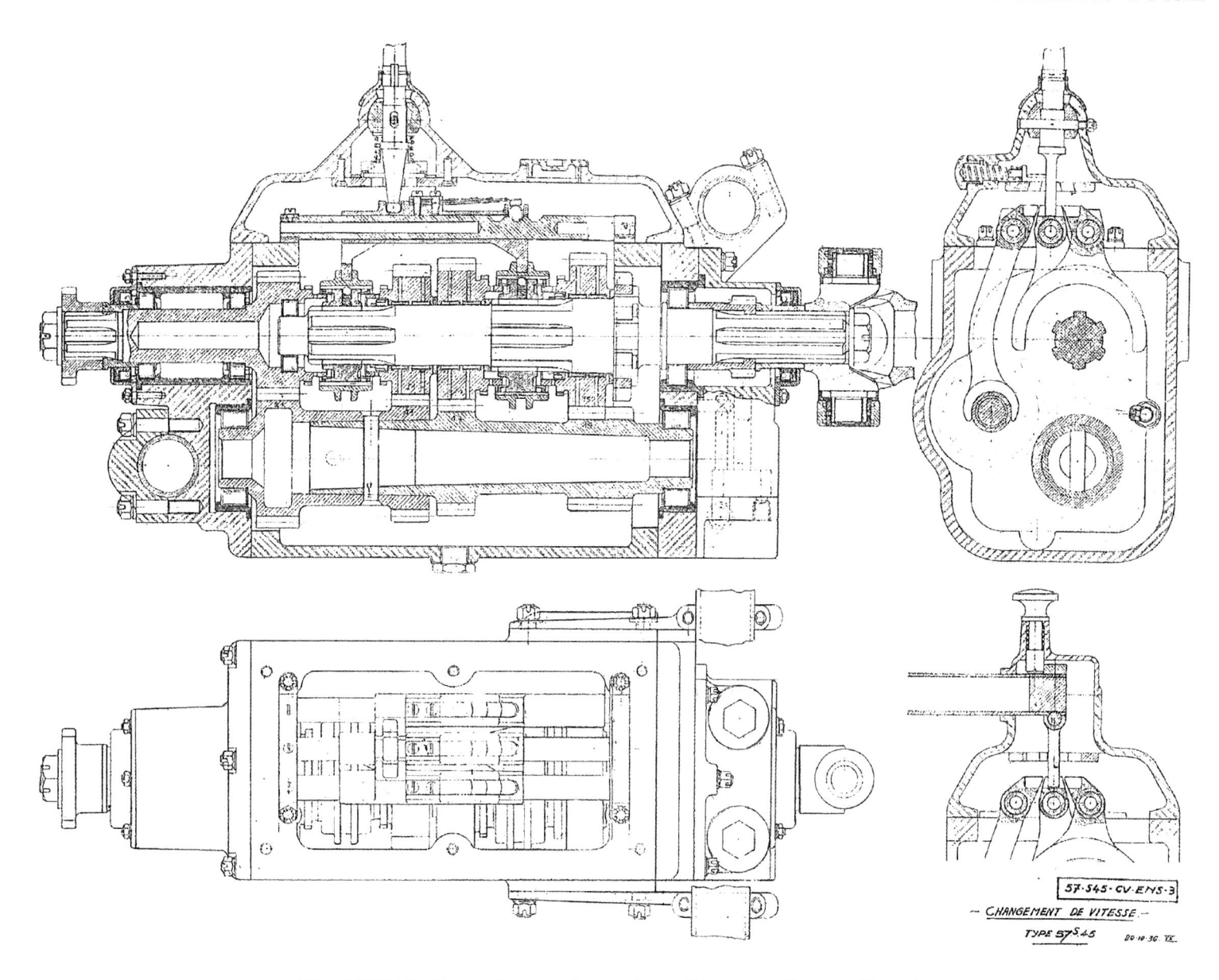

The T57S45 all-synchromesh gearbox. (Courtesy Bugatti Trust)

moved, the cones act as a friction device that tends to rapidly match the speed of the selected gear along with the constant primary and secondary motion shafts, with that of the third motion shaft, before its splined dogs engage fully.

Accordingly, this enables much faster and smoother gear changes without double de-clutching, as well as shorter periods in 'neutral' when racing, and therefore, more power on the road for any given race. However, under competitive conditions the added friction would generate more heat. This could become a problem when the oil is very hot, for internal casing pressure could cause the lubricant to leak. The issue seems to have been resolved by 1936 with a long-tubular breather fitted to the gearbox top cover, dissipating internal pressure that could build up during very long races. A long-range, triple-tank, top-up system was used on the 1937 Le Mans Tanks, being repeated for the 1939 Le Mans car.

Constant mesh gear systems with dog clutches were developed early in motoring history, where their next stage of evolution was synchronised engagement trialled during the 1920s. In America, General Motors' Cadillac manufactured one in 1929, synchronising second and top in a three-speed gearbox, using a simple external cone arrangement. There is no known Bugatti patent application for his T57G gearbox synchroniser, although the system had already been improved by the floating twin-cone, baulked versions anyway. The idea, whilst very compact, was never used for the production T57S models. Perhaps this is because the wear life of the thin bronze cones was not really robust enough for a road-going car. Likewise, Jean was studying what was then considered to be the advanced and futuristic Cotal electro-mechanical gearbox system, viewing the development of this fast-gearchange venture far more enthusiastically than synchromesh.

T57S45 Tank gearbox

Designed by Édouard Bertrand from a sketch by Ettore, this dedicated stand-alone racing gearbox utilised a robust magnesium alloy casing mounted fore and aft on a pair of cross-tubes. It was detailed in a factory drawing, 57.S45.CV.ENS.3, dated October 20, 1936. A version of the gearbox fitted to the King Leopold car, chassis 57248, was superbly described in *The Bugatti Trust Newsletter*, winter 2012. Its power throughput was arranged similarly to that of the T57S gearbox, but employed an all-synchromesh gearchange for all forward gears. It used straight-cut, constant mesh gears to minimise end thrust and mechanical friction, and a twin-pump, dry-sump lubrication system to reduce oil drag. As well as these obvious racing features, it also used well-designed, hollow primary and secondary motion shafts for lightness and reduced inertia, making for faster gearchanges. All gears and bearings were lubricated using spray jets, welded to a 10mm diameter tubular gallery, reprising those on Ettore's Brescia engines. The casing also had fittings for a remote reservoir.

Since the shafts were not subject to any significant internal end-thrust, the bearings are designed for minimal axial loading, using tracked needle and large diameter rollers, a number being un-caged. The geartrain used 19:21 primary to secondary motion shaft pinions, giving reduction ratios of: 0.818 for third, 0.668 for second, and 0.542 for first, with a high 0.714 for reverse. Another conspicuous racing feature to note is the sliding gear reverse mechanism, where, for compactness, and minimum weight, these pinions are only half the width of the others, so clearly reverse had to be applied with caution. For detailed weight-saving, even the gear selector rods and oil pump rotors are partially hollowed. As a result, it is clear that the T57S45 gearbox was wholly designed for racing, and was extremely costly to build.

Intriguingly, an earlier wet-sump model of this gearbox is also apparent, without the rear gear pump section, anticipated for the two 3.3-litre T59/57Gs used in the August 1936 Comminges sports car race, 57.S45.CV.ENS.2, dated June 29, 1936. Curiously, the new gearbox is also reported for the T59/50B single-seater seen at Monaco in April, since photos show that the brake lever axle has been raised to clear it; likely, ENS.1, now missing. Additionally, for the T57S45 gearbox, at least three selector cover versions exist. The earliest form was designed with an external right-hand lever suitable for the Type 59 cockpit using the original chassis mounted bush; used at Comminges. Another version has a central ball-mounted gear lever for a sports car, and finally, a special in-cockpit sliding right-hand version was made for the Grand Prix single-seaters. A similar arrangement was used for the Type 73C. The T57S45 gearbox was never really designed to suit a road-going production sports car, yet it appears to have had commendable service in the King Leopold T59/57G 57248.

Interestingly, the T57S45 gearbox is also associated with significant changes to the rear suspension of the T59 chassis in 1936, which included characteristic long radius arms. The original T59 rear axle suspension movement was determined by the deflection arc of its reversed quarter-elliptic springs and eyes. This geometry required movement in the forward link of the rear axle torque reaction arm, including a degree of travel in the propeller shaft sliding spline. Unlike the forward prop-shaft universal joint, the rear coupling was not affected by angular variation because the torque reaction arm was firmly secured to the differential casing. Consequently, prop-shaft length would change accordingly to suit suspension travel on cornering, bump and rebound. As 3.3-litre engine power increased throughout development, in conjunction with higher racing speeds and faster gear changes, prop-shaft spline 'torque-grab' under load became more pronounced. Under powerful acceleration, the sliding splines effectively seize solid, where, if cornering or riding bumpy surfaces, excessive stress could be placed on torque arm links and prop-shaft drive couplings.

13 T57G Tank chassis detail

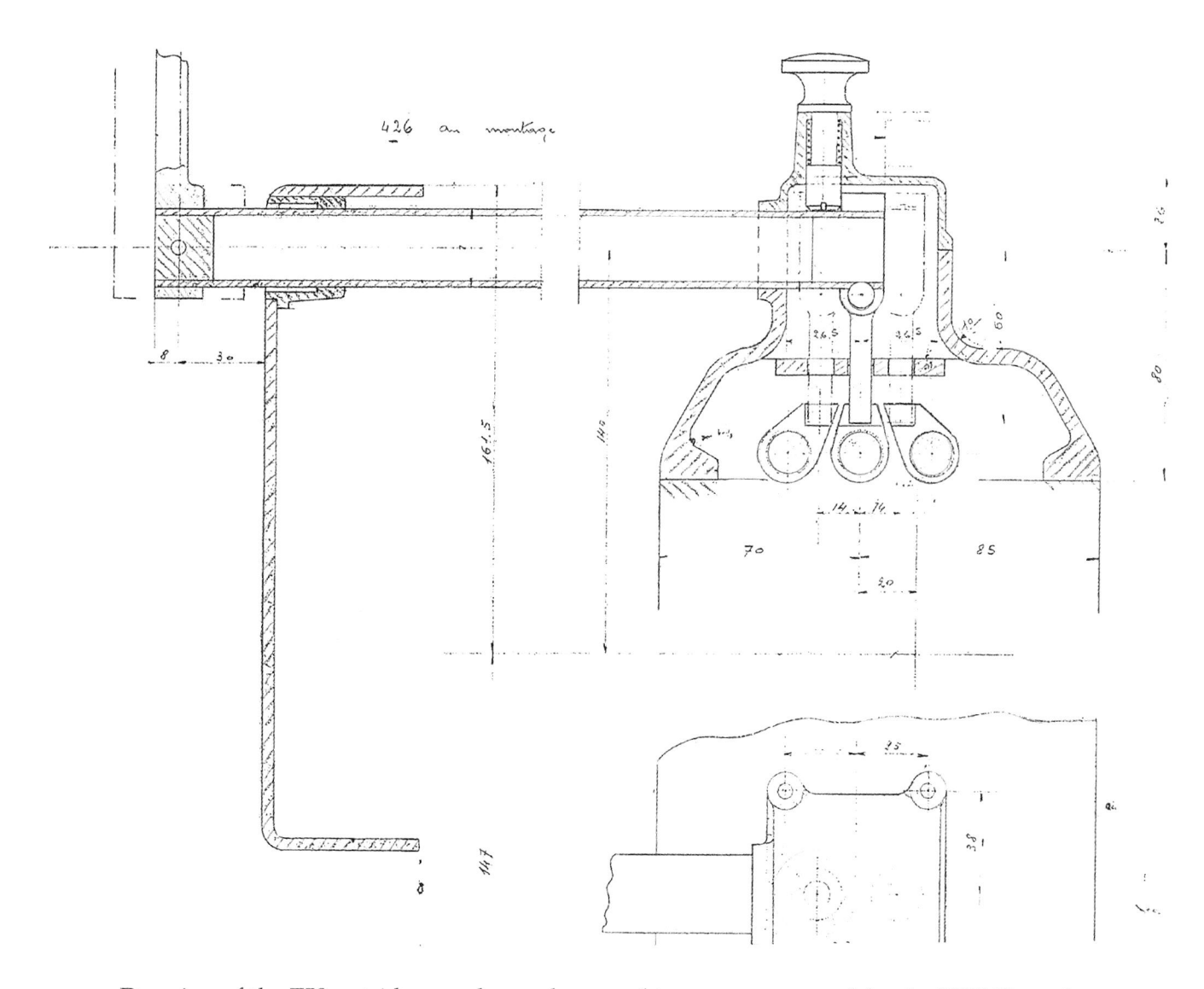

Drawing of the T59 outside gearchange lever and top cover arranged for the T57S45 gearbox.
(Courtesy Bugatti Trust)

It may be observed that when engine power increased after fitting the 45mm valve 'G' cylinder blocks, issues with gearbox, prop-shaft joint and torque arm began to plague the Type 59 between 1935 and 1936. It seems the emerging problem was not fully diagnosed, for even after employing the stronger T57S45 gearbox with its more rigid, metal star and fork coupling, the inability of the prop-shaft spline to plunge under powerful acceleration, due to 'torque-grab,' now placed extreme fore and aft axial thrust directly onto the gearbox third motion (output) shaft. With its limited-thrust roller bearings, this could quickly lead to damaging wear and jumping out of gear. The more powerful T50B engine installation merely exacerbated this deficiency.

The issue was finally resolved by changing the rear suspension geometry and isolating these parasitic loads altogether. Henceforth, the geometry focussed on enabling

Bugatti Type 57 Grand Prix – A Celebration

Photo of the special gearbox top cover for the T73C. (Courtesy NMT Collection)

the rear axle and torque arm to effectively arc from the gearbox output coupling, thus minimising any change in length of the propeller shaft. The revised design to improve control of the rear suspension geometry used new quarter elliptic rear springs, having slide-block bearings (like those on the front) instead of eyes; a shorter prop-shaft; an amended rear axle torque reaction arm and forward link mounting, as well as 950mm long external radius rods similar to the Type 50. Such radius arms appear to have been initially pioneered on the T50B-powered T59s, where Wimille's successful 4.7-litre car, seen at the Vanderbilt Cup in October 1936, is clearly fitted with them. This design was revised between August and September 1936: too late for the Swiss Grand Prix, but ready in time for the Long Island Vanderbilt Cup race; Wimille finished second.

The T50B-engined cars did not have a starter mechanism like the T59, so an alternative was devised, and the T57S45 gearbox is associated with a revised method of side cranking. The 1935 prototype T50S-powered T59 is reported to have used a crude notched pulley arrangement, started by pulling on a wound rope, just like a lawnmower. The new scheme was undoubtedly based upon a similar method devised for the T59/50B car from 1936. A hand-held electric motor with a long shaft was operated externally through a large hole in the left-hand chassis frame. Its driving dog engaged with a spring-loaded 90° bevel gear, which then meshed with another bevel riveted to the annulus-toothed, clutch-shaft-to-gearbox coupling, splined to the clutch shaft. Similar large holes in the chassis frame may be noted on all the T50B-powered racing cars seen during 1936 at Monaco, Turin, Berne, and Long Island. The external electric starter was also used in 1938 at

13 T57G Tank chassis detail

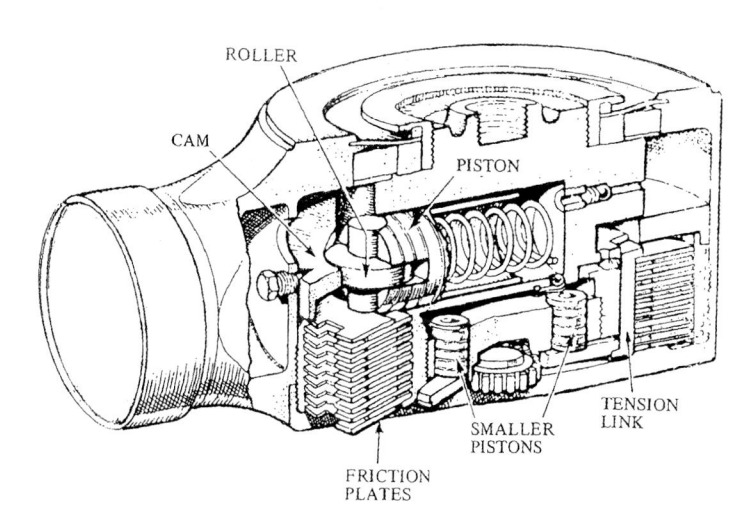

The De Ram damper in partial section.
(Courtesy Bugatti Trust)

Cork, Tripoli, and Reims. It was used again in 1939 with the T50B, 50180, at La Turbie, Montlhéry and Prescott, as well as Paris in 1945. Conversely, the T59/57G Sport (57248), T57S45 Tanks, and 1939 Luxembourg Grand Prix T59/50B sports car used electric self-starter motor systems.

De Ram dampers

Dampers are often popularly called shock absorbers, although technically this is erroneous. Suspension springs are the shock absorbers, whereas dampers merely control bump and subsequent rebound. In their day, De Ram dampers were the most technically-advanced units available to the motor industry, but were incredibly expensive, costing a staggering 15,500f per set to fit. Even when purchased in bulk, they probably represented at least 12 per cent of the total build cost of a Type 57S. Consider that a basic T57 chassis was 73,000f in 1938, which compares with 100,000f for a T57S chassis. Nevertheless, De Rams were extremely well devised, and, when properly adjusted, worked superbly. Conventional friction dampers, like the Hartford scissor or Bugatti brake drum type, used friction materials loaded with a fixed spring; therefore fixed damping. By contrast, more advanced versions utilised adjustable spring pressure, loaded remotely from the dashboard, either mechanically or hydraulically. This would allow compensation to be made by the driver to suit the variety of road surfaces encountered. However, the key limitation of all these types is that the damping resistance force is entirely independent of the bump velocity.

Monsieur De Ram's ingenious, yet somewhat technically complicated, solution to this problem was to load 36 friction plates hydraulically, with an instant reflex action that is proportionate to the bump velocity, all within a completely self-contained unit. That is to say, when the road surface is relatively mild, with long undulations, the damper arm movement is gentle, and so very little hydraulic pressure is applied to the friction discs. However, if road surface irregularities are harsh or fierce, the fast movement of the damper arm will automatically generate a proportionately higher hydraulic pressure to be applied to the friction plates, accordingly increasing the damping force. Therefore, correctly set-up, De Rams will instantly adapt themselves to slow or fast driving, and good or bad road surfaces, so that at high motoring speeds, the harder the bump, the firmer the dampers become.

In the 1930s, De Rams were technologically analogous to the computer-controlled suspension damping systems available for the fastest cars of today. Jean Bugatti appears to have been so confident of their potential success, that the factory produced specialised lightweight housings and operating arms for the Grand Prix Type 59 in 1933. Likewise, special De Ram/Bugatti-housed units were used for the T57S and T57G. Standard De Rams were bulky scissor units, as fitted to the T57GR cars raced in the 1935 Ulster TT, although by then, lightweight housings and arms had already been designed for the Type 57S.

Racing wheels

The extraordinary wheels fitted to all post-1933 racing cars, including the Type 57G, originated from the Grand Prix Type 59. There is a well-known story that during the period when Ettore Bugatti was otherwise completely immersed in the Railcar Project in Paris, he inadvertently discovered cars and components during an unofficial factory visit, probably around October 1932. Utterly incandescent with rage, he immediately ordered the Type 59's destruction, including all patterns and drawings. However, he was eventually pacified by Jean, and famously contributed to it by designing its unique and beautiful radial spoke 'piano' wire wheels, superseding a cast slab-spoke original design. The earliest sketch of the T59 radial spoke wheel by Ettore Bugatti is dated November 1932, and was claimed to be 4.5kg (10lb) lighter than Jean's slab-spoke

Bugatti Type 57 Grand Prix – A Celebration

version, so maybe justified the complication and cost. The essential design features of the wheel became the subject of a French Patent in 1934, number 411019, applied for in the name of Ettore Bugatti. The first formal drawing is 59.CH.32 dated December 9, 1932, and had a rim width of 79mm, followed with 360mm diameter brake drums of 50mm shoe width, and an outside fin diameter of 415mm, dated January 24, 1933.

Ettore's absolute fury about the T59 is clearly understandable, since Jean had neither the mandate nor budget to create these racing cars; especially during the Depression when many workers had been laid off, and all costs had to be carefully considered. However, assuming this story is true, the incident provides a cogent explanation as to why three of the T59s have otherwise inappropriate Type chassis numbers. In this case, for plates 441352, 54208 (also-stamped 59123), and 54213 (also-stamped 59124), none of which are otherwise credibly accounted for in the records. Having previously explored several possible grounds for the atypical numbering, I have had to conclude that Ettore's exuberant and headstrong son deliberately camouflaged the construction of the first three T59 chassis assemblies and their components by billing costs to existing and otherwise sanctioned projects.

The date sequence of the T44 and two T54 numbers coincide late 1932 to early 1933. This is the period when Jean is known to have also tested the prototype T57 engine and transmission in a T44 chassis (44250). Some pretty audacious and creative book-keeping perhaps, but if correct, this would suggest that these three cars were the very first Type 59s built, and that 441352 might well be the archetype. Jean may have been able to hoodwink Henri Pracht, works secretary cum accountant, intensely preoccupied with paperwork, but he could never dupe Le Patron.

The expensive Type 59 light-alloy wheels comprise a number of well-designed and beautifully crafted elements. With this cleverly considered wheel construction, traction and cornering forces are positively separated through components specifically designed for each type of load. The large diameter hub assembly is a 4mm thick Dural alloy machine-spun coned disc, having a 155-gear tooth periphery that engages in a similarly cut, but 8mm wide internally toothed wheel rim. The cone section is riveted to an adapted, but otherwise standard $2\frac{7}{8}$ inches (72.85mm) Rudge-Whitworth, 88-spline steel hub centre initially using an extension ring adaptor, then later a specially manufactured splined hub centre. The nose of the

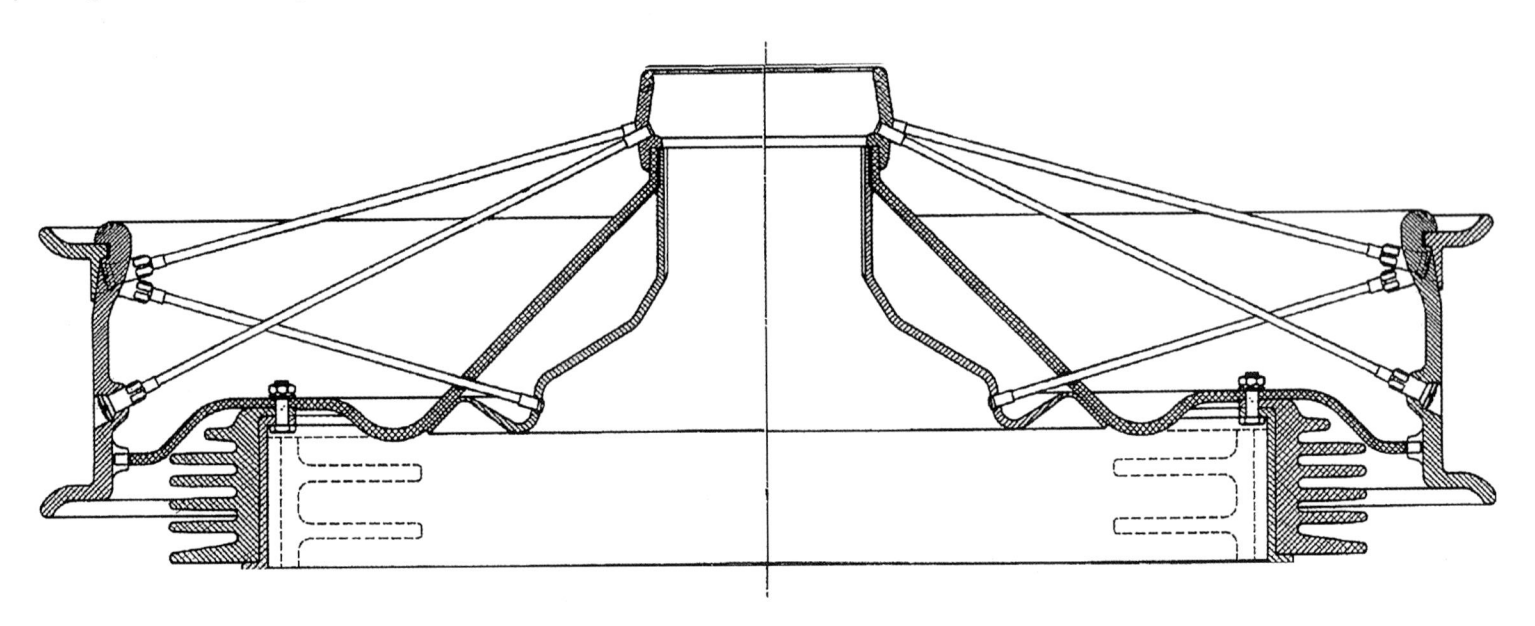

The Grand Prix T59 racing wheel in section, showing the arrangement of the rim, spun disc, brake drum, Rudge hub and spokes. (Courtesy Bugatti Trust)

13 T57G Tank chassis detail

brake drum casting, with a steel-lining insert, is secured to the hub and conical disc assembly with sixteen 5mm bolts and nuts. This construction reinforces the relatively thin driving disc, eliminating flexing under power.

The internally toothed alloy rim fits freely onto the periphery of the hub assembly, where the gear-toothed disc transmits tangential traction and braking forces through to the rim teeth. The tyre is retained on the rim using a split ring, which locates into a groove, and is secured with a plate and two screws that lock it together. The hub and its rim are linked by three different length rows of 2.5mm diameter spokes; 165, 205 and 223mm, respectively. They are all arranged radially and are tensioned for axial cornering forces only. These rows consist of 32 spokes from the front of the hub centre to the front of the rim; combined with a further 32 spokes from the back of the hub to the front of the rim; additionally braced with a sequence of 16 spokes from the front of the hub centre to the back of the rim. The spokes are rather special and lightweight, being made from very high tensile steel, swaged down in the middle by a rolling process, leaving the thread and head portions of larger diameter. The root end is butted to create an anchor, and the other end is roll-threaded to ensure strength, where it has the same diameter at the root of the thread as the reduced mid-span portion. It is apparent from photographs and witnesses that these spokes were initially copper-plated.

It has been claimed by at least two former Bugatti employees that the spokes originated from an existing contemporary light motorcycle, currently unidentified. This assertion has been disputed by some historians because of their expensive, reduced mid-span construction. However, such spokes may have been far more common than is first thought, because similar ones were used by Isotta Fraschini for the wheels of its Tipo 8B 1931-1939; of which, only 30 were ever built. Moreover, specialist wheel maker Rudge-Whitworth employed such spokes for its standard light car wheels, as well as those manufactured for its clients. Given that Rudge-Whitworth produced the T59 inner hubs, it is entirely rational that it also made the exclusive lightweight spokes to order, especially as it had the product volumes and specialised tooling. Besides, consider that as well as wheels, Rudge of Coventry, made light motorcycles. Perhaps this prompted the original tale.

The T59 brakes and drums were subject to experiment and development, upgraded several times after 1935. In May 1935, the original shoe width was increased from 50mm to 55mm,

The Type 59 racing wheel. (Courtesy NMT Collection)

The Type 59 racing wheel as used on 57248. (Courtesy NMT Collection)

steel hub and alloy cone is secured with an alloy sleeve, which also doubles as a hub centre and spoke anchor. A light-alloy

and the overall drum diameter was increased to 430mm, and later to 450mm, having longer fins. These appear to have been designed for the T50-powered T59 driven by Benoist in the 1935 ACF, where the brake backplates were also drilled to aid cooling. The following month, another version with 450mm diameter fins was made, retaining the original 50mm shoe width, 59.CH.314 – June 29, 1935. These also employed new backplates, but with brake cooling air-scoops as well as drilled holes. In December 1936, the T59 wheel assembly was revised with a 13mm wider rim to accept larger section tyres, the drawing finalised 59.CH.465 – December 18, 1936. The change was achieved by increasing the rim width outward beyond where the split ring locates. This was a belated drawing of the design created for the Vanderbilt Cup T59/50B in October 1936, and also the International Record runs at Montlhéry, September-November 1936, both notable for the use of 7.00 x 19in section rear tyres.

Early tyres for the T59 were 5.50 x 19in on all four wheels, but for circuits with long straights, the rears were fitted with 6.00 x 19in, having a larger rolling circumference. Even larger section tyres of 6.50 and 7.00 are also apparent throughout its later history. Similar large section tyres were used for the 1939 Luxembourg Grand Prix T50B sports car. In addition, that year, for all T50B powered cars, brake drum fin diameter was increased, and was 10mm wider, where the winged hub locknuts were flared to 70° in order to reduce mallet damage to the radial-spoke wheels.

Overall, though, the complete wheel is a superb example of innovative thinking, collaborative design, as well as a masterpiece of many skills, representing the individual and united expertise of several different craftsmen. Furthermore, Ettore Bugatti's T59 wheel is a stand-alone beautiful work of art, too. He must have been very proud of them.

Carburettors

The superb updraught American Stromberg UUR-2 twin-choke carburettor was normally fitted as standard to the T57 and T57S, using choke sizes between 26 and 29mm diameter. From 1935, Stromberg carburettors were manufactured in Britain by the Zenith Company, after which the instruments were sometimes known as Zenith-Stromberg. For racing T57Gs and the T57SC, the Bugatti works enlarged the choke to 30mm, informally referring to it as UUR-3, but since the accelerator pump tubes ran in the outside diameter of the choke tube, they had to be specially bent to fit; all a bit of a bodge really. Unhappily, this was the maximum it could be without conceding 'Venturi effect,' which requires a restriction in the inlet pipe that will increase the airflow speed across the jet, causing a sufficiently low-pressure area to atomize fuel. In 1935, when the 'G' engine blocks were revised with 45mm diameter valves and a normally-aspirated induction manifold, it soon became obvious that the carburettor was choking the flow, and, consequently, potential power output in competition.

As a result, Jean Bugatti developed his own twin choke carburettor called the C2, increasing the choke area by 20 per cent. This used a handsome aluminium body and Zenith jets, enabling chokes up to 36mm diameter with correspondingly larger main jet sizes, although in practice for the 3.3-litre, 34mm chokes were normally used. In addition, the C2 carburettor has longer triple-stage atomiser risers, spaced further apart than the UUR-2. The new instrument used 54mm diameter spherical floats, valves, and levers from an American Winfield carburettor. The C2 is characterised by using a revised manifold having six stud fittings instead of the UUR-2/3's four. The new manifold, 57G.MOT.ENS.6-5 May 1936, was specially designed and arranged higher than earlier examples, allowing it to be used for all T57G engines, whether mounted in T57 or T59 frames. The C2 large choke instrument was designed for serious competition; so did have some disadvantages if used on a road car, especially low-speed flexibility.

The T57 2-4-2 array provided superb mechanical balance, but like many straight-8s, they tended to be more difficult to start from cold, especially when compression ratios were high and the C2 carburettor was employed. This rather crude instrument did not have a manually operated choke in the air intake like the UUR-2, instead using a pair of Ki-gas injectors in the carburettor risers. Unfortunately, this simply exacerbated the problem. Here, cylinders one, two, seven and eight tended to be too weak to start, just as three, four, five and six tended to be over rich. In addition, as a result of its spherical floats and unusual valve mechanism, the C2 had a tendency to flood easily, especially when the diaphragm fuel pump pressure exceeded 2.5psi. Float level settings were absolutely critical. Nonetheless, the C2 was used successfully with T57G, and in pairs with the T50B. Unfortunately, only a few of these instruments were ever made, and their drawings appear to be lost.

Evolution – Grand Prix Type 59 to Type 57 Grand Prix

WHEN THE TYPE 57G Tanks first appeared at Montlhéry in June 1936 they had been one of the best-kept secrets at Molsheim. Factory documents barely mention 57G at all, being otherwise always referred to as Type 57S, upon which they are based. This would suggest that the appellation 57GP (Grand Prix), later shortened to 57G, refers to specialised parts and essential modifications to develop a Grand Prix version of the T57S. The earliest 'G' reference to be found is a drawing of a special-material exhaust valve seat dated March 13, 1935. Others mostly relate to cylinder block and valve gear. This date clearly corresponds with Jean Bugatti's announcement of his 'ultimate super sports car,' yet the scarcity of records has meant that development of the T57G has never really been formally interpreted or defined by historians.

The following presentation is an attempt to unravel its history based upon available records, in conjunction with an opinion that components drafted were created and tested. Moreover, in line with prototyping practice, I also take the view that drawings would not necessarily have been finalised for record with the Bugatti 'cartouche' until the item was actually made from earlier drafts and trialled. It is possible to note many examples of parts apparently fitted to prototype cars before they were formally drawn up. This situation is more likely when existing parts are modified for testing. In addition, I believe a key factor to consider in the evolution of the T57G, lies in the systematic and technical transformation of the Grand Prix T59 engine during the period 1934 to 1937. Consequently, we begin with the Type 59's origins.

T59 origins

The T57 touring model and T59 racing car were created concurrently, and, whilst having two discrete functions, their engines share a common architecture and all major dimensions. They also share two valves per cylinder and a 96° valve included angle (VIA), just as the T51, although bizarrely, this is often erroneously published as 94°. Drawing 57S.MOT.51 dated May 1, 1936, show the angles related to VIA for the camshaft drive tower, where: 360-(42+42+90+90) = 96°; conversely, the Bugatti Owner's Club *T57–57S Maintenance & Overhaul Manual* records 94°. Despite their similarities, the T59 and T57 engines were diverse in detail specification where, in fact, they have separate component drawings and numbers, even though often made from common standard billets. Clearly, both are sufficiently close that a union of components was always possible. Other than a supercharger, one major difference is that the T57 engine utilised a 2-4-2-throw crank with a firing order of 1,6,2,5,8,3,7,4, whereas the original Grand Prix Type 59 used a more traditional racing 4-4 array and ignition sequence of 1,5,3,7,4,8,2,6; so why two types of crankshaft?

From a pure design point of view, there are many practical crank-throw arrangements and firing orders for a straight-eight engine. Additionally, since a four-stroke straight-eight produces four power strokes per revolution, most timing forms will run smoothly under load and be free of any odd-order harmonic vibration at low engine speeds. In fact, the intrinsic balance of the straight-eight generally made counterweights on the crankshaft unnecessary. Such qualities made this

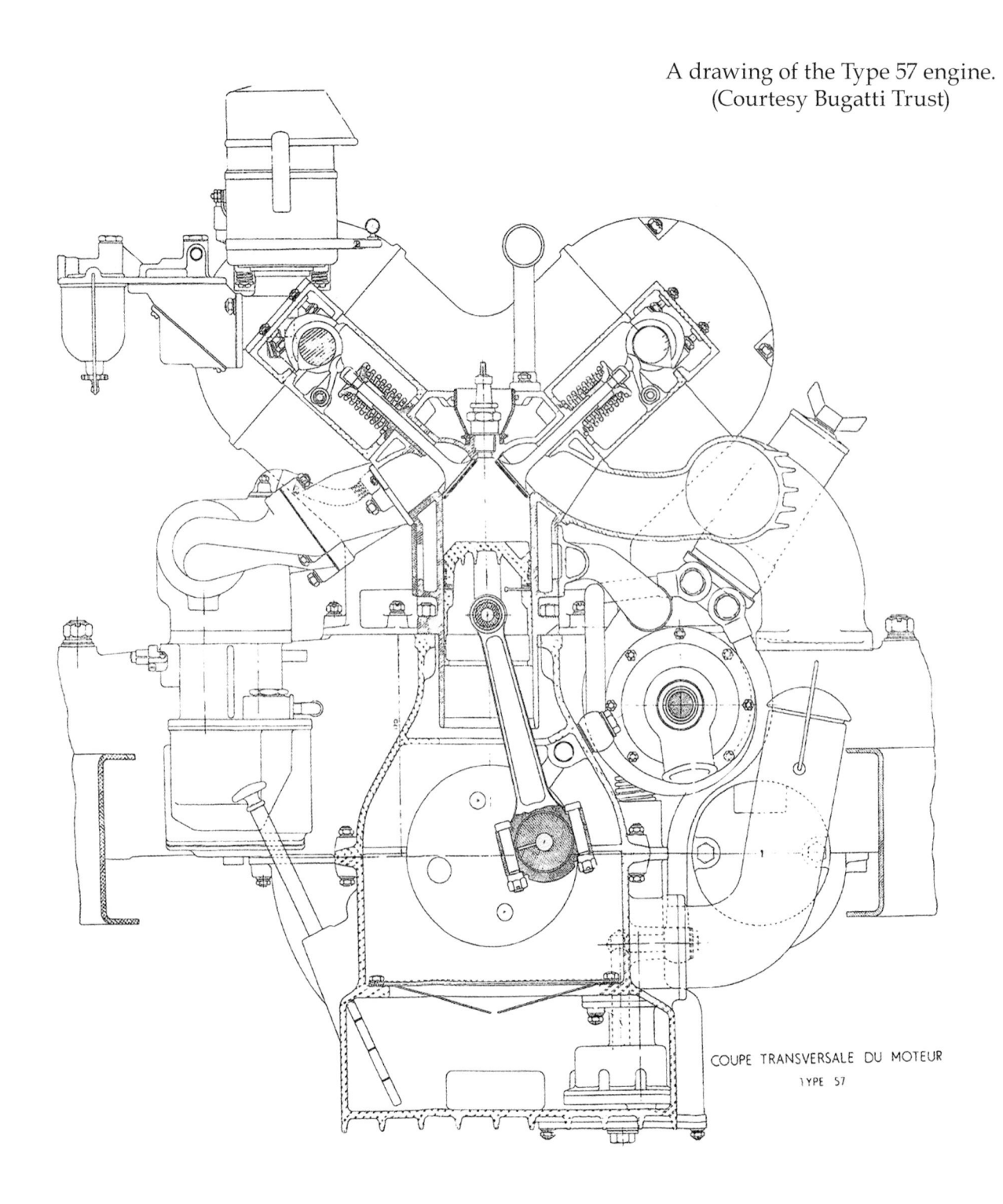

Bugatti Type 57 Grand Prix – A Celebration

A drawing of the Type 57 engine.
(Courtesy Bugatti Trust)

COUPE TRANSVERSALE DU MOTEUR
TYPE 57

14 Evolution – Grand Prix Type 59 to Type 57 Grand Prix

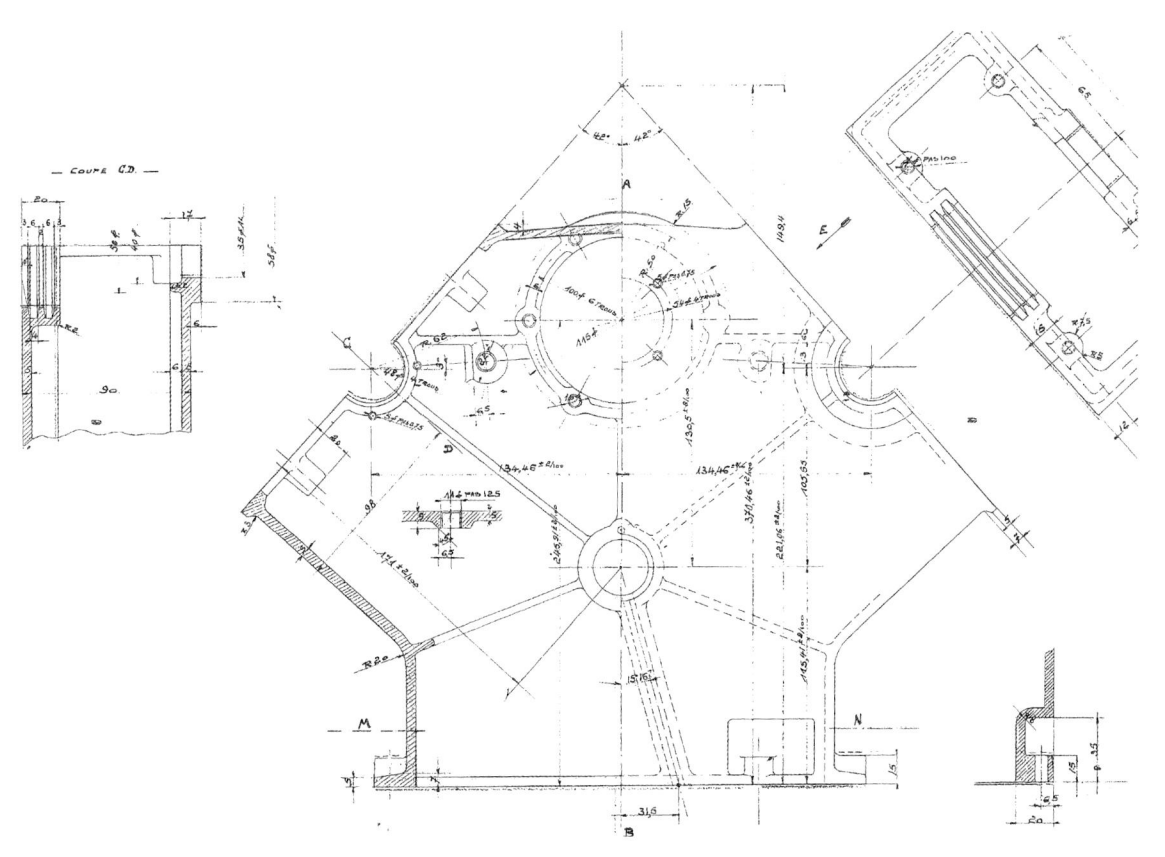

A drawing of the 57G 'Y' camshaft tower showing the angles of inclination from which the 96° valve included angle may be established. (Courtesy Bugatti Trust)

engine popular in both racing and luxury motorcars from the 1920s onward. From the outset of design, a straight-eight may be timed for natural primary and secondary balance, with no unstable primary or secondary moments. Nevertheless, before the modern age of computer analysis, engine designers were hindered by a number of factors. Indeed, the various issues to be considered by the engineer were formidable and demanding. It is not just the dynamic balance of the crankshaft to take into account. There are also important phase considerations regarding carburetion, gas-flow and back-pressures within the inlet and exhaust manifolds for any given timing array and engine speed. With the relatively low-speed of early motorcar engines, such matters were not a priority, since, at these placid rotations, any increase in power was often achieved very simply by enlarging the engine capacity. The 13-litre Type 41 might be considered an example.

Bugatti's first straight-eight

Ettore Bugatti was a pioneer of the straight-eight trend, and had been one of the very first to focus on developing small and more efficient four-cylinder engines for his tiny cars; the 'Pur-Sang' Type 10 of 1909, eight-valve Type 13 of 1910, the Peugeot Bébé of 1911, and then the 16-valve Type 13 of 1914. However, back in 1912, Bugatti successfully tandem-linked two of his Type 13, four-cylinder, eight-valve engines, creating his first straight-eight; installing this into a Type 17 chassis. In this case, the two four-cylinder crankshafts were arranged 4-4, which is to say that one engine's flat crank plane of four was set at 90° to the other's flat plane of four. His experimental straight-eight of 2654cc was a great success, both in operation and smoothness, firmly establishing this particular crankshaft trend for Bugatti. In October 1912, an improved version of the car, now fitted with wire wheels, was trialled at the Gaillon hill-climb, running at 135km/h (85mph); at least until the doubled-up engine torque broke the standard T13 transmission. The special engine is discussed in the July 1927 issue of *Automobile Engineer*, and WF Bradley mentions the car in his 1948 biography.

Advantages

Technically, the maximum to the mean torque for an eight-cylinder engine is about 1.25:1, as compared with 1.4:1 for a six, and 2.0:1 for a four. This simply means that an eight-cylinder engine has more power strokes and torque per revolution than a six or a four. As a result of its extremely even torque, a flywheel was almost unnecessary, allowing rapid acceleration and deceleration, enabling the highest power output with a high level of reliability. During World War I, a four-cylinder engine might run at a maximum of 2700rpm, yet an eight of identical capacity could run at 3500rpm. Comparing eight- and four-cylinder engines of the same capacity, a reduction in the diameter of the engine cylinders can be shown to result in an increase in both engine speed and output. Its smaller cylinders reduced bearing pressures, and the comparatively smaller stroke per cylinder, higher rotations. Such features made the S-8 particularly attractive for powering aircraft. Moreover, with an eight-cylinder racing car engine, a lower centre of gravity can be obtained for the same capacity as an in-line four.

The tandem straight-eight venture was definitely proven for Bugatti, but it was not taken further at this stage. He undoubtedly considered development to be limited by his production tooling and budget. At that time, his workshop was better suited to four-cylinder engines, which, at only three-years-old, was still new and awaiting a return on his banker's investment. Nevertheless, when World War I broke out, the 4-4-array had proven to be an EB design strategy that he readily applied in government contracts. When peace returned, he approached eight-, 16- and 32-cylinder projects with confidence and fervour. Now simply applying modular construction, he recognised that he could create any engine envisaged, even with the very limited tooling available. The earlier designs subsequently transformed, and thereafter his engine projects consisted of cylinder blocks, crankshafts and camshafts in assemblage modules of four. In addition, from 1921 onward, Ettore Bugatti established his instantly recognisable rectangular engine design style, "une forme parallélépipedique"; at least until the emergence of Jean Bugatti's avant-garde Type 57 power unit in 1932.

Technical advances

By the 1930s, engine technology and science had advanced significantly for those with resourcefulness and ambition. Here, the ceiling to further progress was merely the efficient development of engine design, manufacturing technique, advanced materials, and, as always, budget. As engine speeds increased significantly during this period, the intricacies of dynamic balance, manifold gas-flow and torsional vibrations took greater prominence. These technical factors now began to be recognised as impediments to engine efficiency if not scrupulously considered in detail.

With regard to dynamic balance, whilst Ettore Bugatti utilised variations of cylinder timing with his straight-eight engines by rotating individual cranks through 180° (later T51/55 engines, for example), the basic 4-4 crankshaft array endured as one of his key design features for Grand Prix cars. Unfortunately, of the different crank timing options available, the 4-4 array has a fore and aft secondary rocking couple noticeably pronounced beyond 4000rpm, after which energy is lost and the engine becomes more stressed. This also effectively limits engine speed. As rotations rise, the fore and aft rocking couple places increasingly higher loads on the centre crank bearing, as well as imparting detrimental twisting forces at crankcase extremities. Attempts to counteract this couple using balance weights tend to exacerbate destructive forces.

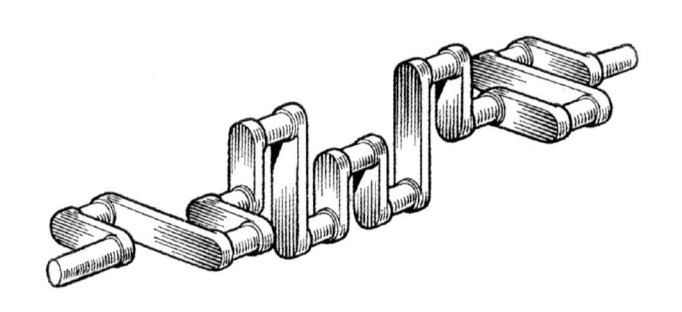

An illustration of a 2-4-2 crankshaft. Here, the journals reflect their throw pattern from the centre outwards, providing a better-balanced array to 6000rpm.
(Courtesy NMT)

Dynamic balance and 2-4-2

For a multi-cylinder in-line four-stroke cycle engine with identical cylinders, the cranks should be placed symmetrically to give uniform firing intervals. However, for couples to balance, the engine should be symmetrical about a plane normal to the axis of the crankshaft. Ideally, this means that the cranks should be arranged in pairs that are parallel to each other, and which are situated at equal distances from the central plane, so that each half of the crankshaft is a mirror image of the other half. Within the straight-eight field, a more-progressive 2-4-2 arrangement was scientifically studied by specialists, and was frequently promoted in automotive textbooks. It was used successfully by EB for touring models, and was clearly encouraged by Jean's T57 design team. This array places the middle four crank throws in the same plane, with the outer pairs at 90° to them, so that the secondary rocking couples of the front and rear pairs are cancelled-out by the four in the centre. Then again, the 2-4-2-array can give rise to complex induction gas flow issues at higher rotations, although is less problematic using a 1-to-8 branch manifold, which tends to balance out the pulses.

Initially, Ettore Bugatti used the more advanced 2-4-2-composition for the T41 Royale engine in 1926, even though his earlier large aircraft engine designs, from which the 13-litre unit derived, used 4-4 cranks. EB also used a 2-4-2 array in the second-series T44 engines from 1929 onward, creating a much smoother-running engine, which was also a notable characteristic of the 2-4-2 Types 49, 46, 50 and 57. These also had the latent benefit of reduced imbalance at increased revolutions, if such speeds could be achieved. Students of technical minutiae may note that the 2-4-2-array was used by Alfa-Romeo for its Tipo B 2.7-litre in 1932, through to the 159-8C Alfetta in 1951, and by Rolls Royce for the straight-8 Phantom IV of 1950-1959. Eminent praise, indeed, for the 2-4-2-crank.

Torsional vibrations

With regards to torsional vibrations, the primary 'node' in a crankshaft system is the flywheel; a point at which there is practically no vibration whatsoever. Given this understanding, it may be seen that a long crankshaft is particularly prone to torsional flexing at the point furthest from the flywheel. The longer the crankshaft, the greater the twist and the rougher and noisier the engine will run. Torsional vibrations are dynamic, spring-like, twisting forces that excite the crankshaft and its drivetrain, usually peaking at specific engine speeds. Many of these vibrations are damped naturally by the friction of the cylinders, or are stabilised by the inertia of camshafts, valve gear, dynamos and superchargers. However, torsional vibrations can amplify harmonically at higher rotations, to a point where they inhibit power and even lead to the fracture of components. Camshafts, especially long ones, are also subject to this in a similar, but far less significant way.

For Jean Bugatti in 1932, the practical compromise and next stage of evolution for the straight-eight's torsional vibration issue was, like Lanchester, to place a flywheel at each end of the crankshaft. So, for the Touring Type 57 engine, his design team did precisely this, and cleverly tackled valve-timing precision by driving the camshafts from the 'primary node,' flywheel end of the engine. The arrangement maintained timing stability at higher revolutions extremely well, and utilised a small, proportional flywheel friction damper at the nose of the crankshaft. This reduced torsional vibrations harmonically, and direct friction damping was used for the camshafts at their driven end. As a result, within the limits of straight-eight cylinder engine design for the period, the Type 57 power unit employed one of the most advanced crankshaft timing arrays, the finest camshaft drive system, and a superior means of minimising torsional vibrations. That is, Jean Bugatti's team of engineers and draughtsmen had produced an advanced engine with plenty of scope for further improvement.

Here, the journals of a 4-4 crankshaft do not reflect each other from the centre outwards, leading to a distinct fore and aft secondary rocking couple over 4000rpm.
(Courtesy NMT)

4-4-Type 59

In contrast, whilst the T59 racing engine design was clearly derived from the general architecture of the T57, internally it was approached differently; utilising the long-favoured Grand Prix 4-4 crank timing. From a gas-flow point of view, this was more compatible with the traditional Bugatti twin-carburettor manifold and paired four-branch exhaust layout; but it was never adopted for the T59. In order to reduce weight, the T59

Bugatti Type 57 Grand Prix – A Celebration

crankshaft and camshafts were not damped at all, although its triple valve springs increased mechanical resistance to stabilize it comparably. Nevertheless, since it retained the 4-4 layout, there still remained the crankshaft fore and aft secondary rocking couple typical of this array, which, at speeds over 4000rpm, would bring about significant, and ever-increasing, component stress, as well as parasitic mechanical losses. In Jean Bugatti's search for increased power and revolutions from the T59 engine, of all the many factors to surmount, its 4-4-array would always hinder successful development, limiting engine speed to little better than 5100rpm.

The original 1932 Type 59 engine crankcase design was based upon many of the principal dimensions of the T57 unit, although without a clutch housing, and was arranged for dry-sump lubrication. Dry-sump lubrication was advantageous for a racing machine, enabling a lower engine centre of gravity, minimising oil starvation on long-curve cornering and allowed increased oil capacity. In turn, this aided engine cooling and extended travel distances. The engine mounting arms were arranged differently too, so that the crankshaft centre-line spans the chassis 161.5mm below the top of the frame, which is 81.5mm lower than the T57. These features had valuable benefits for a Grand Prix car, enabling it to achieve a much lower centre of gravity. Jean Bugatti combined this with a compact multi-plate clutch, separate gearbox, lowered transmission train, and a double-reduction differential in the rear axle.

Drawings indicate that, in June 1932, the T59 engine was initially configured around a 88mm throw crankshaft in union with a 68mm bore cylinder block, giving a capacity of 2557cc (2.6 litres). The twin-lobe supercharger, using 250mm long rotors, was driven at engine speed, and could also displace about 2.6 litres per revolution. In October, the engine was re-configured to accept the 72mm bore cylinder blocks of the T57, providing a swept volume of 2866cc, which is technically 2.9 litres. At this time, the 41mm diameter valves were also T57, as were the con-rods and pistons. Whilst having different clearances and details, they were all machined from the same T57 billets. It is

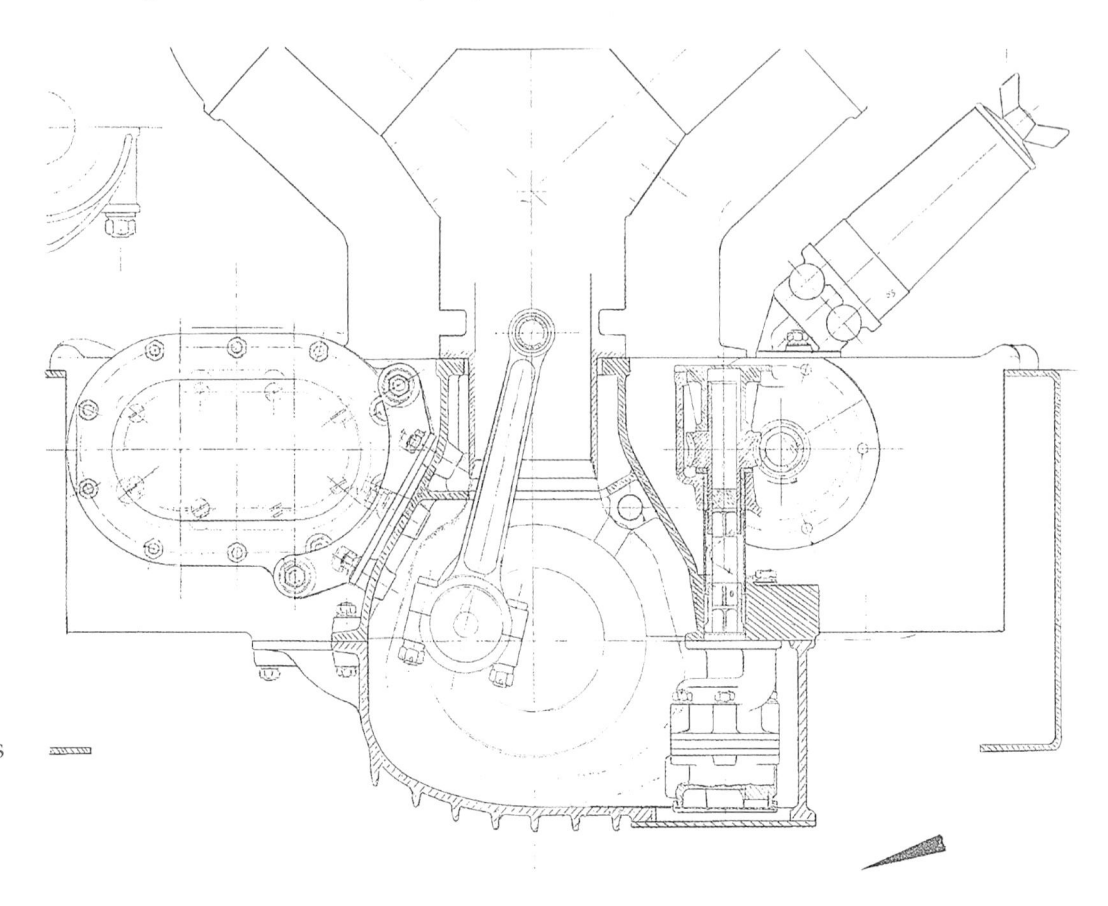

The early T59 crankcase with a 88mm crankshaft and vertical oil pump shaft. This version uses a simple machined billet with un-lightened disc webs. (Courtesy Bugatti Trust)

14   Evolution – Grand Prix Type 59 to Type 57 Grand Prix

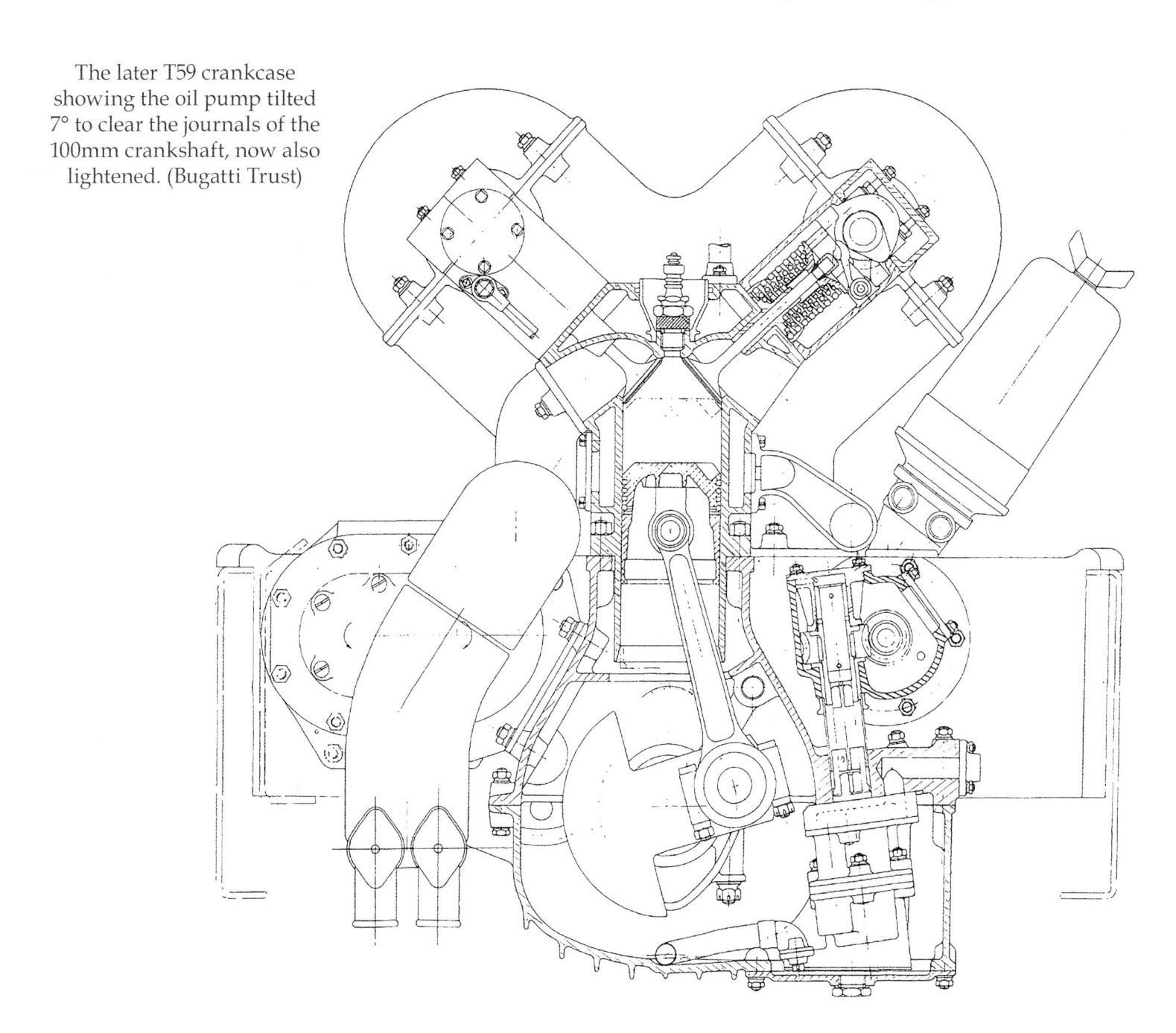

The later T59 crankcase showing the oil pump tilted 7° to clear the journals of the 100mm crankshaft, now also lightened. (Bugatti Trust)

also clear that 2.9 litres was the T59's maximum capacity when drafted using the T57 cylinder block, evident in the design of the original crankcase. In the T59's engine drawings dated October 7, 1932, the dry-sump, twin oil-pump assembly was driven by the horizontal water pump driveshaft through a 90° skew gear to a vertical shaft, exactly as it does for the T57, with comparable dimensions. The T57 oil pump is mounted inside the sump casing, whereas the T59's shallower dry sump necessarily

137

placed the compound oil pumps higher up, at the upper and lower crankcase joint, so was, therefore, much closer to the crank centre line and big-end swing. As a result, this position physically inhibited any prospective enlargement of the engine capacity by increasing crank stroke.

Revised crankcase

In January 1933, a 4-4, 100mm stroke crankshaft was drafted as 59.MOT.41. The following month, both upper and lower crankcase castings were cleverly revised to make room for the longer-throw crankshaft. Here, the design team simply tilted the oil pump, and its drive, 7° outward from the vertical in order to re-locate it further from the swing of the crank, 59.MOT.71 – February 15, 1933. This modification was accomplished surprisingly easily and with the minimum of rework to the wooden patterns, as seen in crankcase drawing 59.MOT – February 9, 1933. It was a superbly well thought-out solution but left a massive bulge protruding from the crankcase. However, by offsetting the oil pump driveshaft, its drive housing flange mounting holes had to be adjusted accordingly, and, since the water pump was mounted on this housing, it, too, was re-aligned to suit the coolant manifold and inlet pipe. As a result, the existence of slots noted in some existing mounting flanges is good evidence that the earlier, 88mm stroke, crankcase version was actually manufactured; without doubt, the first three prototype engines, where the original water pump elements were simply re-used by modifying them to fit the revised crankcase.

Supercharger capacity and speed appear to have remained unaltered. Now with a 100mm crankshaft, a 3257cc (3.3-litre) capacity could be achieved for the T59, yet, possibly for financial reasons, bizarrely it 'appears' this change was not put into practice for seventeen months. Curiously, too, EB's more traditional 68mm x 100mm bore and stroke aspect could also provide a capacity choice of 2905cc, yet this bore/stroke ratio would not necessarily be superior to the potentially faster-rotating, 72mm x 88mm, 2866cc option. Here the larger bore, better gas-flow characteristics and acceleration potential were advantageous, but surely both 2.9-litre options may have been trialled, especially since all the necessary components existed on paper.

Racing debut

The T59 racing cars were initially entered for the ACF in June 1933, but were not prepared in time. Achille Varzi practised just one T59 for the Belgian Grand Prix on July 9, 1933, but did not race. By July 12, 1933, a revised 4-4 array, 88mm-stroke crankshaft was configured to supersede the December 1932 original. Like the Type 57, Type 59 crankshafts were machined from large-diameter forged billets, leaving discs between journals, but the revision saw these discs trimmed down, except for the one nearest the clutch, greatly reducing overall weight, and, subsequently, acceleration inertia. Three 2.8-litre versions of the car were campaigned in September 1933 at the Spanish Grand Prix, in 1934 at Monaco in April, and then again in Tripoli in May. Eminent Bugatti historian, HG Conway, records cylinder dimensions of 72mm x 88mm for this whole period. Nonetheless, the 4-4-array fore and aft secondary imbalance remained at high revolutions. In June 1934, Jean Bugatti evaluated a crank that was balanced outside the works hoping for a solution. However, it must have soon become clear to him that the imbalance was actually the secondary rocking couple of the 4-4-array itself.

3.3-litre capacity

At last, with the revised 100mm crankshaft, the first 3.3-litre versions appeared for the 1934 ACF on July 1. They were still giving problems, however, and two of them retired. Curiously, AIACR race records chronicle that Benoist, who achieved fourth place, was driving a car with a 2.8-litre engine; registered 6548-NV2, whereas Nuvolari and Dreyfus, who did not finish, were driving 3.3-litre cars. This suggests that not all the cars were modified to 3.3 litres at once. Two weeks later, July 15, Dreyfus drove a T59 in the GP de Vichy, coming third in the first heat and fourth in the final. Curiously, this car was also recorded to be 2.8-litre, and again was registered 6548-NV2. At last, on July 29, 1934, the T59 had success at Spa in the Belgian Grand Prix, with a first, second and fourth for René Dreyfus, Tonino Brivio and Robert Benoist, respectively. Of interest, Benoist's car, registered 6548-NV2, was now recorded with a 3.3-litre engine. Whilst numberplates were often swapped about in those days, this one, painted on in the same place, appears to have remained with the same car for the whole month.

By the end of July 1934, the 72mm bore cylinder block, valves, con-rods and pistons of the T59 engine were all essentially T57 items in a T59 casing. Accordingly, the 3257cc (3.3-litre) Type 59 engine had begun its first stage of metamorphosis into the future T57G engine. Yet, this final capacity was still about as

14 Evolution – Grand Prix Type 59 to Type 57 Grand Prix

The T57/T59 cylinder block showing how the cylinders are paired, making increases in size almost impossible without major re-design. (Courtesy Bugatti Trust)

much as this particular arrangement could progress, at least without the re-design of major castings, and alteration of the position of cylinder centres. With further engine enlargement not a practical option, one means of raising power output was to increase the supercharger speed or its swept volume. The T59 blower rotates at engine speed, but unfortunately, its geartrain drive is not easily compatible with any small incremental change. As a result, potential power increase was now only practical by raising the compression ratio and engine revolutions.

However, these requisites are limited by volumetric efficiency, mechanical strength of the cylinder head, crankcase, pistons, connecting rods, crankshaft and main bearing caps; also the dissipation of heat from cylinder heads, as well as the effect of dynamic balance and crankshaft torsional vibrations. However, despite larger 41.7mm valves, improved fuel, carburation, and increased compression ratios, these engines just did not have the mechanical strength and reliability to succeed against the technical superiority of German and Italian racing cars. Engine issues observed in factory mechanics' notebooks are mainly comprised of mechanical failure typically due to overheating, as well as attempts to increase power and raise revolutions. That is, failure of superchargers, crankshafts, crankcases, also bearing caps, pistons, con-rods, valves, cracked cylinder heads and broken camshaft towers. Chassis problems include brakes, and, as power intensified, an increasingly more fragile gearbox.

Factory mechanics' notebooks

Factory mechanics' notebooks provide a record of work carried out on the T59 cars between March 1934 and September 1935. From these notes it is possible to identify a rational sequence of car construction, based upon when first recorded, as well as progressive revision. As previously discussed, Jean appears to have built three prototypes covertly in 1932, without the prior authority of his father. Accordingly, chassis/engine numbers 1, 2 and 3 were campaigned at the Spanish GP in September 1933. The frames of chassis/engine numbers 1, 2 and 3 were replaced with lightened and pierced versions in February 1934, which would have mixed up any previously matched number components. In March 1934, engines 4 and 5 are first mentioned, with 6 and 7 referred to in July 1934. Chassis/engine 8 is not recorded until May 1935. Furthermore, in January 1935, Type 59 engine numbers 1, 3, 6 and 7 are overhauled, after which there is a 'special' rebuild for engines 2, 4, 5 and 8. As we progress through this evidence, the records will become significant to these studies.

Also, as discussed for the T59 engine, at speeds over 4000rpm the fore and aft secondary rocking couple of the 4-4-array exacerbates stresses on the crankshaft and crankcase, creating mechanical losses. Even at 4000rpm the secondary unbalanced force works out at about 70kg (154lb). At higher rotations, the magnitude of this imbalance increases as the square of the speed, tending to focus stress at the crankshaft centre bearing, as well as creating severe twisting forces at crankcase extremities. It is notable that, during 1934, and whilst attempting to obtain competitive engine speeds, several T59 engines broke their crankcases. Mechanics' notebooks record that engine number 1 had three breakages; number 3 two, and numbers 2 and 7 one each. Furthermore, between them, five cylinder blocks and ten camshaft towers broke-off their mounting flange corners.

Whilst some commentators have put the latter down to inept craftsmanship, competent sequential tightening of fasteners was a basic skill for all Bugatti artisans at that time, and racing mechanics were the best in the factory. In reality, such fractures are wholly consistent with excessive twisting forces in the crankcase. Other analysts have suggested this is due to flexing of the chassis, yet no known changes were ever carried out on the frame or crankcase to improve rigidity. Furthermore, there were no comparable breakages reported for engine numbers 4, 5 and 6, which tends to dismiss the notion that the twisting forces were due to inadequate frame stiffness.

In addition, reflect that, whilst it is clear that the Type 35B 2.3-litre engine used a 4-4 crankshaft capable of 5800rpm, recall that this power unit was originally designed for a 2-litre capacity, later enlarged to 2.3. Furthermore, this engine used cylinders that were close together, and therefore a short engine overall. Conversely, the T59 power unit used a cylinder grouping spaced in pairs, and a crankshaft design with an extra bearing, making the engine relatively long. Moreover, contemplate that this crankcase structure was originally stress-configured for 2.6 litres, yet enlarged to 2.8, and then again to 3.3. Given a long engine, enlarged from 2.6 to 3.3 litres, with corresponding increase in power, this placed more strain on its crankcase, and also its original gearbox.

Factory mechanics' notes also suggest that T59 engine number 5 is mostly original, having been constructed with its 2-4-2, 100mm stroke, T57 crankshaft from new in March 1934. Engine number 4 appears to have been similarly assembled.

This might be because the parts were more readily available at the time, given the Depression and budget constraints that held back development. As mentioned, there is a seventeen-month period between the revised 100mm stroke crankcase design and when the first 3.3-litre engines were adopted. Assuming three original 88mm stroke prototypes, surely, it would have been economical to trial an existing Type 57, 100mm stroke, 2-4-2 crankshaft in the revised long-stroke, 7° offset oil pump casing before a special 4-4 Type 59 one.

Given the sequence of date and design change discussed, this might suggest that only the three prototypes ever had 88mm stroke crankcases. Bugatti had his own foundry, so the manufacture of the revised T59 crankcase would not have been too much of an issue. So, if later engines had the revised 100mm stroke crankcase from new, they may have been combined with a T57 crank and 68mm blocks early on. This is to suggest that Jean Bugatti may have been running 88mm crank engines concurrently with 100mm crank versions; also 72mm and 68mm cylinder blocks respectively, both providing 2.9-litre capacity before conversion to 3.3. When changed to 3.3 litres from July 1934, the later engines essentially consisted of T57 elements in a T59 crankcase; being effectively progenitors of the future T57S and T57G, where the three prototype 4-4 Type 59 engines were heading for extinction.

Racing Department disbanded

As discussed, by the end of 1934, Ettore and Jean Bugatti knew they just did not have the financial reserves to compete against the German and Italian challengers, so the Racing Department was disbanded. During a Bugatti Owner's Club dinner in London in December 1934, Jean Bugatti remarked that nine Type 59s had been built at that time, with enough parts made for twelve cars. This concurs with a 1933 *Motor Sport* report: "Bugatti intends to produce in all, a dozen machines." Nonetheless, this was a less than subtle insinuation regarding this Type's prospects for 1935, where Jean clearly intended to sell some. As a result, four of the former Works team Type 59s were sold to British amateur drivers in March and April 1935. These were engine numbers 1, 3, 6 and 7, for Lindsey Eccles, CEC Martin, Noel Rees (for the Hon Brian Lewis to drive), and the Earl Howe, respectively. This corresponds precisely with the factory mechanics' overhaul notes for January 1935. These harsh measures from an otherwise previously successful racing car manufacturer stunned the motoring world at the

14 Evolution – Grand Prix Type 59 to Type 57 Grand Prix

time, so should translate as a sincere statement from Jean Bugatti that he had abandoned Grand Prix racing with the Type 59. Indeed, such an undertaking acknowledged to the racing public that the T59 was no longer viable in International Grands Prix, and so technologically obsolete.

Interestingly, though, an article in the *Autocar*, dated April 19, 1935, titled "A Modern Grand Prix Car," described the car sold to Lindsey Eccles. This was Type 59 chassis, engine number 1. The article states: "The crankshaft is arranged 2-4-2." Given that engine number 1 had three earlier crankcase breakages, it seems this engine finally got a lightened T57 crank, and proved successful. So, it now appears that Jean Bugatti was fully aware that the 4-4 array was limited, and that the T57 had greater prospects for speed and power, especially if supercharged. Consequently, it was around this period in Bugatti history that the 4-4 Grand Prix Type 59 effectively expired, and the 2-4-2 Type 57 Grand Prix was born, both within a T59 crankcase. Hence, Jean Bugatti discarded the redundant 4-4 crank, 100mm stroke T59s, being three of the four cars sold off to private owners.

Having disposed of four of the nine cars built, this left Jean with five chassis to develop, with spares for three more. Historically, one, then later two of these chassis were dedicated to the development of the single-seat T50Bs, whereupon, by August 1935, only three Type 59s were available as 3.3-litre running testbeds. Former Bugatti driver Pierre Marco oversaw much of the work in the factory from its inception, and ran the company post-war. In the 1950s, in response to the question of how many Type 59s were actually built, and assuming he meant 3.3-litre cars, he replied that the total was seven. Given this, and the comment made by Jean in 1934, the two accounts agree, especially as two of the nine chassis were dedicated to T50B prototypes.

From 1936 onward, it seems the factory took the appellation T59 to mean only its chassis frame, where, for example, notes describe T59/57G or T59/50B. Drawings labelled T59 became fewer, and the title T50B increased, now evolving from just engine to whole car. Shortly after receiving a 100,000f machine tool contribution from 'Fonds des Course' toward the development of a French Grand Prix challenger, three more T59-like frames were ordered on December 13, 1935 (in steel with a resistance of between 55 and 65kg). This old-fashioned 55-65kg/mm^2 unit equates to 35-41tons/in^2. Made in good quality mild steel, these frames were intended for T50B-powered cars, being un-pierced and having reinforcements to clear its large supercharger, as well as using a large diameter bracing tube between the frames at the upsweep. Consequently, this should account for a total of fifteen T59 frames, although do not overlook the loss of those following damage in crashes.

Theoretically, in 1935, the five remaining frames should be chassis/engine numbers 2, 4, 5, 8 and 9. However, one was radically modified and fitted with a special T50S engine and bulkheads for the June 1935 ACF, and was undoubtedly never again retrofitted as a T59. Chassis plate 50180 was allocated, corresponding sequentially in the factory register between December 1934 and April 1935, being used for several T50B powered cars. It seems 3.3-litre power units were swapped around between frames, where mechanics' notebooks and Froude records show that T59 engine numbers 2, 4, 5 and 8 were used during 1935 and 1936, seemingly shared between just three chassis noted in competition after August 1935. Curiously, engine and chassis 9 never appears in the notebooks ending September 1935, yet presumably existed. Perhaps frame 9 was that modified for the 1935 ACF T59/50S car, and erroneously stamped 6 instead of 9, since two existing frames appear stamped 6. Recall also that in February 1934, the first three T59 prototypes had their frames replaced with perforated versions, thereby mixing up components. Engine number 9 may have been used for spares or rebuilt as T59/57G number 0, noted in 1936 Froude brake test records. However, despite Bugatti having officially left the Grand Prix arena at the end of 1934, over the next twelve months the Type 59's spirit would continue to haunt active competition and racing, as its 'corpse' was transformed and reborn into an ultimate T57 super sports car.

VISIT VELOCE ON THE WEB – WWW.VELOCE.CO.UK
All current books • New book news • Special offers • Gift vouchers • Forum

15

The Type 57 Grand Prix emerges

AS MENTIONED, THE ACF'S discussions with Bugatti in late 1934, regarding the future of French motor sport, must have hinted about this being for un-supercharged sports cars. The triumphant German and Italian racing cars were generating extraordinary power using supercharger pressure ratios much higher than their French rivals, although, in part, this success also relied on engine strength. Removing some of this benefit, like superchargers, would help the French. Consequently, it is clear that not all the early-1935 financial decisions at Molsheim were unwelcome or particularly dismal. Something new was happening. It's clear that Jean had several options in mind, both for racing and production, that might not only revive his aborted T50S project, but would exploit his existing, yet outmoded, Grand Prix T59 chassis. Clearly, Jean needed a car that was shorter and lighter than the T57GR then under development.

Trade plates

As an aside, regarding vehicle registration plates, before France adopted the 'W,' or formal 'trade' plate in mid-1937, all cars on the road had to be registered and taxed with their local department authorities. This was very inconvenient for manufacturers like Bugatti, which was theoretically impelled to register every vehicle taken out on the roads for demonstration or on test. For practicality, it made sense to simply register a fixed number of vehicles to obtain the equivalent of 'Works,' plates, and to use them accordingly. Consequently, several different cars could be seen to use the same registration number, and sometimes chassis plate. Such practice has, inevitably, led to confusion regarding 'body' and/or 'chassis' swaps. Regrettably, some historians have even encouraged the notion that bodies were actually swapped from one chassis to another. In practice, why spend many man-hours changing over the body of one chassis to fit it to another, when in a few minutes, chassis plates could be swapped and chassis numbers re-allocated in records upon a sale? As a result, I take the view that coachwork tended to stay with the respective unsold chassis, even if engines and other elements were sometimes moved from car-to-car. Exercise caution if trying to relate chassis numbers to Works cars with identifiable numberplates.

T57 engine revised

As revealed in Chapter 1, the faux-sporty T57GR model was merely a temporary hybrid that would bridge development between the T57 and T57S. Jean's T57S 'Marvel' would replace the similarly-proportioned T55 super sports car. The successful T55 was based on the former Grand Prix T47/54 side frames, so it was entirely rational that a new T57 Grand Prix prototype might be based on the former T59 chassis. As evidence in support of this concept, the serial number 57248 was assigned to one of the newly-redundant T59 chassis frames. While the date is not recorded in the factory register, this number is listed sequentially between December 1934 and May 1935: a period which coincides with Jean's formal departure from Grand Prix racing, and his pledge to develop the 'ultimate' T57 sports model. The T57 number was allotted to T59 chassis, engine number 5, which, as shown, was in

15 The Type 57 Grand Prix emerges

effect already a supercharged T57 engine in a T59 crankcase and chassis. The prototype was destined to mature into the Work's competitive, un-supercharged, racing T57 Sport (later supercharged), and now popularly known as 'The King Leopold Car.'

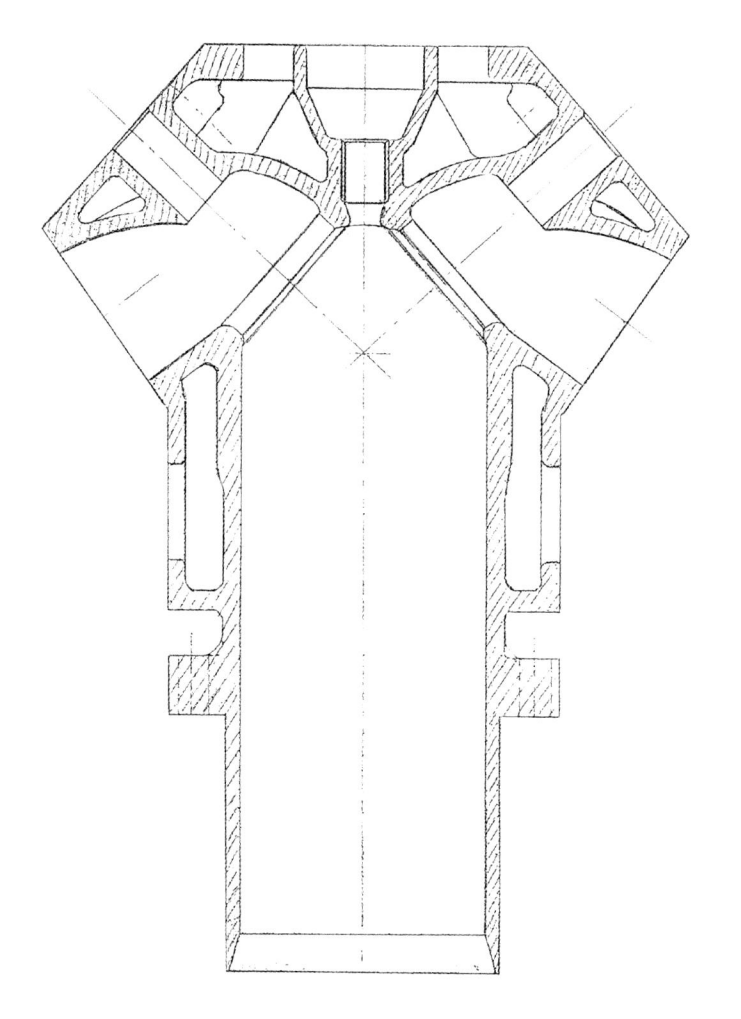

The revised cylinder block. Note the larger ports and valve seats, 14mm sparkplug bosses, as well as the open top casting for a bolted top plate. (Courtesy Bugatti Trust)

True to his word, the first T57 Grand Prix (57G) elements began development in early 1935, consisting of a revised T57 cylinder block casting with cores modified to provide ports enlarged for 45mm diameter valves. Drawing number 59.MOT.195 (also 57G.MOT.1) finalised March 12, 1935 shows this revision, having the crown of the casting open, and specially-machined for a bolted top-plate. Here, the cast sparkplug cup tops are machined with a thread to accept eight castellated bronze nuts, along with 34 Bugatti 5mm square-headed screws to seal a 5mm thick Dural top-plate. This assembly allowed precision alignment and simpler extraction of core materials during the casting process. The top-plate construction provided a further 700cc of coolant volume, by being secured above the open cylinder block crown. Specially designed for increased power and higher rotations, the larger valves were fitted with T59-like triple springs to minimise valve bounce, although the guides varied in material and dimension during maturity. The change to large valves demanded the use of 14mm sparkplugs instead of the earlier 18mm type to avoid block cracking across valve seats. The revised T57G cylinder block now significantly improved breathing and cylinder crown cooling; so was employed universally for all competition T57 and T59 engines thereafter, including the 1939 Le Mans car.

The new AIACR regulations called for un-supercharged engines, so, at the same time, a normally-aspirated manifold was designed, compatible with the enlarged inlet ports of the new cylinder block. Furthermore, the change from supercharged to normally-aspirated racing engine format still demanded high-performance fuels. Here, the use of Benzole and alcohol additives permitted higher compression combustion without knock, and alcohol's characteristic high latent heat enabled relative mixture cooling after supercharging. This trait, though, combined with a normally-aspirated engine, meant that the intake manifold had to be heated using engine coolant. Hence, the revised manifold was cast with a water-heating jacket. Moreover, since the port openings at the block-to-manifold junction were larger, it necessitated a revised version with bigger conduits, and to take a 29mm choke UUR2 Stromberg updraught carburettor. Accordingly, it follows that any engine noted with this revised manifold would be mated to the revised 45mm valve cylinder block; the two are inherently affiliated.

T59 engine revised
Interestingly, this special top end for normally-aspirated T57G engines was fashioned so as to be installable in both T57- and T59-framed cars; the latter engine positioned 81.5mm lower in the frame. Whilst the T57 'Compresseur' concept did not

Bugatti Type 57 Grand Prix – A Celebration

formally emerge until August 1935 (57S.MOT.1), a new forced induction manifold with larger conduits (59.MOT.ENS.BT.90- March 27, 1935) was also designed for supercharged T59 engines to suit the enlarged ports of the Universal Block. This was revised again a few weeks later (59.MOT.ENS.BT.101-17 May 1935), now having 'buffer' end chambers at cylinders one and eight. These manifolds did not need to be jacketed, because supercharge action inherently heated the mixture. A baffle was also introduced into the oval opening of the manifold to slow mixture velocity and increase pressure. This helped to convert the velocity head of the flow into a pressure head. These changes indicate tuning options to harmonically control gas-flow instabilities in the manifold system, especially given the higher engine rotations being sought.

As discussed, the factory mechanics' notebooks mention that, after the sale of four 1934 Works cars, four remaining T59 engines were subject to a 'special' rebuild, being Nos 2, 4, 5 and 8. From the records reviewed above, these would appear to have been revised as T57G in their T59 crankcases, trialled with the large valve T57G cylinder block and new T59 blower manifolds.

In summary, Jean Bugatti now had a revised high-performance top-end, universal for both normally-aspirated T57 and T59 power units, as well as for supercharged T59 engines; now all developed to T57G design. On Jean Bugatti's limited budget, it is entirely rational that this expensive investment, suitable for both engine versions, should be trialled by the Works in all 1935 competition opportunities. It would not be economically viable to do otherwise. The Grand Prix 4-4 T59 was dead, yet the 2-4-2 T57 Grand Prix was brought to the fore, alongside the development of the T57S and SC, whose power unit has close affinities with the 2-4-2 T59 engine. Of course, the existing T57GR and redundant T59 chassis were ideal testbeds for engine and component development at that time. Significantly, once the shorter and lighter T57S was presented at the Paris Salon in 1935, the heavy two-seater T57GR was no longer listed for sale, naturally superseded by the new T57S, T57SC and, eventually, T57C models.

Faster supercharger

An unnumbered draft exists dated March 15, 1935, showing a modification to the T59 blower drive, having an off-centre 40-tooth idler, rather than 39, and a 24-tooth final gear, giving a supercharger speed of 1.125 times that of the engine, or 2.9 litres per revolution. The individual components are properly numbered, so must have been made and trialled, but the reduction of the original 27-tooth final wheel to 24 made it very fragile, especially after heat-treatment, having a root thickness only three-fifths of gear tooth depth. It does not appear to have been a success. Just a few months later, the T57SC blower drive gearing was tackled differently in the new crankcase design, enabling its blower to run upwards instead of downwards, and at 1.17 times engine speed.

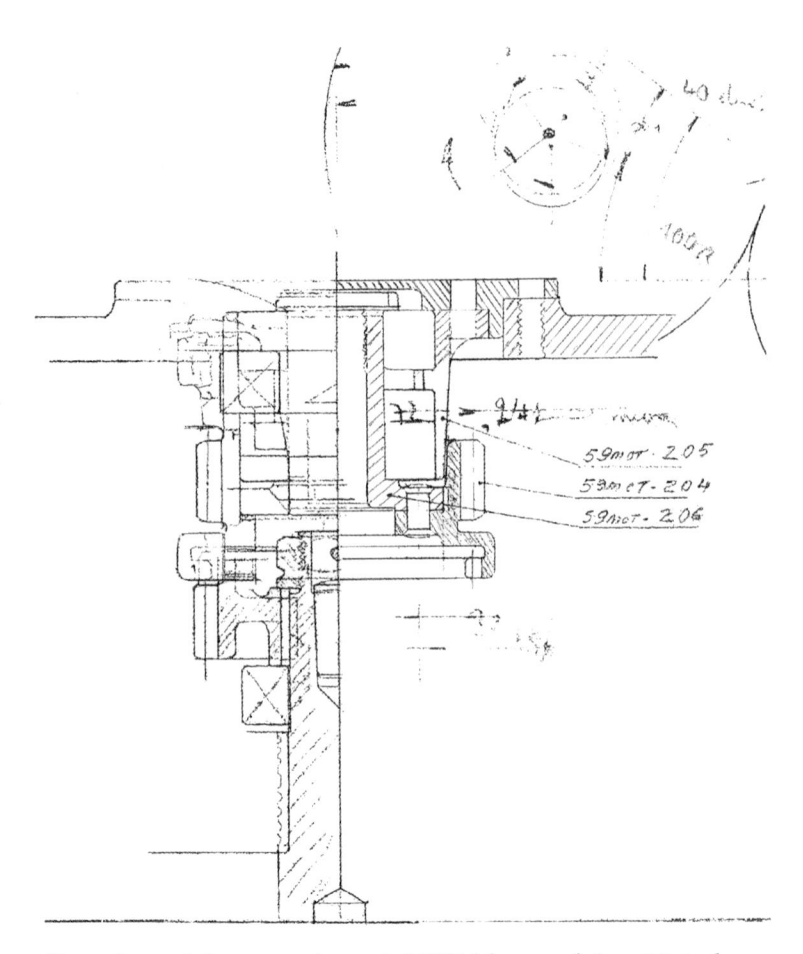

Drawing of the experimental T59 blower drive. Note how thin and fragile the gear root is with the new 24-tooth gear, 59MOT-204. (Courtesy Bugatti Trust)

T57G engine is trialled

As discussed, the development of the extraordinarily successful and reliable T57G engine used in the June 1936 Tanks was a carefully kept secret throughout 1935, never

15 The Type 57 Grand Prix emerges

explicitly recorded in factory notes. Conversely, given all the above technical details, the following competition history appears to illustrate the T57G engine's evolution based on the existing records available.

The very first use of the revised T57G engine block and manifolds appears to be for the Paris-Nice Rally, April 13-15, 1935, where Gaston Descollas achieved second place in the un-supercharged works T57GR, fitted with the water-jacketed induction system later seen on the TT cars. Now, at last, the faux-sporty GR was showing some real vitality. On April 14, Robert Benoist won at the Chavigny Hill Climb, near Nancy, driving a Works T57GR in the 5-litre class. This car was fitted with the large-valve cylinder block, where, following trials, mechanics' notes record this engine receiving 49mm crown height pistons with Bollé rings on April 11. It was also fitted with an appropriately low ratio, 12:54, 4.5:1 final drive. A few days later, April 18, Wimille drove a supercharged T59, and achieved the fastest time at the La Turbie Hill Climb, breaking the hill record by 2.2 seconds. On May 5, again in T59s, Wimille achieved second place in the Tunis Grand Prix, and, by now probably with the second blower manifold design, Benoist was first in the Picardie Grand Prix on May 26. The new T57G engine format was clearly demonstrating some success.

That summer, Piero Taruffi, a 28-year-old development engineer employed by Bugatti, raced in the Eifelrennen on June 6, but his T59's propeller shaft front joint deranged causing the car to polevault and crash. Notes show that the car was fully restored by July 16. On June 9, Benoist drove the Paris Salon T57GR in the 450km endurance rally, the Circuit des Vosges. Registered 9219-NV2, with entry number 87, the car used a higher, 12:50, 4.16:1 axle, and trialled brake drums designed for the T57S. Additionally, the heavy streamlined front wings were replaced with light cycle-type mudguards. Later in June, Gaston Descollas achieved second place in the Criterium de Tourisme, Lorraine GP meeting, again in the works Paris-Nice T57GR. It was the fastest of all in practice, and twice broke the 5-litre Class lap record. On June 30, Wimille attained second fastest lap before spinning off in the Lorraine three-hour race driving a T59 with a bonnet fitted with two different sizes of louvres, like the 1933 prototype.

For the Gran Premio del Valentino on July 7, Taruffi led the first circuit, but retired on lap 25 with a broken gearbox. For the Belgian Grand Prix on July 14, Bugatti presented three T59s plus a non-running spare; presumably the earlier crashed Taruffi car. Only three engines, 2, 4 and 8 were actually Froude tested on July 6, prior to this race. The cars attained only fifth and sixth places over the 508.3km, 34-lap race, with the third retiring on lap seven with a dead engine. For the Dieppe 2-Hour Grand Prix a week later, Wimille achieved the fastest lap, but paid for it with a cracked piston, being finally placed third, and Benoist retired on lap three with a broken supercharger drive, damaging a rotor. This component failure may be evidence that the fragile March 1935 design, 24-tooth final gear was actually trialled to destruction. The remaining four T59s in the race were run by the English drivers Howe, Eccles, Martin and Lewis; the latter three retiring. Taruffi drove a T59, now featuring a box above the carburettors, along with a cool air intake bonnet scoop for the Grosser Preis on July 28, but the car spun off on lap three. Here, the scoops brought in cold air directly, instead of from under the bonnet, further improving volumetric efficiency. On August 4, for the Comminges Grand Prix, Wimille ran a T59, finishing fifth in the 15-lap final, although this race did not count for him in the Driver's Championship. Benoist was listed DNA (Did Not Arrive).

Ulster TT

On Saturday, September 7, 1935, the Works entered two T57GR models for the Ulster Tourist Trophy held at the Ards circuit; a 35-lap, six-hour race. The cars bore Bugatti Works Bas-Rhin District registered Nos, 9219-NV2 and 9294-NV2, and were driven by the Earl Howe and the Hon Brian Lewis, respectively. Later known as the T57T model, the cars were fitted with engine Nos 223 and 224. Photographs of the cars suggest they still had 'wet' sumps, even though a dry-sump conversion had been designed for the Series 1 T57 crankcase in May 1934. The identities of standard and early 'S' dry-sumps are difficult to separate. Whilst not strictly T57S prototypes, these engines were clearly embryonic T57Gs because they used the revised manifold and Stromberg carburettor, and so, inherently, the T57G large-valve cylinder blocks. They were also fitted with pistons giving an 8:1 compression ratio. Froude test records for engine 223, dated August 22 and 23, show tuning for 158bhp at 5250rpm. The cars were fitted with a higher 12:47, 3.9:1 rear axle ratio and inelegant standard De Ram dampers. The subsequent T57S models were to use compact and lighter Bugatti-made housings and levers for their internals.

The Works T57GR Bugattis were the fastest cars in the TT,

145

Bugatti Type 57 Grand Prix – A Celebration

and quickly held first and second places, with Howe breaking the lap record for un-supercharged cars. Howe and Lewis took the lead, alternating several times, but the strain and demanding Ards circuit took their toll on their experimental 'S' twin-plate clutches, both slipping badly. Howe managed to finish in third place at an average speed of 128km/h (79.72mph), but Lewis was forced to retire, his clutch slip by now terminal. Nevertheless, Howe and Lewis were left astonished by the TT cars' overall performance. As an aside, believed to be un-supported by the works, a privately-entered T57GR with a Corsica body was driven jointly by Philip Dwyer and Hugh McFerran from Belfast. The car retired on lap ten after crashing into sandbags outside Newtownards Town Hall. The following day at Monza, September 8, Taruffi and Wimille drove T59s in the 502.97km Italian Grand Prix, where both had the intake air scoops seen in July. Taruffi achieved fifth place, but was still some 14 laps behind Hans Stuck in the super-fast winning Auto Union. Wimille retired on lap 27 when his engine failed.

BARC 500

On September 21, Jean Bugatti entered an un-supercharged T59 into the BARC Brooklands 500-Mile race; a drive shared by the Earl Howe and the Hon Brian Lewis. It was formally entered as a T57S, and had a 2-4-2 throw crank engine (number 5), chassis number 57248, and was fitted with the 'G' design, large-valve cylinder block, heated manifold, and Stromberg UUR2 carburettor. Despite looking like a T59 with a Brooklands silencer, it was the very first normally-aspirated T59/57G prototype to be entered as a Type 57S. It was running well, and might have won, until the carburettor flooded and Lewis became confounded by the T57 fuel system, finally finishing third.

San Sebastian, Brno, East London and Pau

The day after the 500, Wimille and Benoist, with Taruffi as reserve driver (since the third car was still in England), drove two T59s with air scoops in the Spanish Grand Prix at San Sebastian, where they achieved fourth and sixth places, respectively. A week later, on September 29, Wimille drove a T59 in the 495.4km Masarykuv Okuh held in Brno, but the engine failed on lap six after just 170km. A T59 with an air scoop was shipped to South Africa for the Grand Prix held on January 1, 1936, where Froude test house records suggest this car used engine number 2. Robert Aumaître accompanied the car to the Prince George Circuit, East London, missing Christmas with his family, since he and the car left Southampton at the end of November on the MV Warwick Castle. Accompanied by many European teams, Whitney Straight and Dick Seaman sailed, too, where Robert's company was greatly appreciated by them. It was said that he learned English on this trip. Wimille was a qualified pilot, so flew his Farman aircraft from France, and, after a slight mishap, finished his journey by train. Upon completion of 18-laps of the 17.75km (11-mile) circuit, Wimille's car had the fastest lap, but was placed only second on handicap because of its supercharger. On March 1, 1936, Wimille drove a T59 with an air scoop at Pau, having the fastest time in practice and best lap, but he retired with brake problems on lap 30 after just 82km.

Lightened crankshaft and pistons

The T57 crankshaft was further lightened in accordance with drawing 57G.MOT.8 finalised on February 5, 1936, where the main webs were reduced in the interests of speed and acceleration. This component was destined for the T57G Tanks, but undoubtedly must have been trialled in both T59 and T57 competition cars. For the first time, new pistons were made from billets of Elektron magnesium alloy, and over the next few months, machined with different crown heights (57G.MOT.9 and 57G.MOT.59).

Paris-Nice Rally

For the Paris-Nice Rally, April 4-9, 1936, Bugatti entered a T57GR with a 1934 Bas-Rhin Department (Works) registration, 3738-NV3, and entry number 10, crewed by Pierre Veyron and Lucian Wurmser. The car did not finish. According to Wurmser's biography, this car was chassis 57335 fitted with a Gangloff body. Factory records indicate it used engine 223, which was a 158bhp prototype 'G' used previously in Lewis' Ulster TT car. Records also indicate the car was fitted with an 'LS' engine in May, although no one recalls what LS meant. Curiously, drawing 57G.MOT.1, dated January 9, 1936, illustrates an experimental T57 cylinder block, otherwise similar to 57.MOT.1, but made from bronze and fitted with steel liners. This version utilised a bolted top-plate, but also separate sparkplug cups. Nothing else is known about this block, and it does not appear to have been a success; but I wonder, did LS mean 'Laiton Sommet,' Brass Top in Alsatian vernacular.

15 The Type 57 Grand Prix emerges

Two Type 59s in the 1935 Monaco Grand Prix, race numbers 16 and 18. Note the large air scoops. (Courtesy Bugatti Trust)

La Turbie, Monaco, Tunisia and Spain
At the La Turbie Hill Climb on April 9, 1936, Wimille drove a T59 that was first in its class and had second fastest time. For Monaco, on April 13, Benoist took a T59/50B single-seater, but did not run in the race after practice, although Wimille and Williams ran T59s with air scoops, attaining sixth and ninth places respectively. These cars had bolted top plates with seven-tube risers instead of four (*L'Actualite Automobile 1936* and also *Bugantics* Vol.11/1). Wimille drove a T59 in the 381.42km Tunisian GP on May 17, taking third place. On June 7, Wimille raced a T59 in the Gran Premio de Penya Rhin, but retired when his gearbox failed on lap eight.

New carburettor
For racing purposes, the otherwise excellent UUR2 Stromberg carburettor was limited by its 29mm choke. This unit was still too small, even when opened out by the Works to 30mm, where this special version referred to in Works notebooks as UUR3 seems to be. However, for the T57G, Jean also developed a factory-designed, 36mm choke, C2 updraught, triple-diffuser carburettor. This relatively crude racing instrument undoubtedly evolved as a result of the T50B project, although, for the 3.3-litre T57G, was usually choked to 34mm. As with any racing carburettor on a high-compression engine, it was developed for power, so would have been an absolute menace starting from cold. No doubt the Bugatti racing mechanics developed their own start-up practices and rituals. This new instrument had chokes set 63mm apart, with a broader flange that necessitated six mounting studs instead of the usual four, so required a revised normally-aspirated manifold, but otherwise very similar to the water-jacketed version from 1935. This revised manifold – 57G.MOT.32 dated May 1936 – was raised slightly so that the wider instrument was higher, permitting the complete block and manifold assembly to be applied universally in T57, T57S, and T59 frames.

147

Bugatti Type 57 Grand Prix – A Celebration

T57G Tank debut

Now we come to the test days, June 8 and 9, 1936, when the super-streamlined T57G Tank made its spectacular debut into the sports car Grand Prix arena at Montlhéry. The motoring press was astounded by its futuristic appearance, as well as its spectacular performance and reliability, and wondered how these new cars were developed in secret. Retrospectively, given the technical transformation of the T59 and T57 engines at the beginning of 1935, we can see how a fourteen-month program of trial and contest had honed the competitiveness of the T57G engine. The successes and failures in the events entered by Bugatti with the T57GR and T59 cars had allowed him to explore the limits of the T57 Grand Prix engine, and to rectify issues. The information gathered included details regarding clearances, fits and tolerances for all moving parts, as well as material strength margins. The programme clearly covered both supercharged and normally-aspirated versions, whether in T57GR or T59 frames, so would provide a database of excellence toward its successful application to the T57G Tanks. Jean Bugatti would now know the precise limits of compression ratio to use for his revised T57 large-valve engine blocks, whether supercharged or normally-aspirated.

Despite Jean having great success with the T57G 'Tank' in June and July (ACF and Marne), he continued to develop the T57G engine.

Spa, Deauville and Nürburgring

Now a sports car race, for the 24-hour Francorchamps at Spa July 11-12, 1936, the Works entered a T57GR Torpedo, race number 32, a drive shared by Yves Giraud Cabantous and Roger Labric. This car was recorded with engine 224; having a 45mm valve block used formerly in the Ulster TT, and clearly one of the Ulster TT Torpedo-bodied cars. Undoubtedly, this was now installed with the 1936-revised manifold and Bugatti

T57GR number 32 at Spa, July 11, 1936. This car is clearly an Ulster TT model developed as a 'G,' and now likely fitted with the new C2 carburettor. (Courtesy Bugatti Trust)

C2 carburettor. Alas, after just four hours, Labric went off at Stavelot, the bumpy right-hand bend following the fast downhill section of track, badly damaging the car's radiator and losing all coolant.

On July 19, two T59s were entered for the 372km Deauville GP, a perilously narrow course straight through the town itself and along the promenade. Wimille won the race at an average speed of 124.6km/h (77.86mph). A photograph shows his engine using the bolted top-plate and seven-tube riser seen earlier in the year. Benoist also raced, but he crashed into sandbags quite early on, the front left dumb-iron badly bent. Of the sixteen starters only three finished, with many other cars crashing. In the case of Marcel Lahoux and Raymond Chambost, both former Bugatti drivers, their crashes were fatal.

As a result of these tragedies the track was never used again. A week later, following his success at Deauville, Wimille drove his T59 with immense optimism in the Grosser Preis at the Nürburgring, but, regrettably, he was forced to retire with a broken gearbox on lap two. With increases in power over the year, the gearbox had become an escalating liability that Jean was keen to resolve.

Outrage at St Gaudens

The Comminges GP held on August 9, 1936 at St Gaudens, was a race for un-supercharged sports cars. As discussed earlier, the regulations laid down by AC du Midi allowed Bugatti to enter two specially-prepared T59/57G cars, looking just like un-supercharged T59s, but employing the most advanced and proven engine elements from the T57G Tanks. These included, magnesium pistons, new C2 carburettor, 57G 'Y' camshaft tower, and upgraded, centrally-mounted ignition system. Froude records dated July 29, 1936 show engines 59/57G No 0 and 59/57G No 8 'Preparation Comminges.'

With 9:1 compression ratios, the engines could develop 170bhp at 5600rpm. The cars also appear to have been fitted with wet-sump T57S45 gearboxes, fitted with an external change lever, although the cars pre-date the revised rear suspension geometry associated with this unit. The cars also utilised an aircraft type, seven-layer oil cooler stack between the front dumb-irons, protected from stones by a grille in a frame below the coolant radiator. Naturally, without blowers, the cars were actually lighter than supercharged T59s. Pierre Veyron told reporters that the cars had reached 230km/h (143mph) on test.

Car, race number 14, registered 8265-NV2, was driven by Wimille, and the second car, number 16, was driven by Benoist. As with the BARC 500, they were not just T59s with supercharger removed. Clearly, the engine internals were otherwise identical to those fitted in the Tanks at the ACF and Marne, but in a T59 crankcase.

Although very fast during practice, the Bugatti drivers ensured they did not both get pole position on the starting grid. However, once away, the Bugattis made rapid progress. After the first lap, Wimille was 200m ahead, and then, by lap two, 300. By the third lap, Wimille was 600m ahead of the pack, with Benoist in second place, only 15 seconds behind him. Halfway, the end of the tenth lap, Wimille was a full minute ahead of Dreyfus in his Talbot. At the finish of the first heat, the Bugattis were first and second. After a break to allow mechanics to service the cars, heat two began. Now both in pole position, once away the two Bugattis quickly took the lead again and held it, although on lap 11, Benoist's car began to trail smoke that steadily worsened until he was forced to retire on lap 14 with a cracked piston. Wimille, however, maintained his blistering pace and won easily. His overall race average between the two heats was 152.58km/h (95.36mph), proving the normally-aspirated T59/57G's performance was little worse than that of the supercharged T59 two years before.

T59/57G

Historians have strongly criticised Jean Bugatti for this passing off a Grand Prix T59 as a T57 sports car, but as we have seen in this analysis, from Jean's point of view, it was a T57 Grand Prix car. The original T59 evolved alongside the T57 in 1932 with distinctive and different engine applications, yet mechanically, it began to merge with the T57 throughout 1933 and 1934, until, by 1935, it became a T57 engine in a T59 crankcase. At least one even obtained a T57 chassis number. By 1936 it was a refined T57G in a T59 crankcase, and in 1937 went on to become the hugely successful T57 'Sport,' super sports car. Eventually superseded by the T59/50B sports car, 57248 was detuned, revised, and then acquired by King Leopold of Belgium.

16

Three Tanks or four

FOR MANY YEARS BUGATTI historians have been rather undecided about the existence of a fourth T57G Tank, especially since only three have ever been identified or seen together at one time. However, as explored by the late Anthony Blight in his

The Bugatti pit counter. In particular, note the allocation of four pit bays: Bugatti 88, Bugatti 86, Bugatti 84, and Bugatti 82. (Courtesy *The Autocar*)

superbly researched book *The French Sports Car Revolution*, the source of the four-car story derives from a dinner in Paris, shared by Bugatti's principal works driver-cum-sales director Robert Benoist and motoring journalist Maurice Henry. Here, the very first revelation about the T57G Tanks' existence and their entry into the June 28, 1936 French Grand Prix (ACF), was made known through a small note published in the May 25 edition of *L'Auto*. Here Benoist acknowledged:

"Yes, it's true, we are building four cars of the current 57S model, and you will see three of them at the Grand Prix next month."

Such a public assertion should be reliable, for Benoist was highly placed within the organisation to know whether this was correct; and he was well regarded by the motoring press as an emissary for Bugatti, having previously acted as a spokesman on several occasions. Additionally, Jean Bugatti's plan to build four cars in time for the French Grand Prix is supported

The upturned Tank behind the western banking of the Montlhéry Autodrome. Note the absence of the rear quick-lift jacking bars. (Courtesy Bugatti Trust)

June 29, 1936 at Montlhéry. Note the differences between the bonnet lip, retaining straps, oil cooler air intake shape, wheelarch air intakes, and two-tone paint flash. (Courtesy Bugatti Trust)

151

Bugatti Type 57 Grand Prix – *A Celebration*

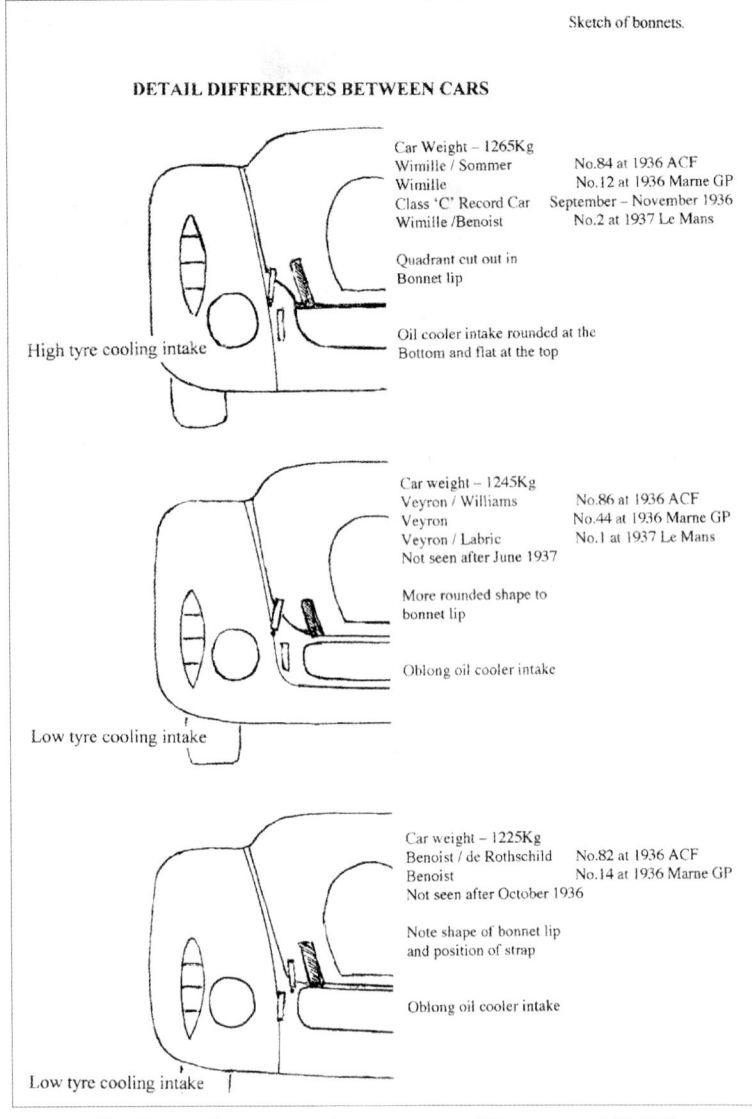

DETAIL DIFFERENCES BETWEEN CARS

Sketch of bonnets.

Car Weight – 1265Kg
Wimille / Sommer — No.84 at 1936 ACF
Wimille — No.12 at 1936 Marne GP
Class 'C' Record Car — September – November 1936
Wimille / Benoist — No.2 at 1937 Le Mans

Quadrant cut out in Bonnet lip

Oil cooler intake rounded at the Bottom and flat at the top

High tyre cooling intake

Car weight – 1245Kg
Veyron / Williams — No.86 at 1936 ACF
Veyron — No.44 at 1936 Marne GP
Veyron / Labric — No.1 at 1937 Le Mans
Not seen after June 1937

More rounded shape to bonnet lip

Oblong oil cooler intake

Low tyre cooling intake

Car weight – 1225Kg
Benoist / de Rothschild — No.82 at 1936 ACF
Benoist — No.14 at 1936 Marne GP
Not seen after October 1936

Note shape of bonnet lip and position of strap

Oblong oil cooler intake

Low tyre cooling intake

Bodywork comparison notes. (Courtesy NMT)

by photographs taken of the board above the pit counter during the contest. These illustrate 'Bugatti 88, Bugatti 86, Bugatti 84, Bugatti 82.' Compellingly, it establishes that the frequently under-funded Racing Department had committed entry fees, and formally registered four cars several months earlier. Given the evidence that four race numbers and four pit bays were officially allocated to the Bugatti team by the ACF Montlhéry race committee, then, in the context of the 'four-car' announcement made by Benoist, four Bugatti Tanks must have been built, even if only numbers 82, 84 and 86 were actually used. Consequently, would it be that irrational to judge that race number 88 was for a fourth, or a 'spare' car?

Moreover, Froude test house records support at least five T57G engines at around this time. In particular, they document four T57G engines just prior to the ACF. Here, 57G No 1 was tested on June 21, 57G No 2 on the 22, 57G No 3 on the 23, and 57G No 4 on the 24, each tuned to yield around 157bhp at 5000rpm. Only 57G No 1 has a Froude history earlier than June 21, 1936, being for May 27, with Nos 2, 3 and 4 apparently newly built. An even earlier 'G' development prototype, engine 238 'prep Montlhéry,' was tested as early as March 28, 1936, producing an amazing 183bhp at 5600rpm. Whilst 'G' engines were also used in several T57GR cars, this test record denoting the sequence 1 to 4, establishes that at least four 'G' engines had been specially-made at this time, further implying that four T57G Tanks had been built.

Enthusiastic research

On the other hand, despite enthusiastic research by many, to date it remains an almost certain fact that only three Tanks have ever been photographed together. Even more problematic, only three chassis numbers were allocated to T57Gs by Bugatti's accountant, these being: 57454, 57455 and 57456. Henri Pracht, accountant and company secretary, entered these numbers into his notebook for Saturday June 27, 1936; practice day prior to the ACF. None of the chassis numbers are ever related to engine numbers, so it is difficult to allocate them to a particular car. T57G racing engines were certainly swapped around anyway. The note is amongst some of the very few factory records known to exist about the T57G. Clearly, such conflicting evidence is not easy to reconcile, hence many Bugatti historians tend to support the view that only three Tanks were actually constructed. Intriguingly, photographs exist of a crashed Tank, one of which shows the car upside-down and quite badly damaged behind the western banking of the Montlhéry Autodrome. These photos have never been formally dated, and are a mystery since there are no records of such a serious crash. Nevertheless, interesting conclusions may be drawn from these pictures to identify a car, ascertain a precise crash site, and to focus on a date for the incident.

Bodywork studies

Firstly though, it is essential to study minute exterior details of the three Tanks photographed during the ACF and Marne

152

16 Three Tanks or four

Montlhéry map showing Virage de la Ferme and site of the crash. (Courtesy NMT)

MONTLHÉRY – LINAS
Circuit 12.5km (7.8 miles)

Epingle du Faye
AUTODROME
Virage du Gendarme
Virage de la Ferme
Site of crash

Grands Prix, as well as to compare similarities with the crashed car and the one seen during the two-day functional and performance tests three weeks before the ACF. Regard the famous line-up of Bugatti Tanks photographed at Montlhéry on June 29, 1936, this having been taken the day after the ACF. Consider their respective differences, especially in the shape of the bonnet lip and the position of retaining straps. Note that the Wimille/Sommer car, number 84, has high, front-wing cooling air intakes, and that the oil cooler intake is flat at the top but has a rounded lower edge. Also, study the bonnet shape at the retaining points where concave quadrants are visible on the bonnet lip, as well as noting the position of the leather straps and retaining spring clips. Note that the darker paint flash begins at the lower front edge of the body. The Veyron/Williams car, number 86, has the distinctive, low-position, front-wing cooling air intakes, as well as a notably-rounded, convex, bonnet lip shape. Its bonnet retainer positions are similar to car number 84, except the oil cooler air intake has an oblong shape. In particular, note the darker paint flash, which begins at the oil cooler intake. The Benoist/de Rothschild car, number 82, has the same low-position, front-wing cooling intakes and oblong oil cooler intake as car number 86, but its bonnet lip is angular, being neither rounded nor quadrant shaped. It also has unique retaining spring clip and strap positions, and the darker paint begins at the front lower edge. In summary, it may be seen that all three cars can be individually identified from their respective front views.

Thus prepared, contrast this with the line-up of Tanks recorded six days later at the Marne Grand Prix. It may be noted that the Wimille car, race number 12, was number 84 earlier; the Benoist car number 14 was previously number 82, and the Veyron car, number 44, was formerly 86. Consequently, it follows that from these highlighted details, it was the Wimille car photographed at Montlhéry during the Class 'C' World Record runs in October and November 1936. Moreover, it was the Benoist car, modified with a second cowl, that was displayed on the stand at the Paris Salon in October 1936, declaring to be the holder of the 'Hour' record broken in September 1936. During 1937, the two cars presented for the Le Mans 24-Hour Endurance Race on June 19 and 20 were the Veyron car with

153

Bugatti Type 57 Grand Prix – A Celebration

race number 1 (ex-86 and 44), and the Wimille car with race number 2 (ex-84 and 12), although now both with doors and enlarged radiator openings, and tail-mounted spare wheels. Curiously, though, the Benoist car (ex-82 and 14) was never seen again after the Paris Salon; so could this have been the crashed Tank?

Froude records

Regarding the above analysis in conjunction with Froude records: on September 19, 1936 prior to the Paris Salon and record runs, 57G No 4 was tested and produced 163bhp at 5500rpm. The same engine was tested again on November 12, 1936, prior to the International Record 24-hour run, then again on January 22, 1937, tuned for 150bhp at 5500rpm (prep LM). Engine 57G No 1 was tested on June 9, 1937, prior to the Le Mans race, as, too, was 57G No 3 (prep LM) with a C2 carburettor and tuned for 140bhp at 5000rpm. Presumably, 57G Nos 1 and 3 were used for the 1937 Le Mans race, and so 57G No 4 was used for the 24-hour record run between September and November 1936, later overhauled, run-in, and held in stock as a spare. Could this have been the TA Roberts' engine perhaps?

Crashed car

Referring back to the photograph of the up-turned Tank, the view is clearly the rear of the Montlhéry banked Autodrome; more specifically, the western end of the bowl, identifiable as an area just off a sharp left-hand curve in the Road Circuit known as Virage de la Ferme. This bend is at the end of the fast straight on the return from the forested section after passing the water tower. Of particular interest, though, note that the under-shield of the car has a panel fitted over the rear axle. This cover was permanently removed during the ACF and Marne events to improve cooling when the rear brakes became too hot, which, in turn, heat-expanded the rear hubs making the wheels difficult to remove. Notice too, the plain-sided rear wheel cover hanging open, and crucially, the absence of the unique rear quick-lift jacking bars. Compare these features with the views of the pristine prototype Tank recorded at the Autodrome during testing on June 8 and 9, 1936, where clearly, the crashed car is a pre-ACF version of the Tank, if not the actual test car itself.

Another photo also provides clues, this time showing the crashed car turned back on to its wheels and badly damaged.

The crashed Tank turned back on to its wheels. Crucial to dating, notice the absence of the bonnet retaining strap and its slot in the bodywork. (Courtesy Bugatti Trust)

As a general observation, several people seen in the photos are in shirtsleeves, suggesting a warm period of the year, although one is wearing a raincoat as if there had been a recent shower of rain. The headlamp arrangement seen on the car is clearly an early version; a June-July 1936 pattern as seen during performance testing at Montlhéry, and later at the ACF and Marne events. Note, in particular, the high position of the front-wing cooling air intake. Additionally, take note of the concave quadrant in the bonnet lip, as well as the oil-cooler air intake shape; rounded at the bottom and flat at the top. As before, these are distinctive and unique features of the test car, or, more specifically, what appears to be the Wimille car, rather than those of the Benoist and de Rothschild car missing after the Paris Salon. Crucially for dating, note the absence of a small slot cut into the bonnet for the leather retaining-strap, and compare with later photographs.

Therefore, given the noted detail features of all-three cars at the ACF, such as: the removal of the rear under-shield; retaining-strap slots; louvred wheel covers; and rear quick-lift jacking bars; it follows that the crashed Tank in the photos pre-dates the ACF. However, the Tank's only known earlier visit to the Autodrome was on its premier outing for testing on June 8 and 9. Consequently, it may be reasonably concluded that

154

the wrecked car appears to be the Wimille Tank, and that the crash occurred during its performance testing on Monday 8 or Tuesday, June 9.

Having narrowed the crash down to this two-day period, can it be pinpointed further? From the photographs of the damage to the car at the Montlhéry crash site, the scenario suggests the car has spun-off anti-clockwise through 180° at Virage de la Ferme, struck the ditch sideways, turned over once before sliding through the grass upside down and coming to rest. Every portion of the bodywork has suffered some degree of damage, and clearly appears to be a write-off. Obviously, it would have been impossible to continue with any further testing. Bizarrely, though, this is contrary to test-day publicity, where given that the contemporary news reports for both trial days were so detailed and positive about the car, it seems almost inconceivable to believe that the incident did not become a special news item on its own accord. Therefore, this fact would suggest that the incident could only have occurred late into the afternoon of Tuesday, June 9, when all the official testing was over and everyone had more or less packed up for the day. For this reason, too, it is the only realistic time window when Bugatti might have escaped an unpublicised accident, especially as it would remain reasonably light until 9.00pm in the evening.

Scrap or repair

Having linked the crash to a specific date and time, and apparently identified the car, this situation now poses the question: Could the Wimille Tank have been perfectly repaired in the next fifteen days leading up to the ACF?

Ponder, for example, that in order for repairs to be carried out, it would have been necessary for the panels to be cut into several pieces before re-work and welding back together. Obviously, it would have been easier and faster to completely rebuild the body. Yet, even assuming minimal damage to the chassis and running gear, repairs of this calibre today would take several months. Given that it appears so doubtful that the very thin alloy bodywork could have been restored to an immaculate finish in such a short time, it should be seriously considered that Jean Bugatti judged the crashed car to be beyond economical repair and wrote it off. This measured and informed reasoning reconciles much of the apparently conflicting evidence, too.

In combination with the photographic analysis discussed, as well as Benoist's revelation to the press that four cars were being built, and that four cars were registered for entry into the ACF, even though only three have ever been seen together, it may be concluded that in May 1936 there must have been four Bugatti Tanks originally constructed; at least before one of them was wrecked. Furthermore, because the crashed Tank was written-off three weeks before the ACF, it provides a cogent explanation as to why only three T57G cars were actually in existence when Henri Pracht recorded his entries for June 27, 1936; the day before the ACF. This study not only shows there were four Tanks constructed, but, significantly, from the details emphasised identifying individual cars, the Wimille Tank must be one of identical twins. If this interpretation of the photos and records is accepted, it is possible to re-evaluate the cars and other events at that time in the light of this. If there were originally two identical cars with high, front-wing cooling air intakes, as well as two with low air intakes, this would suggest two distinct build periods. Put another way, a pair of early prototypes as well as a pair of later models; but if so, which pairs were early and which late?

The more obvious visual disparity between the three remaining cars has prompted Bugatti historians to suggest early and late versions before; some interpreting the differences in the height of the front-wing cooling air intakes to imply chassis variations. Technically, though, this approach seems to be rather tenuous, for the intakes are nothing more than very simple openings in the leading edges of the bodywork; their sole purpose being to admit cool air to the tyres and brakes. Logically, it could be argued that the lower opening version might admit slightly more airflow to the brake drum than the higher, simply because it is at a point of the greatest aerodynamic pressure when the car is in motion. In practice, though, there is probably very little between the two variants. Ultimately, this might possibly suggest the high intake version is earlier than the lower; but that is about all.

Of much greater significance, the three dissimilar car weights, verified at the Marne Grand Prix, definitely appears to be evidence of the use of three unique chassis arrangements at that time. The weigh-in recorded the Wimille car as the heaviest at 1265kg; Veyron's was 1245kg; and Benoist's the lightest at 1225kg. This weight difference of exactly 20kg between cars, with 40kg between the heaviest and lightest, appears to be noteworthy, so surely must be indicative of differences in chassis detail. Putting this into perspective, the

Bugatti Type 57 Grand Prix – *A Celebration*

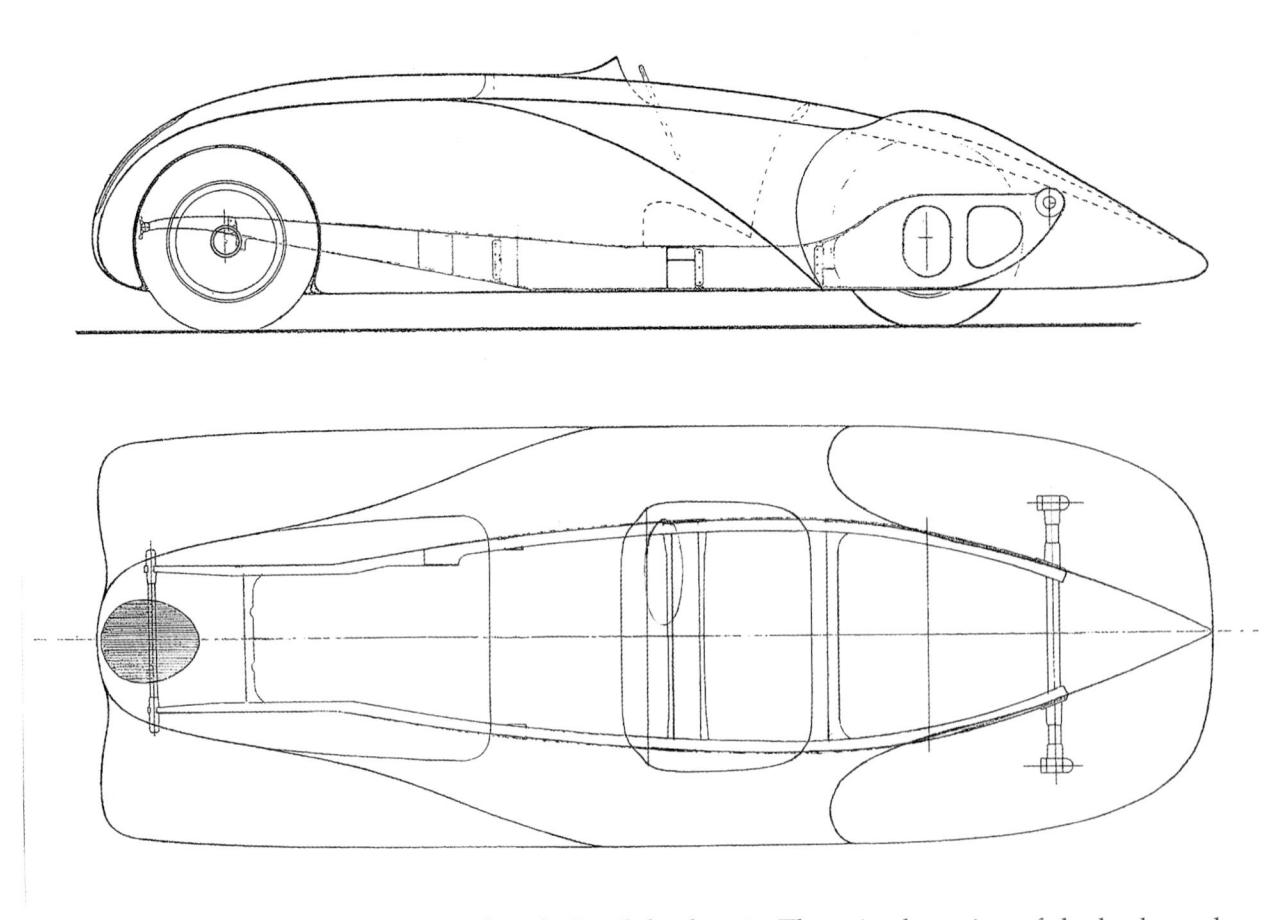

Body drawing 1078 superimposed with Gondola chassis. The raised portion of the bodywork exactly mirrors the chassis, confirming their simultaneous design. (Courtesy Bugatti Trust)

weight saving in perforating a T59 GP chassis is estimated to be 7.7kg: enough to influence racing performance; so a difference of more than five times that has to be of major consequence. It is known that a great deal of effort went into making the cars lighter, although such changes would take time.

The surviving Type 57G 'Tank' undoubtedly appears to be the Wimille car, and uses a lightened 'parallel' chassis frame, the sides of which have been perforated to reduce weight. It also employs light-alloy crossbeams. A number of other components, including the gearbox and differential casing, were reportedly made from magnesium alloy, and some transmission parts have been made lighter by using stronger materials. Nevertheless, it is clear that its current form was not necessarily always so, where it now represents the culmination of the Type 57G Tank's evolution.

A summary might be useful at this point. Weight differences would almost certainly suggest that the heaviest car was an early prototype, whereas the lightest would be a later and more technically-advanced version. But is there any additional evidence to suggest early and later versions of the Tank?

In hindsight, of course, Jean-Pierre Wimille and his car proved extraordinarily successful in the 1936 ACF, Marne Grand Prix, Class 'C' World Records, as well as the 1937 Le Mans race. However, whilst he had been a member of the Bugatti racing team since 1934, in comparison with some of his extremely distinguished colleagues and guest drivers in various race events, even in 1936 he seems to have been regarded by the Racing Department as a relatively junior Works driver. By contrast, Robert Benoist was a veteran of high esteem, having been awarded the Légion d'honneur in 1927 in recognition of his motor racing successes. Robert Benoist was, to all intents and purposes, a World Champion driver long before the title existed. Furthermore, consider the hierarchy of drivers during tests at Montlhéry prior to the Marne Grand Prix. The pecking-order being: Benoist – principal works driver – then Veyron and Sommer, before a cloudburst stopped proceedings; Wimille did not even get a look-in. Also, reflect on the relative senior and junior status of paired drivers at the ACF, through identifiable shades of racing overall, white senior and light brown junior. In the same vein, even by 1937, Bugatti's entry for the Le Mans race placed the two experienced d'Endurance drivers, Roger Labric (who entered the cars) and Pierre Veyron as predominant, with racing number 1, thereafter assigning the 'veteran' – Benoist, and the 'kid' – Wimille, with racing number 2. For these reasons, therefore, it might be convincingly argued that, for 1936, as Bugatti's principal driver, Benoist's lightest car was the more technically-developed, and, conversely, Wimille's heavier car would suggest a base prototype.

Considering the 20kg and 40kg difference in weight between the heaviest and lightest cars, it may be estimated that the major variation can be accounted for in their respective components and their weight-saving modifications. From the historical records, it is clear that Wimille's car began life as the heaviest 'Tank' and improved over time; where its chassis is now fully upgraded. Therefore, it is reasonable that the changes noted today represent a 40kg weight difference from its original form, and that a 20kg difference would represent an intermediate phase of development.

In retrospective analysis, and given the driver pecking order, it is evident from the weight considerations that Benoist's lightest car was the most newly built; a 1936 Series 2 frame, with perforated chassis and alloy crossbeams. Veyron's, the next lightest car, was also a 1936 Series 2 chassis, with a perforated chassis but without alloy crossbeams. Then Wimille's car, the heaviest, and therefore earliest, was a 1935 prototype 'gondola' chassis with an un-perforated frame. Likewise, the crashed Tank was its identical twin, both of which must have been mainly constructed during 1935.

Given the discussed technical evolution of the T57S chassis and engines throughout 1935, it follows that the two earlier T57G prototypes would have used the gondola surbaissé T57S frames in conjunction with prototype T57G engines. In fact, the raised panelling style of the Tank body exactly mirrors the gondola chassis profile in plan, evoking their parallel design origins. This is especially prominent at the rear, where the inner wing cleavage shows lines of rivets that could attach to brackets fitted directly to the curved gondola chassis frame. The two later 'Tanks,' constructed after the frame revisions, would have used the 'parallel' surbaissé chassis assemblies only delivered late February or early March 1936. Such a timeline, beginning September 1935, allows a schedule for two T57G Tank prototypes to be initiated with T57S gondola chassis, around the period when the two Paris Salon cars were being assembled. Given that Bugatti's chassis requisitions were for batches of four, and that four narrow firewalls currently exist, it follows that four gondola chassis were probably constructed; two for the Paris Salon, and two prototype T57G Tanks.

Coachwork practice

Let us also contemplate coachwork prototyping practice. Historians have explained that the outline sketches initially produced by Jean's design office were passed to specialist Joseph Walter in the body shop. He was a highly skilled woodworker, metal craftsman and draughtsman, being largely responsible for translating a body sketch into reality. He also made necessary detail changes to drafts as the full-size skeleton body progressed, being occasionally interceded by Jean who had the final word. Walter, along with three specialist woodworkers, carried out this prototyping work. It was usual practice that templates were placed on the actual chassis required. Once the skeleton or buck was complete, it was then delivered to the sheet metal specialists. Assuming this operation required few changes, Joseph Walter would then finalize the drawings for record with a coachwork reference number endorsed by the Works. To summarize, it may be seen that the final coachwork drawing was only finalised after the frame or buck was complete and the body finished in metal. In turn, Walter's task could not begin until a suitable running chassis was presented to the body shop.

Timeline

The reality of this may be judged by comparing the timeline of the Paris Salon cars' coachwork drawings with their public appearance. The earliest GA Type 57S chassis drawing is dated August 7, 1935. The Torpédo body drawing number 1075 is dated September 7, 1935, and the Coupé Spéciale, No 1076, is dated September 16, 1935. Yet the 1935 Paris Salon opened on October 1, 1935. Whilst it is clear that

Bugatti Type 57 Grand Prix – A Celebration

the Coupé Spéciale (l'Aérolithe) was not fully finished, the Torpédo was sufficiently complete, developed and tested, to be a fully operating Works demonstrator. It surely stretches credibility to believe that the task of building the chassis, making the bucks and alloy bodies of these two cars, fitting them to their frames, and delivering them to Paris, could have been carried out in just 23 and 15 days respectively. Clearly, the formal factory coachwork drawings were completed after the body was actually made, and likewise, earlier chassis drafts must have existed before the finalised versions were drawn up in August. Such a revision of reasoning would allow a more sensible minimum 53- and 45-day build period. Given such conclusions, it follows that the only existing chassis frame, upon which the Tank coachwork No 1078, dated January 10, 1936, could have been based and finalised, was the gondola T57S frame. Moreover, since the raised panelling of the Tank precisely follows the gondola chassis shape, the two were obviously designed concurrently. As a result, at least one prototype T57G Tank must have been built by early January 1936, and that a second body construction would have been well advanced before the revised T57S chassis were delivered to Bugatti by the Brunon-Vallette Forge at the end of February.

Weight differences

Regarding weight differences, the gondola chassis rear suspension crossbeam is more robust and heavier than that of the parallel version, and additional brackets were required for its rear De Ram dampers. Also, the 1935 prototypes used normal Type 57 front and rear axles before the lighter T57S versions were developed. As a result, most of the variations in weight would be due to differences between a prototype T57S gondola chassis frame and one which has been systematically lightened with holes, fabricated with light-alloy crossbeams, magnesium alloy castings, as well as stronger and, therefore, more lightly-made, steel components. On this basis, it would appear that the two prototypes were the heaviest because they were built with standard, un-modified, early T57S components. The two later models were based upon the revised T57S engine and chassis, with perforated frames, utilising lighter castings and components. The Benoist car, the last to be built, was lightened further, with alloy crossbeams and magnesium castings. This analysis and its conclusion would reconcile a number of otherwise unexplained mysteries.

Two dashboards

Curiously, given the previous conclusions, why was the lightest and most developed Benoist Tank not seen after the October 1936 Paris Salon? What might have happened to it? A photograph of the Wimille Tank's dashboard during the 1936 Class 'C' World Records shows a completely different switch and instrument layout to that of the post-war car. I think this is of great importance, for the Wimille car's dashboard was basic at the ACF and Marne, so had only just been specially upgraded for the record runs. The October 1936 dashboard layout is clearly earlier than the 1937 Le Mans version seen post-war, but why change it unless absolutely necessary? Besides, I have discussed the various chassis options and concluded that the two prototype cars' chassis must have been early and un-perforated T57S gondola versions of the surbaissé frame. This is because they were the 'S' frames in existence when the first two cars would have been assembled between September and December 1935. Their crescent-shaped chassis bulkheads would have been narrower than the two later cars with the 1936 Series 2, 'S' frames. Modern studies of the surviving Wimille car show that it has 1936 standard, but perforated, chassis frame sides with light alloy crossmembers. Clearly, this transformation must have occurred during its preparations for the Le Mans 24-hour endurance race.

The Wimille car's dashboard, at that time mounted in the heaviest and least developed car, changed between the October/November 1936 World Record runs and the 1937 Le Mans in June. At the same time, the lightest and most technically-advanced Tank disappeared immediately after the October 1936 Paris Salon, never to be seen again. As a result, I propose that during their pre-Le Mans rebuild, the two cars were united into the one we know today. That is, the three Tanks were disassembled during the winter of 1936-37 and rebuilt using the lightest and most up-to-date components in order to complete two 1937 Le Mans entries. Here, we have one 1935 un-perforated gondola chassis, and two perforated 1936 revised ones. Given that only two cars were required to enter, it is rational that the un-perforated frame should be returned to the production line, and that the two lightened ones should be re-used for competition.

Therefore, I suggest that the unique front bodyshell of the successful Wimille car was re-constructed with the most up-to-date and lightweight Benoist chassis, running gear, and engine assembly. This would aptly create a composite car,

16 Three Tanks or four

crescent-shaped bulkhead, as well as an equivalent, but more developed dashboard layout. If it is accepted that Wimille's and Benoist's cars merged to evolve into the winning Le Mans car, and subsequently the surviving one, it accounts for the fact that Benoist's Tank was never seen again. This is because much of its revised chassis and running gear became the basis of the new car. The 1935 un-perforated gondola chassis taken from Wimille's car would have been disassembled and reworked to 1936 'S' pattern, and re-assigned to the production line. Curiously, there has long-existed an otherwise irrational rumour that a Type 57S was built employing the chassis from Wimille's Tank. Might this explain the story? But where is the car now? It has been suggested that a car with an ex-Tank chassis No.57456 is the former Wimille car, although this is actually a long-wheelbase T57 Atalante, so this must be wrong.

Veyron car

The Veyron car, of course, already had a semi-lightened 1936 'S' frame, but would undoubtedly have been further lightened

Dashboard of the Wimille car during World Records, November 1936. (Courtesy Bugatti Trust)

Dashboard of Wimille car post-war. Compare the spacing of the small dials and the positions of lighting switches with November 1936. (Courtesy Bugatti Trust)

T57S Étoile filante and Jean at Montlhéry 1936. Note this car has 'G' specification front and rear axles for T59 wheels, as well as 'G' oil radiator. (Courtesy Bugatti Trust)

satisfactory to both Benoist and Wimille from the components of their respective 1936 cars. The more advanced Benoist Tank chassis already had the revised 'S' frame design, and wider,

and upgraded prior to the Le Mans race. This car was not seen after the end of 1937, and, for economy, was undoubtedly returned to the production line, once the perforations had been

159

Bugatti Type 57 Grand Prix – A Celebration

plated and welded. If such a chassis exists amongst collectors with this detail, and its production date coincides, it may very well be the ex-Veyron chassis.

Shooting star

The written-off Tank's beautifully-made alloy body was irreparable, yet its chassis and running gear were probably not seriously damaged at all. Being a heavy car as discussed, I believe it utilised an early, standard T57S gondola chassis, in which case most of its workings could have returned to the production line. Naturally, with its special 'G' engine modifications it could have re-emerged as one of the skimpy-bodied Works cars, or as a demonstrator. Interestingly, a photo exists of Jean Bugatti driving a special open-wheeled T57S with a V-radiator at Montlhéry in 1936, often ascribed to chassis No 57222. Commonly known as 'Étoile Filante' or Shooting Star, it appears to have some of the attributes of the 1935 Paris Salon T57S 'Torpédo,' including a gondola chassis. This car also has T59 racing wheels, as well as the unique T57G oil cooler between the front spring-hangers. Why re-make specialised parts when they already exist in a chassis with a damaged body? Given the special and costly modifications to the front and rear axles required to fit Grand Prix wheels and brakes, might this have been the fourth Tank's resurrection? It would have been relatively easy to re-body the crashed Tank's gondola chassis using the ex-Paris Salon Torpédo coachwork, lowering it all by 78mm to suit the 1936 reduced V-radiator line.

Summary

In summing up, it is apparent that four Bugatti Tanks were originally built, although one of the prototypes crashed badly and was written off. Its chassis and components would have been returned to the production line or rebuilt as a Works competition car. The distinctively-bodied second prototype, driven by JP Wimille, was unexpectedly successful, so, prior to the 1937 Le Mans race, the bodywork was re-assembled with the lightweight upgraded chassis and running gear from the Benoist car. The heavy chassis and running gear from the Wimille car could have been disassembled and re-worked into a production car, or a Works demonstrator.

The Tanks' chassis numbers were undoubtedly allocated in the factory records for legal purposes and insurance. Moreover, it should also be remembered that factory chassis numbers and road registration plates were swapped about on many occasions for Works cars within specific Type. When no longer required, the former Works chassis numbers would be re-allocated to production models. On June 27, 1936, three chassis numbers were allocated to the ACF Tanks: 57454, 57455 and 57456. On June 2, 1937, Nos 57454 and 57455 were allocated to two 'G' cars in Paris, just prior to Le Mans. Given this documented sequencing, and a view that the numbers allocated were in some semblance of order with the identification of the cars, then the planned usage of the four Tanks might have been: 57453, 57454, 57455 and 57456. Hence, in 1936, it could also be taken that 57453 was intended for the Montlhéry Trials prototype that crashed; 57454 for the Wimille car; 57455 for the Veyron car; and 57456 for the Benoist car. When the three cars were disassembled in preparation for Le Mans, Benoist's latest chassis obtained some bodywork from Wimille's car, where 57456 then officially disappeared and 57454 remained with what looked like the Wimille car. Chassis No 57455 remained for the rebuilt Veyron car.

Chassis number 57453 was allocated to a Works demonstrator for Veyron, with engine No 2SG and 'Aero' coachwork on June 1, 1937. This is believed by some to be the Black Atlantic. Interestingly, this date is the day before the two Le Mans Tanks were noted, and, as mentioned in the Froude records, 57G No 1 and 57G No 3 were tested prior to that race. Curiously, engine 57G No 2 disappeared from the record, maybe detuned slightly to become a more road-friendly 2SG. Demonstrators would almost certainly have used the 'G' large valve cylinder block with higher than normal performance; recall Benoist's incident at Montlhéry over the T57S45 Tank on July 2, 1937, when he qualified in the Works demonstrator. Later, the three 'G' chassis numbers were re-allocated. 57454 may have been used for the 1939 Le Mans 'Tank' with the Works No 1244-W5. After the car's destruction on August 11, 1939, it went to the Black Atlantic ex-57453, and later still, to factory coach T101. 57455 was allocated to the car delivered to Willy Toussaint in Namur, and 57456 assigned in December 1938 to a long T57 Atalante, engine 392, for actor Albert Préjean. Since the surviving Tank was never officially sold and registered for the road, it does not really have a formal chassis number, although 57454 must be closest.

Who was driving?

Finally, in this analysis, another important question arises:

160

why did the crashed Tank at Montlhéry not become public knowledge? Driver error is usually pardonable, for only catastrophic mechanical failure with fatal consequences would be very bad publicity for a manufacturer prior to a race. The accident, whilst appearing serious enough to injure its driver, does not appear to justify any extraordinary lengths to keep it muted. Even Bugatti's leading mechanic Robert Aumaître, although quite clearly identifiable in one of the photographs, has never mentioned it in his reminiscences. Therefore, perhaps the question aught to be: who was driving the car when it crashed?

The four drivers who shared the test car on June 8 and 9 appeared unscathed at the ACF on June 28. Sommer, of course, joined the racing team only days before the race itself, and Wimille ran a T59 in Barcelona for the Gran Premio de Penya Rhin on Sunday June 7. His race did not last long, for the gearbox failed on lap 8. With his race over, given the menace of political turmoil and lawlessness in the country, just 40 days prior to the start of the Spanish Civil War, it would have been prudent for the team to leave promptly. Whilst France was suffering her own political unrest, with strikes and fuel shortages, it would not have been too incredible, or demanding, for Wimille to travel the 1090km (678 miles) in his fast-touring T57 Ventoux, to arrive at Montlhéry by the late afternoon of Tuesday June 9 for a practice. Whether he actually got to drive the test car is not recorded, but if he did, he, too, appeared completely unscathed at the ACF.

Interestingly, however, it is reported that about twelve days before the ACF event, Jean Bugatti became unwell. His situation deteriorated considerably, and he was rushed into hospital, gravely ill and diagnosed with peritonitis due to acute appendicitis. Jean's condition was serious enough to last until well after the Marne Grand Prix, where his father, Ettore, scarcely left his side during this harrowing three-week period. Both of them missed the great successes of the Tanks, although Ettore was seen and briefly photographed trackside before the start of the Marne.

On the other hand, peritonitis can also present as a result of delayed treatment of internal injuries following trauma, especially at a time before seat belts, when the steering wheel was the main means of restraint for a driver in a shunt. Jean's severe illness, commencing less than a week after the two Montlhéry test days, is possibly coincidental. However, if he had been driving the Tank, it would have been a very sound reason why the accident was kept quiet, for Ettore strictly forbade Jean to race, even though it is well known that he was a compulsive daredevil who frequently defied his father in such matters. Thus, with all the performance tests at the Autodrome completed successfully by the end of the second day, I wonder, might Jean Bugatti have taken his triumphant car out for a jaunt around the track, but following a light shower of rain, crashed it? This is pure speculation, of course, and, unless someone has recollections or documents, we shall probably never know ...

VISIT VELOCE ON THE WEB – WWW.VELOCE.CO.UK
All current books • New book news • Special offers • Gift vouchers • Forum

17

Tail lights

HAVING TAKEN THIS JOURNEY through the complex history and development of the Type 57 Grand Prix cars, and evaluated the many facts, figures, errors and rumours surrounding these incredible racers, we come to the book's closing. Hopefully, the conclusions identified here will have unravelled and clarified the presently uncertain account of its evolution. As discussed, the Type 57 Grand Prix cars embodied elements of the T57 Touring model and the Grand Prix T59, as well as influences from the Type 50B and P100 Aircraft projects. Jean Bugatti obviously considered the Types 57 and 59 to have been one and the same family, and this basic truth is frequently demonstrated in all the Bugatti publicity and advertising that celebrated their racing successes.

Dated August 3, 1937, Type 57S Bugatti publicity leaflets detail the 1936 and 1937 race successes of the model, without differentiating between those of the T57G Tanks 1936-1937, T59/57G cars at Comminges 1936, or the T57 'Sport' at Pau, Bone and Marne in 1937. It is markedly evident that Jean Bugatti and the Works considered the T59 to be a close brother of the T57, where their development was closely interrelated from 1935. Moreover, the early 1935 revised G engine block and normally-aspirated induction manifold were specifically designed to be compatible with each chassis variation of the Types 57GR, 57S and Grand Prix 59. This fact confirms that the Type 57G engine was anticipated for all three models, and was tested in many of the competition opportunities that season, reinforcing the concept that the Type 59 was just another variation of the Type 57 family of cars.

Within the technical sections, the history and development

Souvenir postcard of Bugatti T57S, celebrating performance results. Note that under Type Sport 57-S, it covers T57G Tanks and T59/57G. (Courtesy Bugatti Trust)

162

17 Tail lights

Drawing of the winning ACF Tank, commissioned by *The Autocar* magazine July 22, 1936, and illustrated by F Gordon-Crosby.

Drawing of the Le Mans-winning Tank, commissioned by *Motor* magazine, December 7, 1937, and illustrated by Frederic Nevin.

of the T57S chassis has been discussed, with suggestions as to why the design changed. Additionally, a detailed examination of the 'G' engine, gearbox, dampers and T59 racing wheels has shown how the T57S and T59 integrated to become the successful sports racing car of 1936 and 1937. Furthermore, the vital significance of different crankshaft arrays has revealed how reliability at higher revolutions can win Grands Prix.

The rumours about a fourth T57G Tank have been explored and illuminated, where I trust the evidence ratifies the case for four original 1936 cars; two prototypes based on 1935 T57S gondola chassis frames, and two using 1936 revisions. In turn, the existence of four cars accounts for other rumours in conjunction with evidence that the existing one is a composite of Wimille and Benoist's racers. In future,

perhaps the ex-Wimille 1936 Tank chassis will be identified, along with the 1937 ex-Veyron Tank frame. In addition, I trust the story of the two T57S45 cars has been clarified, and will prompt more research into their likely whereabouts today. Furthermore, that the true 'G' composition of the 1939 T57C Le Mans car has been settled, and why Jean Bugatti chose to keep this knowledge unpublicised. Finally, the circumstances surrounding Jean Bugatti's fatal crash have been explored and established, where it was quite clearly a tragic accident during functional and performance testing.

There will inevitably be some oversights, but the aim of this book was to publish just about everything known about the Type 57 Grand Prix cars, and to celebrate their triumphs,

Bugatti Type 57 Grand Prix – A Celebration

as well as highlight those many individuals who should be credited and acknowledged for their efforts leading to the cars' extraordinary success. Some of the fastest sports racing cars of their time, the T57Gs were celebrated by the magazine *Autocar* which commissioned artist F Gordon-Crosby to illustrate the ACF-winning Bugatti Tank in the July 22, 1936 edition. Likewise, the December 7, 1937 edition of *The Motor* celebrated the success of Jean-Pierre Wimille with an illustration by Frederic Nevin, showing the Le Mans winning car racing dramatically at night.

The Type 57G cars were celebrated by toy makers of the time, and reverence has endured to the present day through scale model manufacturers from many countries of the world. They have been made in many materials, including wood, plastic, tinplate, white metal, resin, zinc, ceramic, blown acrylic, and multi-media materials, in all scales from 1/8 to 1/86. They span fine scale static models, slot-car racers and simple toys.

In the 1950s and '60s, before scale models became more widely available, artisans handcrafted wooden commissions for enthusiasts. Some were sold through Jacques Simonet's shop 'Manou Auto Sport' in Le Mans, under the 'Racing' brand. Some of the model-makers were anonymous, although known French craftsmen included Monsieur Leguet, André Caffiaux, and Raymond Daffure of Marmande. In the UK we had Barry Lester (later of Auto Replicas fame) in Salisbury, and John Shelford in Plymouth. In 1969, Gordon Tapsell of GT Models produced vacuum-formed acrylic versions for slot-car racing enthusiasts. When white-metal kits rose to prominence in the 1970s, model Bugatti 'Tanks' were manufactured in the John Day series, as well as Brian Harvey's Grand Prix Models. Swiss modeller, Manuel Schmid adopted polyester-resin, and distributed his fine models through Michael Sordet's Ma Collection in Switzerland, and the Lang Brothers' Spielwaren Danhausen of Aachen, Germany. Czechoslovakian Hynek Knopp's Bohemia Models also used this material for its model Bugatti 'Tanks.' Resins improved over time to enable more precision and detail, with companies such as Starter, Sprint, Provence Moulage, Le Mans Miniatures, Vroom, Profil 24, MMK Productions in France, and Ruby Models in Italy, all celebrating the T57Gs.

As Rex Hays wrote, "Models are trophies in tribute to the success of a particular car, and are endowed with the capacity to invoke the spirit of the automobile as well as to inspire the imagination of the viewer." Clearly, the T57G Bugattis were the most amazing sports cars of their time, demonstrating incredible performance with reliability in racing, where this successful history has endured through the generations to the present day, and will undoubtedly continue long into the future.

1936-37 T57G Tank models celebrated in a scale of 1/43, from different makers, periods and countries.
(Courtesy NMT Collection – photo by D Roberts)

17 Tail lights

939 Le Mans-winning T57C Tank models celebrated in 1/43, from different makers, periods and countries. (Courtesy NMT Collection – photo by D Roberts)

Bugatti T57Gs celebrated as electric slot racing cars in 1/32 scale. Left to right: GT Models, Le Mans Miniatures and MMK. (Courtesy NMT Collection – photo by D Roberts)

165

Bugatti Type 57 Grand Prix – A Celebration

1937 Le Mans-winning Tanks in different scales: 1/18, 1/24, 1/32, 1/43 and 1/86.
(Courtesy NMT Collection – photo by D Roberts)

1939 Le Mans-winning Tanks in different scales: 1/18, 1/24, 1/32 and 1/43.
(Courtesy NMT Collection – photo by D Roberts)

17 Tail lights

T57S models by Spark and CMC.
(Courtesy NMT Collection – photo by D Roberts)

T59 model made from a wood, card, paper and wire kit, designed by master model-maker Rex Hays, manufactured by Modelcraft in 1947.
(Courtesy NMT Collection)

Bugatti Type 57 Grand Prix – *A Celebration*

Rear view of the Modelcraft T59 model. (Courtesy NMT Collection)

Bibliography & further reading

Books

57 – The Last French Bugatti Price, B (Veloce Publishing 2003)
Amazing Bugattis, The Haslam, Garner, Harvey and Conway (The Design Council 1979)
Autodrome Collins, SS, & Ireland, GD (Veloce Publishing 2007)
Automobile Electrical Equipment Young, AP (Iliffe & Sons 1944)
Automobile Engineering Tonkin, CW (Arnold & Co 1936)
Automobile, The, Vol 1 Hasluck, PN (Cassell & Co 1906)
Bugatti – A Racing History Venables, D (Haynes 2002)
Bugatti – by Borgeson Borgeson, G (Osprey Publishing Ltd 1981)
Bugatti – Doubles Arbres Jarraud, R (Editions de l'automobiliste 1977)
Bugatti – Evolution of a Style Kestler, P (Edita 1977)
Bugatti – From Milan to Molsheim Hucke, U, and Kruta, J (Monsenstein & Vannerdat 2008)
Bugatti – La Gloire Zagari, F (Automobilia 1993)
Bugatti – le pur-sang des automobiles Ed5 Conway, HG (Foulis/Haynes 1997)
Bugatti – The Man and the Marque Wood, J (The Crowood Press 1992)
Bugatti – Yesterday and Today Mathews Jnr, LG (Editions SPE Barthélémy 2004)
Bugatti Book, The Eaglesfield, B, and Hampton, CWP (Motor Racing Publications 1954)
Bugatti Magnum Conway, HG, and Sauzay, M (Haynes 1989)
Bugatti Memories Cesari, G (Private 2013)
Bugatti Story, The Boddy, W (Sports Car Press 1960)
Bugatti Story, The Bugatti, L (Souvenir Press 1967)
Bugatti Type 57 and 57S Maintenance and Overhaul Manual Borgenstam, C, and Symondson, RC (The Bugatti Owners Club 1977)
Bugatti Type 57S, The Simon, B, and Kruta, J (Monsenstein & Vannerdat 2003)
Bugattis of Jean de Dobbeleer, The Fawcett, C (Private 2011)
Chequered Flag, The Rendall, I (BCA/Weidenfeld & Nicolson 1993)
Classic Racing Cars Posthumus, C (Hamlyn 1977)
Classic Racing Engines Ludvigsen, K (Haynes 2001)
Classic Sports Cars Posthumus, C (Hamlyn 1980)
Complete History of Grand Prix Motor Racing, The Cimarosti, A (Motor Racing Publications 1990)
Concise Dictionary of Motorsport, The Bishop, G (Bison 1979)
Das Grosse Bugatti Buch Tragatsh, E (Motor Buch Verlag 1986)
Duesenburg: The Mightiest American Motor Car Elbert, JL (Private 1951)
Dynamics of Mechanical Systems Prentis, JM (Ellis Horwood Ltd 1980)
Ettore Bugatti – A Biography Bradley, WF (Motor Racing Publications 1948)
French Grand Prix, The Hodges, D (Temple Press 1967)
French Sports Car Revolution, The Blight, A (Foulis 1999)
Grand Prix Bugatti Edition 3 Conway, HG (Haynes/The Bugatti Trust 2004)
Grand Prix Car, The Pomeroy, L (Motor Racing Publications 1949)
Grand Prix Saboteurs, The Saward, J (Morienval Press 2006)
History of Motor Racing, A Lurani, G (Hamlyn 1972)

Bugatti Type 57 Grand Prix – A Celebration

History of Sports Cars, A Georgano, GN (Nelson & Sons 1970)
History of the World's Racing Cars, A Hough, R, and Frostick, M (Allen & Unwin 1965)
Jean-Pierre Wimille – A bientôt la revanche Paris, JM and Means, D (Drivers 2002)
Le Mans 24-Hour Race, The Hodges, D (Temple Press 1963)
Le Mans Clausager, AD (Barker 1982)
Automobiles et Autorails Lot, A (Jean-Pierre Gyss 1979)
Lucien Wurmser – Mécanicien de Grand Prix Wurmser, A (Private 2002)
Metallurgy for Engineers Rollason, EC (The Chaucer Press 1939)
Modern Motor Cars and Commercial Vehicles Vol 1 Judge, AW (Caxton 1936)
Montlhéry – The Story of the Paris Autodrome Boddy, W (MBE) (Veloce Publishing 2006)
Motor Manuals Vol 1, Automobile Engines Edition 4 Judge, AW (Chapman & Hall 1942)
My Two Lives Dreyfus, R, with Klimes, BR (Aztex 1983)
Practical Automobile Engineering Abbey, S (Odhams 1945)
Racing Car Development and Design, The Clutton, C, Posthumus, C, Jenkinson, D (Batsford 1956)
Sports Car, The Stanforth, J (Batsford 1957)
Sports Racing Cars Pritchard, A (Haynes 2005)
Theory of Machines, The Beven, T (Longmans, Green & Co 1939)
Thoroughbreds from Molsheim Dumont, P (Edition Pratique Automobiles 1975)
Tribute by Trophy Hays, R (MacGibbon & Kee 1959)
Vanishing Litres, The Hays, R (MacGibbon & Kee 1957)

Journals/magazines

Autocar, The Magazine – Various
Bugatti Trust Newsletters – Various
Bugatti Owners Club – *Bugantics* – Various
Classis and Sportscar Magazine – Various
L'action automobile Journal – Various
L'actuallite automobile Journal – Various
L'Auto Journal – Various
La vie automobile Journal – Various
Motor, The Magazine – Various
Motorsport Magazine – Various
Omnia Journal – Various

BARRIE PRICE & JEAN-LOUIS ARBEY

BUGATTI

THE 8-CYLINDER TOURING CARS 1920-1934
TYPES 28, 30, 38, 38a, 44 & 49

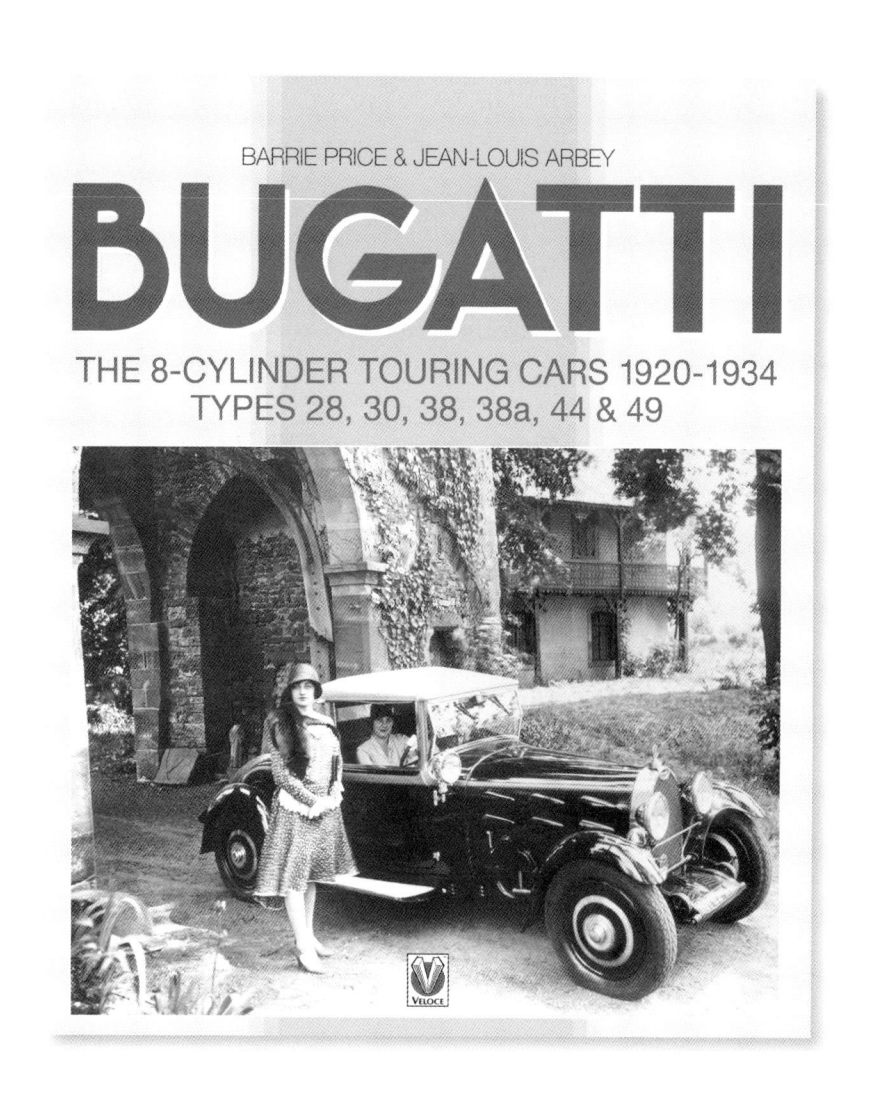

Detailed study of the 8-cylinder touring cars built by Bugatti following the 1914-18 war. Illustrated with over 200 contemporary illustrations of cars, components and chassis. Performance in competition is irecorded, as is a survey of the fall and rise in values over eight decades.

ISBN: 978-1-901295-95-5
Hardback • 25x20.7cm • £30* UK/$59.95* USA • 160 pages • 231 colour and b&w pictures

For more info on Veloce titles, visit our website at www.veloce.co.uk • email: info@veloce.co.uk • Tel: +44(0)1305 260068
* prices subject to change, p&p extra

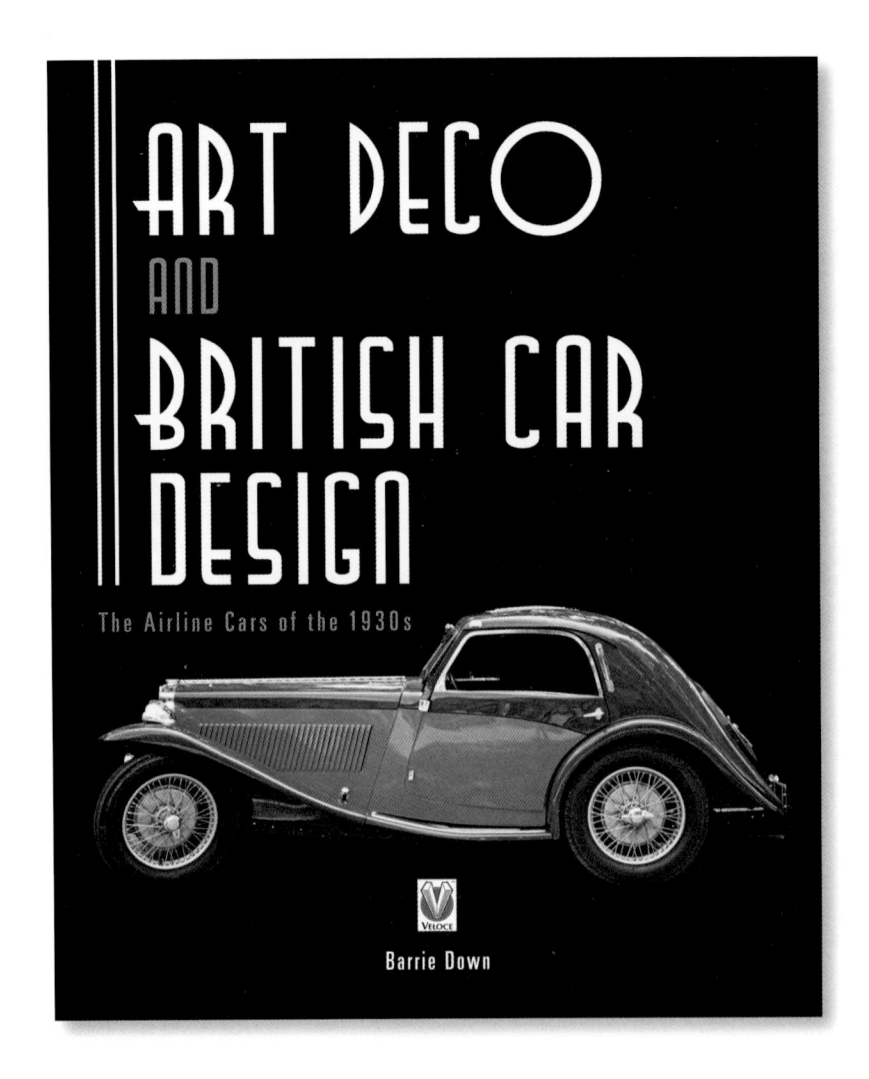

Art Deco and British Car Design
The Airline Cars of the 1930s
Barrie Down

The Art Deco movement influenced many different industries in the 1930s, and the British motor industry was no exception. Featuring a comprehensive examination of Art Deco styling elements, and a beautifully illustrated portrayal of British streamlined production cars, this is a unique account of a radical era in automotive design.

ISBN: 978-1-845845-22-3
Paperback • 25x20.7cm • £19.99* UK/$34.95* USA • 144 pages • 215 colour and b&w pictures

For more info on Veloce titles, visit our website at www.veloce.co.uk • email: info@veloce.co.uk • Tel: +44(0)1305 260068
* prices subject to change, p&p extra

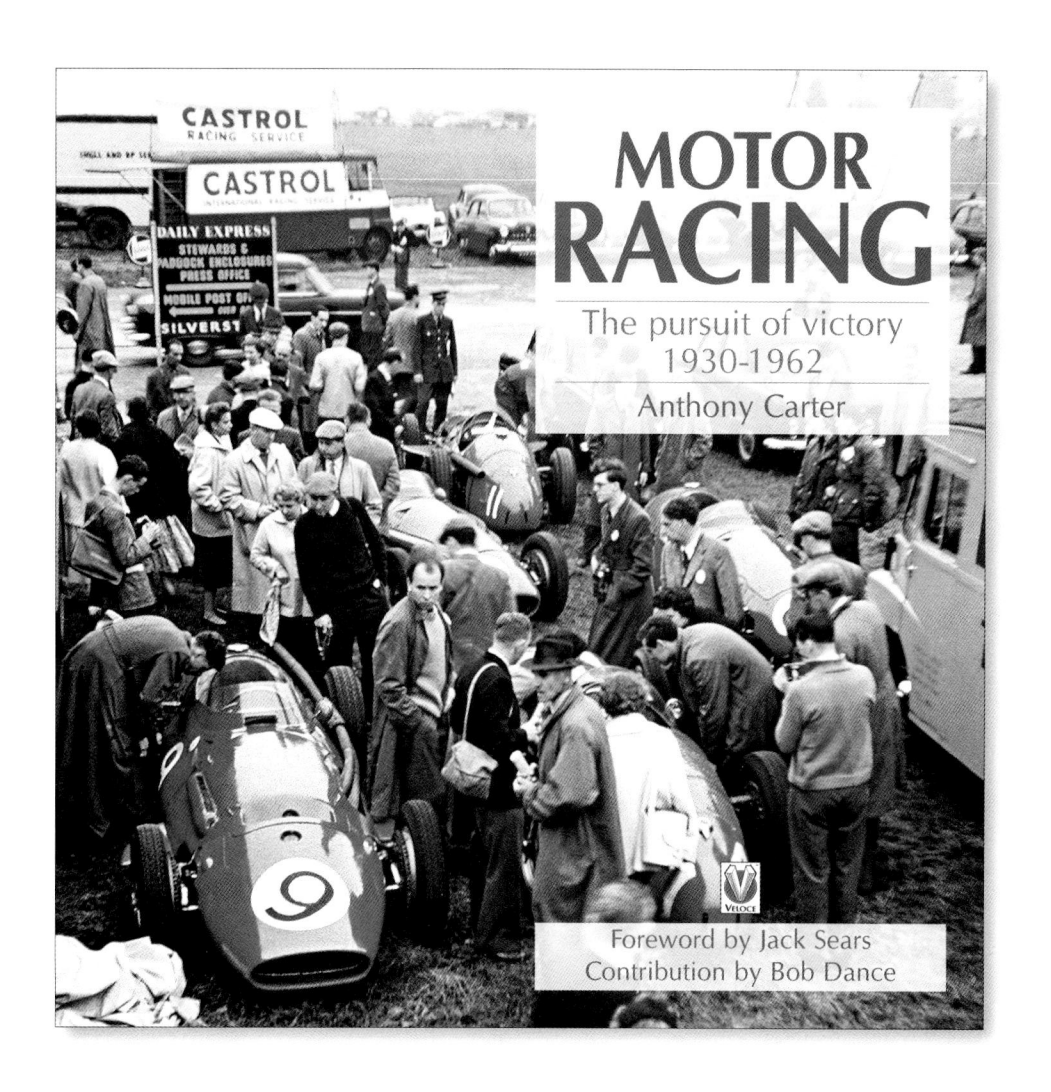

MOTOR RACING
The pursuit of victory 1930-1962
Anthony Carter

Foreword by Jack Sears
Contribution by Bob Dance

Previously unpublished stunning photographs from motor racing history, in a book that examines the many facets of Grand Prix racing before the dominance of television. A beautiful look at a fascinating time in motor racing.

ISBN: 978-1-845842-79-6
Hardback • 25x25cm • £30.00* UK/$59.95* USA • 176 pages • 218 colour and b&w pictures

For more info on Veloce titles, visit our website at www.veloce.co.uk • email: info@veloce.co.uk • Tel: +44(0)1305 260068
* prices subject to change, p&p extra

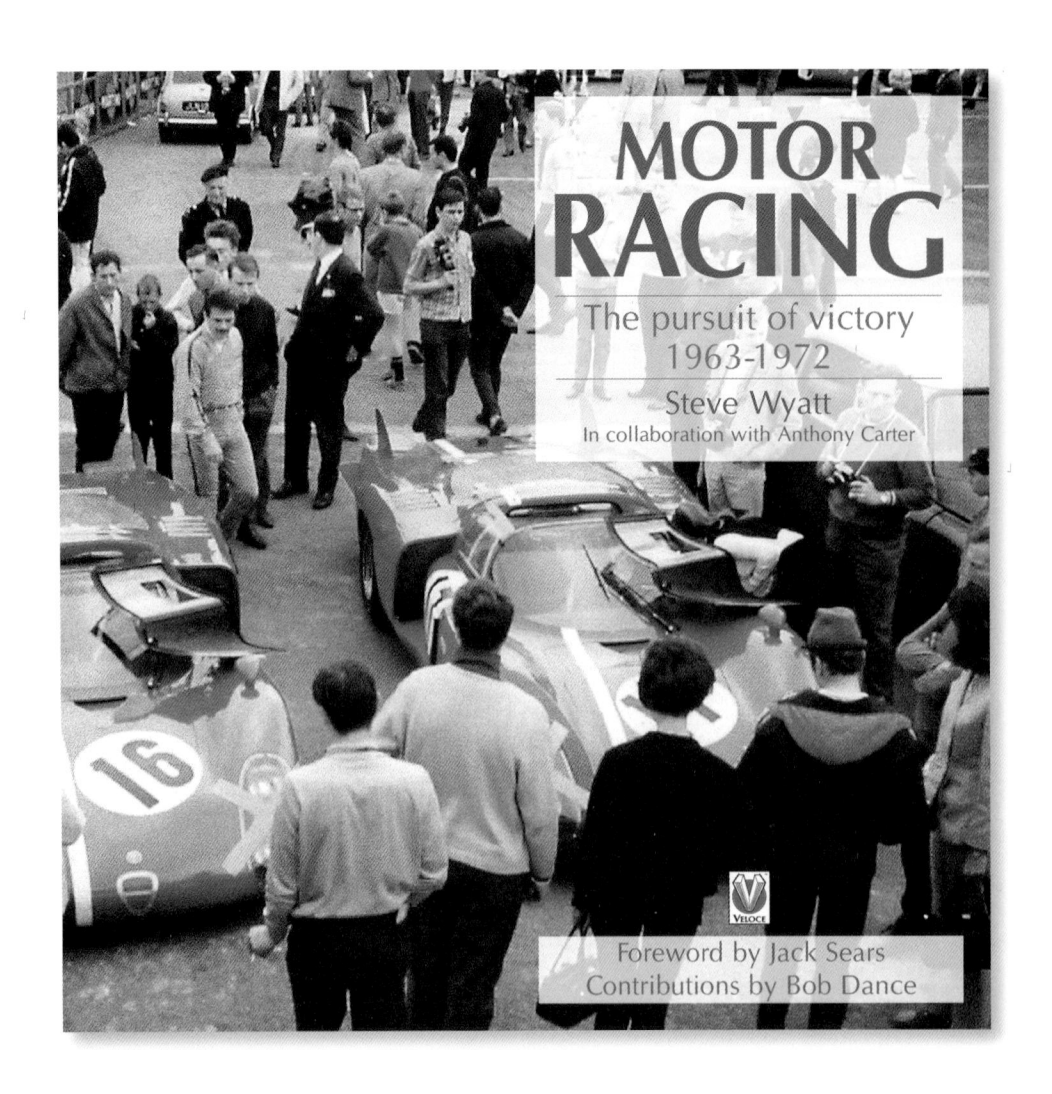

MOTOR RACING
The pursuit of victory 1963-1972
Steve Wyatt
In collaboration with Anthony Carter

Foreword by Jack Sears
Contributions by Bob Dance

Picking up where the first volume left off, this is a beautifully illustrated journey covering a period of ten years in motor sport. Moving year by year, this book is written from the perspective of a passionate motor sport enthusiast of the day. Features many previously unpublished photographs.

ISBN: 978-1-845842-85-7
Hardback • 25x25cm • £45* UK/$89.95* USA • 272 pages • 427 colour and b&w pictures

For more info on Veloce titles, visit our website at www.veloce.co.uk • email: info@veloce.co.uk • Tel: +44(0)1305 260068
* prices subject to change, p&p extra

Index

ACO See Ouest
Adler 52, 94
Aérolithe, l' 16, 158
Aircraft, P100 See De Monge/ Bugatti P100
Alfa Romeo 52, 55, 86, 94, 96, 135
AIACR (Allience Internationale des Automobile Clubs Reconnus) 14, 17, 25, 32, 61, 76, 78, 138, 143
Ariztegui, Monsieur 115
Aston Martin 52, 94
Aumaître, Robert 35, 65, 86, 92, 98, 101, 119, 146, 161
Austin 52
Autocar, The 18, 34, 55, 141, 164
Autodrome 26, 35, 42, 47, 65, 152, 154, 161
Automobile Club de Basco-Bearnais (ACBB) 76
Automobile Club de France (ACF) frequently mentioned
Automobile Club du Midi (ACM) 74, 79, 149
Automobile Engineer (Journal) 133
Automobiles Bugatti 10, 11, 16, 25, 26, 27, 58, 86, 99, 101
Auto-Union 11, 12, 146

BARC (British Automobile Racing Club) 69, 72, 74, 146
Barnato, Woolf 57
Bartlett, Helen Blair 113
Beer, George 109,
Belgian GP 138, 145,
Belgians, HM King of See Leopold
Bendix 61
Benoist, Robert Frequently mentioned
Bensoussan, Edgar 110
Bentley, WO 96
Berne See Swiss GP
Bertrand, Édouard 49, 124
Bira (Prince Birabongse Bhanubandh of Thailand) 94, 96

Blanchard, André 109
Blight, Anthony 14, 61, 150, 151
BMW 32, 52, 55, 94
Bône 79, 80, 162
Bordeaux 7, 86, 97, 103, 106, 108
Bosch (magneto) 74, 78, 83, 88-90, 111
Bradley, WF 7, 18, 23, 25, 26, 48, 58, 100, 133
Brivio, Antonio 138
Brno 146
Brooklands Automobile Racing Club See BARC
Brunet, Robert 32
Brunon-Vallette 17, 25, 116, 118, 158
Bugantics 92, 111, 118, 147
Bugatti, Ettore frequently mentioned
Bugatti, Jean frequently mentioned
Bugatti, L'Ébé 25, 26, 57
Bugatti, Lidia 92, 101, 102
Bugatti, Roland 101, 102
Bugatti C2 Carburettor 49, 74, 76, 88, 106, 114, 130, 147, 149, 154
Bugatti cars
  Peugeot Bébé 133
  Type 10 133
  Type 13 133, 124
  Type 17 133
  Type 32 18, 22
  Type 35 117, 140
  Type 41 27, 133, 135
  Type 44 52, 55, 128, 135
  Type 46 103, 106, 135
  Type 47 14, 142
  Type 49 10, 11, 14, 135
  Type 50 11, 48, 99, 126, 135
  Type 50B 60-62, 68, 75, 76, 82, 114, 125, 127, 130, 141, 147
  Type 50S 11, 16, 60, 141, 142
  Type 51 11, 14, 99, 131
  Type 54 14, 128, 142
  Type 55 14, 69, 142
  Type 56 92
  Type 57 frequently mentioned

Type 57C 17, 87-92, 94, 100-102, 108, 113, 163
Type 57G frequently mentioned
Type 57GR 14, 16, 17, 19, 69, 73, 87, 109-114, 121, 127, 142, 144-148, 152, 162
Type 57S frequently mentioned
Type 57SC 17, 88, 89, 130, 144
Type 57 Sport 69, 73, 76, 79, 80-83, 124, 127, 142-149, 162
Type 57S40 60
Type 57S45 59, 60-62, 64-66, 68, 74-76, 78, 82, 89, 123-125, 127, 149, 163
Type 57T 145
Type 59 frequently mentioned
Type 59/50B 61, 68, 82, 88, 124, 127, 130, 141, 147, 149
Type 59/50S 121, 130, 141
Type 59/57G 69, 72-74, 76, 78, 80, 89, 114, 115, 124, 127, 141, 146, 149, 162
Type 73C 124, 126
Bugatti Owner's Club 68, 118, 131, 140
Bugatti Book, The 8, 59
Bugatti Magnum (book) 101
Bugatti Trust, The 60, 61, 68, 124
Buick 11

Cabantous, Yves Giraud 109, 148
Cadillac 124
Carrière, René 52, 79, 82
Celeron 89, 111
Cesari, Gene 106
Chaboud, Eugène 86
Chambost, Raymond 149
Chavigny, Côte (Hill Climb) 145
Chénard et Walcker 52
Chinetti, Luigi 96
Chiron, Louis 82
Chrysler 49
CIJ 34
Cobb, John 52

Comminges, GP du 69, 74, 76, 78, 82, 124, 145, 149
Comotti, Gianfranco 80
Conway, Hugh G 60, 101, 109, 138
Conway, Hugh RG 7, 101
Coquille, Emile 48
Coupé Spéciale See Aérolithe
Costantini, Bartolomeo (Meo) 49, 99
Cotal Gearbox 124
Crosby, F Gordon 164

Deauville, GP de 78, 113, 149
Delage 52, 55, 65, 94, 96
Delahaye 32, 36, 41, 52, 55, 76, 78, 82, 86, 92, 94, 96
De Monge/Bugatti P100 27, 90
De Ram (damper) 17, 24, 88, 117, 119, 121, 127, 146, 158
Depression, France 10, 26, 34
Depression, Germany 11
Descollas, Gaston 145
Dieppe, GP de 145,
Dobbeleer, Jean de 106, 111
Domboy, Noël 11, 49
Don, Kay 35
Dreyfus, René 28, 32, 39, 41, 74, 77, 78, 82, 138, 149
Dunlop (tyre) 24, 48, 75, 78, 82, 92
Durand, Georges 48
Dwyer, Philip 146

Eaglesfield, Barry 7, 59
Eccles, Lindsay 140, 141, 145
Eifelrennen 145
Elektron 76, 89, 110, 114
Enthusiastes Bugatti 102
Essen Motor Show 109
Esso 96, 101, 102
Étancelin, Philippe 39
Étoile Filante 160

Fairfield, Pat 55
Faroux, Charles 48, 55
Federation Nationale de Clubs

175

Automobiles de France 13
Ferodo 121
Fonds des Course 13, 61, 78, 141
Ford 52
Forestier, Raoul 55
Frazer-Nash 52, 55
Francorchamps 110, 148
French GP See ACF
French Sports Car Revolution, The See Blight
Froude, Heenan and 25, 49, 61, 74, 76, 78-80, 82, 114, 121, 141, 145, 146, 149, 152, 154

Gaillon (Hill Climb) 133
Gerard, Louis 96
Giles, GM (Colonel) 118
Giraud-Cabantous, Yves See Cabantous
Gondola 117, 118, 157-160, 163
Goodrich-Colombes (tyres) 82
Gordini 52
Gresley, Sir Nigel 23
Grosser Preis 145, 149
Grover-Williams, William (see Williams)
Gueux, Circuit de See Marne
Gulinelli, Counts 25

Hampton, CWP (Peter) 7, 59, 118
Hartford (Damper) 88, 127,
Hays, Rex 8, 164
Henry, Maurice 19, 35, 79, 151
Hitler, Adolf 11, 101
Hobson Telegage 82
Howe, The Earl 69, 72, 73, 121, 140, 145, 146
HRG 52, 94
Hucke, Uwe 108-110

Isotta-Fraschini 129
Italian GP 146

Jaeger 76
Jaguar 23
Jarraud, Robert 74
Jones, Ray 61
JP Cars 34
JRD 34

Kippeurt, René 52, 55
Kortz, Felix 49

La Baule 98, 101
La Chanzi, MV 79
La Turbie (Hill Climb) 127, 145, 147
L'Actualite Automobile 147
L'Auto 19, 28, 35, 151
Labric, Roger 49, 52, 55, 86, 148, 157
Lagonda 32, 36, 52, 55, 94, 96

Lanchester 135
La vie Automobile 48
L'Express 99, 101
Lehoux, Marcel 149
Le Mans 24-Hour Race (Grand Prix de'Endurance) Frequently mentioned
Leopold, King (formally Prince) of the Belgians 83, 98, 124, 143, 149
Léoz, Genaro 52, 55, 80
Lewis, The Hon Brian (later Lord Essendon) 69, 73, 74, 121, 140, 145, 146
Lockheed, French 88
London Motor Show , 16, 121
Long Island See Vanderbilt Cup
Lovejoy-Delco 88
Lucas 90
Lucé, Le Grand 52, 92, 103
Luxembourg, GP 127, 130
Lyons, William 23

Mallard 23
Marco, Pierre 93, 141
Maison Blanche 55, 92
Marne GP de la 26, 35, 36, 39, 74, 82, 110, 149, 153, 154, 155, 156, 157, 158, 161, 162
Marseille, GP de 79, 82
Martin, Charles 140, 145
Mathieson 96
Mazaud 96
McFerran, Hugh 146
Mercedes Benz 11, 12
Meteorite See Aérolithe, l'
Metz, Joseph 99
MG 52, 94
Michelin (tyre) 48
Miller, Harry 11
Miramas 79
Molsheim 10, 11, 18, 25, 26, 59, 68, 79, 80, 92, 93, 98, 100-102, 106, 116, 131, 142
Monaco, Grand Prix de 113, 138,
Montlhéry frequently mentioned
Monza 145, 146
Morel, André 39
Morgan 94
Morys, David 61
Motor, Magazine 164
Motor Sport 23, 65, 121, 140
Mulhouse, National Museum 68
Musee d L'Automobiliste 110

Napier-Railton 73
Nevin, Frederic 164
Novo, Henri 115
Nice 80
Nuvolari, Tazio 55, 57, 138

Olympia See London Motor Show

Ouest, Automobile Club de l' 48, 52, 59, 106

Pathé 73
Paris, Michel (Henri Toulouse) 41
Paris-Nice Rally 145, 146
Paris Salon 14, 16, 17, 43, 60, 118, 119, 121, 144, 145, 153, 154, 157, 158, 160
Paris Showroom 26, 27
Patrick, Robert 111
Pau, GP de 76, 146, 162
Penya Rhin, Gran Premio de 147, 161
Peugeot 52
Picardie, GP de 145
Pitchetto, Antonio 23, 49, 89, 91, 122
Poulain, René 52
Pracht, Henri 28, 128, 152, 155
Préjean, Albert 160
Prescott (Hill Climb) 127
Price, Barrie 17
Prize, 400, 000f 77, 78

Rees, Noel 140
Reims See Marne
Ricardo, Harry 25
Richardson, Eri H 106, 108
Rieger, René 92
Riley 52, 55, 73, 94
Roberts, TA (Bob) 111, 114, 115, 154
Rolls-Royce 61, 89, 114, 135
Roots 89
Rost, Maurice 48
Rothschild, Baron Philippe de 17, 21, 28, 30, 34, 153, 154
Rudge (motorcycle) 129
Rudge-Whitworth (wheel) 48, 92, 128, 129
Rudloff, Alfred 99

San Sebastian, Gran Premio do See Spanish GP
Saugé de Estrez, Raymond de 52, 55, 77, 78
Sauzay, Maurice 101
Schell 55
Schlumpf, Fritz 106
Scintilla Vertex (magneto) 83, 97, 106
Seaman, Dick 146
Seydoux, Nicholas 110
Seyfried, François 111
Sherman, Jerry 106
Shooting Star See Étoile Filante
Simca 94
Simca-Fiat 52
Simeone, Fred 110
Simeone Foundation Automotive Museum 110
Singer 52, 94

Sommer, Raymond 28, 30, 34, 35, 55, 66, 77-80, 82, 94, 96, 153, 157, 161
South African GP 146
Spa-Francorchamps 24-Hour Race See Francorchamps
Spanish GP 138, 139, 146
Straight, Whitney 146
Strike 26
Stromberg (carburetor) 72, 130, 143, 145, 146, 147
Stuck, Hans 146
Symondson, RC 6
Synchromesh 17, 121, 122, 123, 124, 125
Swiss GP 62, 126

Talbot 32, 36, 39, 41, 52, 55, 66, 74, 76, 77, 79, 80, 82, 94, 96, 149
Taruffi, Piero 145, 146
Thomas, Percy (Tommy) 72
Tourisme, Criterium de 145
Tourist Trophy See Ulster TT
Toussaint, Willy 102, 160
Trémoulet, Jean 86
Tripoli, Gran Premio di 138
Trippel, Hans 102
Trippel Werke GMbH 102
Truslow, John 106
Tunis GP 79, 145, 147
Tunisie, Grand Prix de See Tunis
Turin GP 75

Ulster TT 69, 127, 145, 148
Une forme parallélépipedique 134

Valentino, Gran Premio del 145
Vanderbilt Cup 42, 62, 126, 130
Varzi, Archille 138
Veyron, Pierre frequently mentioned
Vichy, Grand Prix de 138
Vosges, Circuit de 145

Walter, Joseph 23, 157
Warwick Castle, MV 146
Werner, Klaus 110
'Williams' (William Grover-Williams) 21, 28, 30, 32, 34, 43, 47, 52, 118, 147, 153
Wimille, Jean-Pierre Frequently mentioned
Winfield (carburetor) 130
Wurmser, Lucian 79, 92, 101, 146

Zenith (carburettor) 83, 130
ZF (Limited Slip Differential) 62, 76

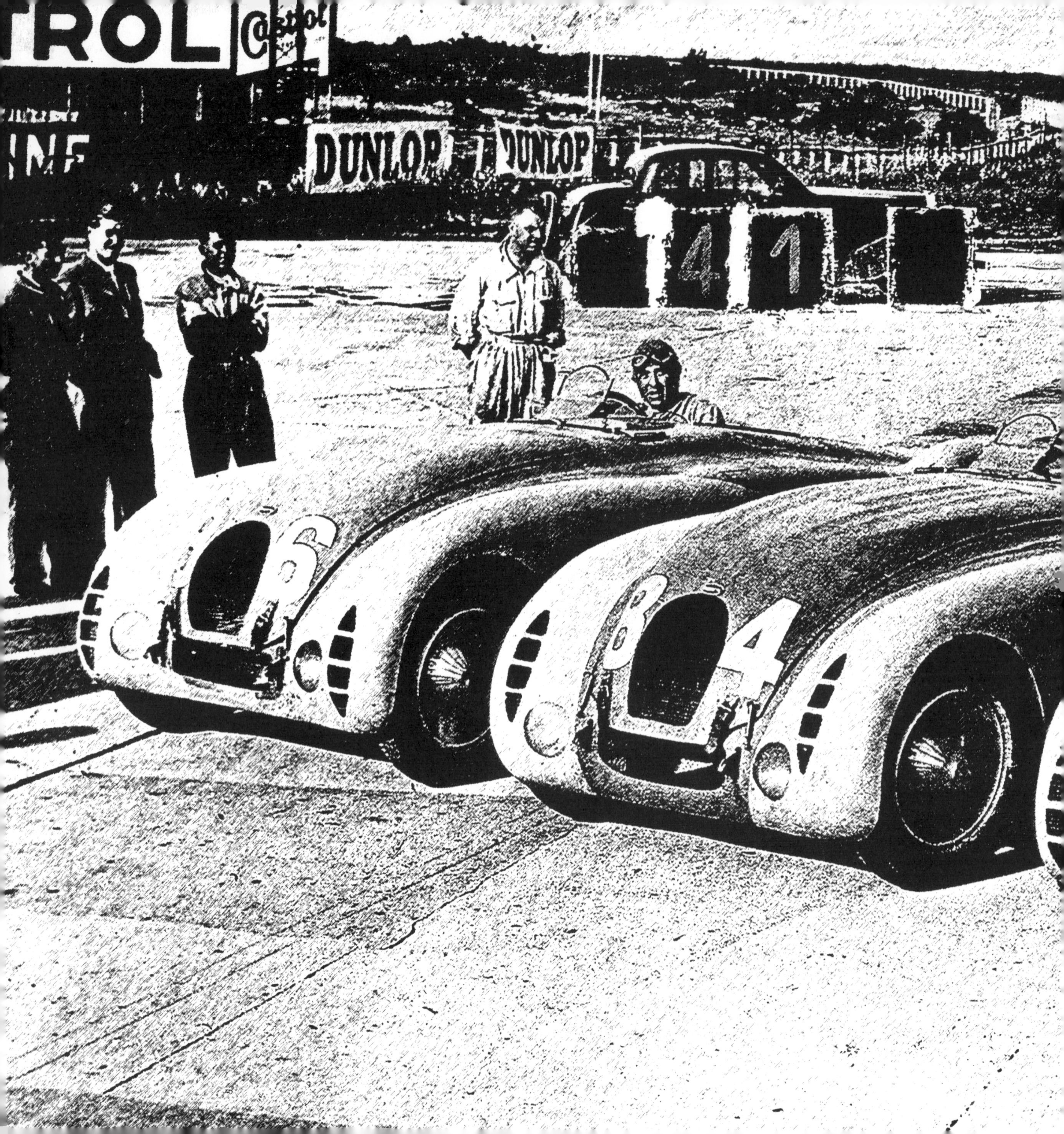
TROL
DUNLOP
DUNLOP